# The Historical Jesus

## BLOOMSBURY T&T CLARK GUIDES FOR THE PERPLEXED

T&T Clark's Guides for the Perplexed are clear, concise and accessible introductions to thinkers, writers and subjects that students and readers can find especially challenging. Concentrating specifically on what it is that makes the subject difficult to grasp, these books explain and explore key themes and ideas, guiding the reader towards a thorough understanding of demanding material.

**Guides for the Perplexed** available from Bloomsbury T&T Clark:

*New Testament and Jewish Law: A Guide for the Perplexed*,
   James G. Crossley
*The Origin of the Bible: A Guide for the Perplexed*,
   Lee Martin McDonald
*Paul: A Guide for the Perplexed*, Timothy G. Gombis

# The Historical Jesus

## HELEN K. BOND

Bloomsbury Academic
An imprint of Bloomsbury Publishing Plc

BLOOMSBURY
LONDON • NEW DELHI • NEW YORK • SYDNEY

**Bloomsbury T&T Clark**
An imprint of Bloomsbury Publishing Plc

Imprint previously known as T&T Clark

50 Bedford Square      1385 Broadway
London      New York
WC1B 3DP      NY 10018
UK      USA

**www.bloomsbury.com**

**BLOOMSBURY, T&T CLARK and the Diana logo are trademarks
of Bloomsbury Publishing Plc**

First published 2012 by the Continuum International Publishing Group Ltd
Reprinted by Bloomsbury T&T Clark 2013 (twice), 2014

**British Library Cataloguing-in-Publication Data**
A catalogue record for this book is available from the British Library.

ISBN: HB: 978-0-567-03316-1
PB: 978-0-567-03317-8

**Library of Congress Cataloging-in-Publication Data**
A catalog record for this book is available from the Library of Congress.

Series: Guides for the Perplexed

Typeset by Newgen Knowledge Works (P) Ltd., Chennai, India
Printed and bound in Great Britain

*To Keith*

*And our angels, Katriona Sophia and Scott Alexander*

# CONTENTS

# PREFACE

I have a long-standing interest in the Jewish world of Jesus and the social and political realities of first-century Palestine. In the course of several publications, I have looked at Roman governors, the Jewish priesthood, Herodian rulers and the Gospel passion narratives. The historical Jesus always featured in these to some extent – he is, after all, the main focus of most New Testament scholarship – but often in a rather shadowy way and with little attempt on my part to form any kind of coherent portrait of the course of his life. I would like to thank Harris Naaqvi at Continuum for allowing me the chance to rectify that omission by approaching me to write this volume in the *Guides for the Perplexed* series. I have enjoyed the challenge of transforming the historical Jesus from a more distant scholarly acquaintance to an abiding preoccupation, though sometimes I have to admit that the task was truly daunting. I'd also like to thank Harris's successor, Dominic Mattos, who had the unenviable task of rearranging deadlines when the manuscript failed – yet again – to materialize. Many thanks, too, go to Dr Paul Middleton: our competition not to be the slowest writer in the series spurred me on (even if, in the end, his fine volume on martyrdom preceded my own).

Books are seldom the work of only one person. I would like to thank all those who have stimulated my interest in the historical Jesus over the years, both as teachers and students. As always, the New Testament team at Edinburgh have given me strong support, especially Prof. Larry Hurtado and Dr Paul Foster. Special mention has to go to my Historical Jesus honours class of 2009–10, who read through some often rather scanty versions of the following chapters and always responded with intelligent and challenging questions (the 'apocalyptic continuum' always reminds me of you). The Edinburgh New Testament postgraduate reading group read through the penultimate draft of the book and always made perceptive comments. I'd also like to remember here, with some sadness, Prof. Robin McL. Wilson, who taught me briefly as an undergraduate and who more recently generously engaged in electronic discussion of the *Gospel of Thomas*. Mark Goodacre made a number of extremely useful comments and suggestions, particularly relating to double and triple traditions and my heavy reliance on Q! And on a wider level, the academic group who keep me sane and smiling, most especially my dear friends Drs Lloyd Pietersen and Bridget Gilfillan Upton.

Thanks, too, go to Rosemary Hoskins for babysitting, baby walking and for more kindnesses than I can list here. My parents, as always, lent their support to the project: my Mum cast her expert proofreading eye over the whole manuscript and my Dad drew yet more maps. I owe a particular debt of gratitude to my darling husband, Keith Raffan, who takes my strange fascination with ancient men in his stride. Most of all, I'd like to mention my beautiful children, Katriona and Scott, without whom this book would have been finished much sooner, but life would have been immeasurably duller.

# Introduction

Jesus of Nazareth was arguably one of the most significant men ever to have lived. It is hardly surprising that more books, meditations and plays have been written about him than any other person. Some are devout and pious: Julian of Norwich's mystical devotions, the mediaeval mystery plays or Mel Gibson's brutal *Passion of the Christ*. Others have caused more of an outcry: *The Last Temptation*, in which Jesus, close to death, imagines what life would have been like had he married Mary Magdalene; the *Holy Blood and the Holy Grail* in which he really does marry Mary and produces a child; and, in a similar vein, *The Da Vinci Code*.[1] The runaway success of the latter doubtless indicates a great deal about early twenty-first century society – a love of conspiracy stories, a general disaffection with 'organized religion' and a strange, almost perverse, desire to believe outlandish theories, despite a complete lack of evidence – but at the heart of it all is a fascination with an enigmatic character who still exerts a curious attraction over modern individuals.

Most people in the Western world, even those with no particular Christian commitment, find it almost impossible to escape the legacy of Jesus. Time itself, ever since the calculations of Dionysius the Small in the sixth century, has been reckoned according to whether events occurred before or after Jesus' birth. The yearly calendar, still followed by schools and universities, is punctuated by holidays commemorating events in his life. Jesus' ethics, enshrined in the Sermon on the Mount, are regarded by many as a truly good and honourable way to conduct their lives, particularly his advice to love one's enemies (Lk 6.27) or to turn the other cheek in the face of adversity (Mt 5.39). And it is impossible to exaggerate the impact of Christianity, the movement founded and inspired by Jesus, on Western religion, culture, art, music and politics.

For Christians, of course, the study of Jesus is particularly significant. Fundamental to Christian belief is the Incarnation, the idea that God became human in one historical person, a man who lived at a definite time (the early first century C.E.) in a definite place (Galilee). Christianity, then, is grounded in a historical person, and historical research can help to bring the human Jesus to life. It can illume the geographical places where events took place (Nazareth, Capernaum, Jerusalem); introduce the people he encountered (tax collectors, Pharisees, chief priests); and explain the significance of first-century institutions and beliefs (the Temple, messianic hopes, and beliefs in some kind of resurrection). Attempts to understand the life of Jesus can also help the believer to imitate Jesus, to lead his or her life in a manner reminiscent of his.

Jesus' followers believed that he was raised from the dead three days after his crucifixion and they quickly began to proclaim that God had inaugurated a new means of salvation for the whole of creation through his death and Resurrection. After Easter, Jesus was regarded in ever more exalted terms – as the pre-existent Son of God, the Saviour of the World who died for humanity's sins and as the resurrected redeemer now ascended to heaven. By the time the Gospels were written in the late first century, Christian specu-lation had created a wide gulf between the 'risen Lord' and the man from Nazareth, and most scholars make a distinction between the 'historical Jesus' (the man who breathed the air of first-century Galilee) and the 'Christ of Faith' (the risen Lord as he was remem-bered by the Church). Of course, we cannot drive too firm a wedge between the two. As we shall see in the following chapters, we only have access to the historical Jesus through texts deeply shaped by post-Resurrection reflection on the Christ of faith. And, despite the huge transformative power of the Resurrection, the Christ of the Church must have some level of continuity with the historical man at its origin. Nevertheless, it is as well to make it quite clear from the outset that this book is not concerned with the theological significance of Jesus as his followers came to understand it over the next few centuries (what scholars call 'Christology'[2]), but with the historical man who died on a Roman cross.

But what exactly do we mean by 'historical'? Superficially, of course, we all know that history is the study of the past, the reconstruction of 'what actually happened' in a time prior to our own. Yet history is never a straight forward, disinterested activity. Historical reconstruction is fundamentally an imaginative attempt to understand our own present, to create shared memories which

reinforce our sense of who we are. And those embarking on reconstructions, the historians, bring their own questions and concerns
to the project. The very fact that others and I have chosen to write
books about Jesus, to spend many hours pondering his life and
violent death, shows that we think that his story is important to
the modern world in some way or other. Above all, history is interpretation: we depend on sources which are selective interpretations
and from them create our own interpretative narrative. When the
project is a biographical one, the study of a particular character, the
problems are compounded: how can we ever understand another
person's life, particularly when the sources offer a variety of opin-
ions? And when the subject of our enquiry lived 2,000 years ago
and quickly became the object of religious devotion, the fragility of
any portraits, and the scope for distortion are all too obvious.

This does not mean that the search for the historical Jesus is
bound to fail, only that we have to be extremely careful about
the way in which we go about it. We shall see in subsequent chapters that a 'full portrait' of Jesus is beyond our grasp. Most of the
details of his life are now lost, including the precise dates of his
birth and death, details of his family life and anything of his life
before about 30 years of age. Furthermore, we will never know
anything of his character, his private feelings, inner emotions or
psychological motivations. Our sources simply do not furnish us
with this data. We shall have to be content with an *impression* of
the historical man, with broad brushstrokes on a canvas indicating
some of the major contours of his life and the central elements of
his teaching, some of what others thought about him and possible
reasons for his death. Much else is lost in the chasm that separates
his time from ours.

Like other *Guides for the Perplexed*, this book is designed for
upper-level students or interested readers who have some general,
though not detailed, knowledge of the matter at hand. Chapter 1
will both introduce readers to the major questions and concerns
of historical Jesus scholarship and present them with a range of
answers and reconstructions. We shall pay particular attention to
the work of a number of prominent modern Jesus scholars: Geza
Vermes, E. P. Sanders, Richard Horsley, the Jesus Seminar, J. D.
Crossan, David Flusser, J. P. Meier, N. T Wright, J. D. G. Dunn
and Dale Allison. Next we shall turn to an analysis of the *sources*
for the life of Jesus (Graeco–Roman, Jewish and Christian). We

should not expect a first-century peasant to have left much of a mark in contemporary history, but how much attention should we pay to the brief comments of Tacitus, Suetonius or Josephus? How historically reliable are the Gospels? And what about writings not contained in the New Testament, non-canonical works such as the Gospels of *Thomas* or *Peter*? Might they contain older and more reliable traditions, or are they red herrings in historical Jesus research? Once we have considered the question of sources, the second half of this short guide will present key elements in the life of Jesus. I imagine this section as a series of snapshots, each exploring key elements from the life of Jesus (his Galilean upbringing, his relationship with John the Baptist, his preaching the Kingdom of God and so on). The topics explored are all ones which most Jesus scholars would accept as broadly historical, and in each case I have tried to arrange the material so that readers can clearly identify the main areas of dispute. My hope is that by the end of the second part of the book, readers will have enough information to start to construct their own portraits of the historical Jesus. We need to begin, though, by seeing how the Quest for the Historical Jesus started in the first place.

# PART ONE
# Background

# CHAPTER ONE

# In quest of the historical Jesus

Like knights in search of the Holy Grail, biblical scholars have been attempting to reconstruct the historical Jesus for well over two hundred years. Christians, of course, have always had an interest in the life of their founder: the Gospels present their material in biographical terms, the Gospel harmonies of the second century and beyond show at least some desire to work the often divergent Gospel accounts into a coherent and seamless life of Jesus, and the surge of Holy Land pilgrimage from the third century onwards indicates an interest in the very stones and paths touched and walked by Jesus. But modern *academic study* of the historical Jesus only really began in the wake of the eighteenth-century Enlightenment, with its appeal to rationalism as the basis of scientific enquiry and its rejection of a God who intervenes in history in supernatural ways. The emergence of historical criticism in the nineteenth century allowed distinctions to be made between the 'Christ of faith' and the 'Jesus of history', distinctions that have underpinned the Quest ever since.

The path of the Quest has not been altogether smooth. Modern scholars tend to divide it into four rather uneven phases: the Old Quest; the period of No Quest; the New Quest; and the Third Quest. We shall see in the course of this chapter that reality was often rather more untidy than this four-fold schema suggests. Nevertheless, these divisions are still broadly useful and will enable us to see some of the major trends over the last two hundred years.[1]

# The Old Quest
## (Reimarus, 1778–Schweitzer, 1906)

The person most commonly credited with inaugurating the Quest was a respected Hamburg professor of oriental languages, Hermann Reimarus.[2] Outwardly professing an orthodox Christian piety, Reimarus kept his real views on Christian origins hidden. It was only after his death that the *Wolfenbüttal Fragments*, part of a longer work known as the *Apology*, were published anonymously by G. E. Lessing. Of particular interest are two treatises: 'On the Resurrection Narratives' (published in 1777) and 'On the Intentions of Jesus and His Disciples' (1778). In these, Reimarus argued that Jesus was a political claimant who hoped to be made king, but in the end his hopes were frustrated and he died on a Roman cross. The disciples, however, had invested everything in him and, in an attempt to obtain power and worldly esteem, stole the body from the tomb, concocted the story of a resurrection, and transformed Jesus into a universal saviour who would return in glory. Christianity, therefore, was based on apostolic fraud rather than divine revelation.

Not surprisingly, the *Fragments* caused an outcry. It was not so much that Reimarus's ideas were new: he drew heavily on emerging Enlightenment scepticism regarding miracles (the Resurrection, in particular), and was especially indebted to the controversial views of the English Deists who had already argued, amongst other things, that the Gospels were full of inconsistencies, that Jesus saw himself as a political saviour, and that the apostles altered the original Gospel after their master's death. What was striking about Reimarus's contribution, however, was that he gathered all of these ideas together into a complete account of Jesus' life, situating it firmly within a first-century Jewish context, and transforming a story of the supernatural and revelatory into one based on reason, natural origins and, ultimately, deception. Reimarus had cut the link between the historical Jesus and the Gospels; the latter were no longer faithful accounts of their founder's life, but attempts to propagate the disciples' fraud. After Reimarus, it was no longer possible simply to ignore the contradictions in the Gospels, to take miracles at face value, or blandly to assume a continuity between Jesus' message and Christian preaching. The quest for the Jesus of history had truly begun.

Some tried to reconcile Reimarus's views with more traditional beliefs. A theologian from Heidelberg, H. E. G. Paulus, attempted a 'rational' explanation of the miracles, arguing that they were in fact natural events mistakenly taken to be miracles by the rather gullible disciples. Most famous is his explanation of the feeding of the five thousand: by sharing his own loaves and fishes, Jesus prompted others to do likewise. Thus, the feeding was not a miracle but a story of what can happen when everyone pools their resources. The most important publication of this period, however, came from a young Zurich academic by the name of D. F. Strauss. In his *The Life of Jesus Critically Examined* (1835; ET 1846), Strauss accepted the rationalist outlook of his day but saw that attempts to retain the historicity of biblical accounts by removing miraculous elements (as Paulus had attempted to do) destroyed the whole point of the stories. The resulting accounts were congenial to rational minds but had been shorn of any religious significance. Strauss's great contribution was to introduce the category of *myth* into the discussion. He argued that the Gospels were not historical reports of the life of Jesus, but rather mythical accounts of Christian origins, composed by the evangelists largely on the basis of their Hebrew scriptures. Sometimes, mythical elements were simply added to actual events (such as the details of the dove or the heavenly voice in the baptism story); sometimes, stories were completely mythical (such as the Transfiguration, in which the appearance of Moses and Elijah were entirely derived from Scripture). For Strauss, the historical Jesus was so deeply buried under later Christian myth that it was virtually impossible to reconstruct his life. This, however, was of no great concern – he was much less interested in the historical Jesus than in the Christ of Christian faith, the ideal 'God-man' who transcended the limitations of his own space and time and spoke to modern people. Strauss may have jettisoned the historical nature of the Gospels, but he had reclaimed the deep religious convictions which inspired their composition.

The category of myth had already been used in large parts of the Old Testament narrative, and had also been applied by some to the birth and resurrection narratives. What was striking about Strauss, though, was his application of myth to *the entire gospel tradition*. The reaction to his work was immediate and largely hostile. By positing a 'third way' of understanding the Gospels, he had managed to antagonize both rationalists (who preferred

to explain away the miracles on natural grounds) and also tradi-
tionalists (who did not like rationalist explanations, but who were
certainly not prepared to regard the Gospels as myth). His critique
was significantly more devastating than Reimarus's because it was
clearly a work of exceptional scholarship and careful argument.
His opponents might not like his claims, but they had to take them
seriously.

Strauss's work ended his academic career, but it inspired a flurry
of scholarly analyses of the Gospels and their sources. Strauss had
argued forcefully that John's gospel was never intended to be historical (a view endorsed by F. C. Baur in 1847), but what of the synoptic
Gospels (Matthew, Mark and Luke)? How might we explain the so-
called Synoptic Problem, the literary relationship which undergirds
these three Gospels? And which Gospel is the oldest? By the mid-
nineteenth century, the answer to these questions had emerged in
what was known as the 'Two Document Hypothesis'. Mark, it was
argued, was the first Gospel to be written and had served as a major
source for both Matthew and Luke (hence, the presence of passages
where all three Gospels are virtually identical). But the two later
evangelists had also used another written source known as Q (the
first letter of *Quelle*, the German word for 'source'), which explains
why sometimes these two Gospels are in close agreement. The identification of Mark as the earliest (and therefore, it was assumed, the
most historically reliable) Gospel was to play a significant role in
the next wave of books on Jesus, the Liberal Lives.

In a reaction against rationalism, the late nineteenth century
saw the emergence of Romanticism, an artistic movement associated with figures such as William Wordsworth, Franz Schubert
and Ludwig van Beethoven, who stressed emotion as the source
of inspiration and creativity and the essential goodness of human
beings. Positioning themselves within this general outlook, the
(largely German Protestant) writers of the Liberal Lives were particularly interested in Jesus' religious feelings, and confidently dis-
cussed both his 'inner life' and 'messianic consciousness'.[3] They
took it for granted that advances in historical criticism (particularly the pre-eminent position now enjoyed by Mark) would enable
them to extract the historical core of the Gospels, revealing the
'real Jesus of history', and that this figure would have something
relevant to say to their own age. Rejecting the Christ of Christian
creed and dogma, they aspired to liberate the simple, timeless and

universal message of Jesus, expressed at its simplest in the fatherhood of God and the brotherhood of man. Jesus became a rather
sentimental teacher of timeless morality, the first Christian rather
than the Christ, and the model of Christian behaviour.

These psychological and moralizing studies enjoyed a great deal
of popularity in their day, but one of the sharpest criticisms levelled
against them concerned their *subjectivity*. As Albert Schweitzer
was to note in 1906,

> each individual created [Jesus] in accordance with his own
> character. There is no historical task which so reveals a man's
> true self as the writing of a Life of Jesus.[4]

And soon afterwards, George Tyrell famously declared that what
the authors of the Lives reconstructed was 'only the reflection of a
Liberal Protestant face, seen at the bottom of a deep well'. What
the authors of the Liberal Lives had done was to project their own
ideals onto Jesus, dressing him as a nineteenth-century German
liberal, who could then provide a relevant example for their own
day. (The modernizing of Jesus, as we shall see, is a perennial problem in Jesus research).

The influence of the Liberal Lives was to wane considerably in
response to three events. First was the publication in 1901 of a
book by W. Wrede on the 'messianic secret' in Mark's gospel, in
which he argued that the secrecy motif so prevalent in that Gospel
did not go back to the life of Jesus but was a theological construct
of the evangelist.[5] Mark might be the earliest Gospel, but it was
no less theological than any of the others, and historians put their
faith in it at their peril.

The second challenge came in the reintroduction of *eschatology* (the view that Jesus was concerned with 'the last things'). This
had been there to some extent in Reimarus (though he tended to
politicize it), but it had lost its dominance in the work of Strauss
and the liberal Protestants. The eschatological Jesus was defended
first by Johannes Weiss and then even more powerfully by Albert
Schweitzer in his highly influential publication of 1906, *The Quest
of the Historical Jesus*.[6] Schweitzer argued that the key to understanding the historical Jesus was not his ethics but his eschatology – his obsessive, almost fanatic belief that the end of the world
was about to dawn. In contrast to Wrede, Schweitzer took the

Gospels as broadly accurate in their portrait of Jesus; what they revealed, however, was a misguided figure who was utterly wrong in his predictions. Initially, Schweitzer argued, Jesus expected God to bring the present world to an imminent end through the agency of a figure known as the Son of man (an expectation outlined in Mt 10.23). When this failed to happen, Jesus realized, on the basis of the suffering servant in Is 53, that he had to become the Son of man himself, and hoped that his violent death on the cross would force God to act. Again, the eschaton did not arrive, and Jesus' prediction failed to materialize. Schweitzer concluded that the historical Jesus was a 'stranger and an enigma', a failed first-century Jewish prophet with little to say to the early twentieth century.

Schweitzer's criticism of the liberal Protestants was not so much that they had missed the eschatological dimension in Jesus' teaching (it was all too prominent in Mark's gospel for that), but rather that they had set it to one side. The writers of the Liberal Lives tended to differentiate between the 'culturally conditioned' and the 'enduringly valid' within Jesus' life. Eschatology belonged to the former and could be safely ignored, while Jesus' moral and ethical teaching belonged to the latter and was made central. Schweitzer argued that this division was incoherent and called for 'consistent eschatology' in which Jesus' apocalyptic outlook coloured everything. The Lives, he argued, had modernized and domesticated Jesus, ignoring his radical message and social critique in favour of a set of timeless moral truths. When eschatology was made central, everything about the historical Jesus was seen to be time-bound and alien. The enduring significance of Jesus for Schweitzer could not be found in the historical man from Nazareth, but in the 'Spiritual Jesus'. The relationship between Jesus and the believer takes on an almost mystical quality in the famous final paragraph of his work:

> He comes to us as One unknown, without a name, as of old, by the lakeside, He came to those men who did not know who He was. He speaks to us the same word: 'Follow thou me!' and sets us to the tasks which He has to fulfil for our time. He commands. And to those who obey him, whether they be wise or simple, He will reveal himself in the toils, the conflicts and the sufferings which they shall pass through in His fellowship, and, as an ineffable mystery, they shall learn in their own experience Who He is.[7]

Essentially, then, for Schweitzer, it is the Christ of faith who holds contemporary meaning for Christians, not the historical Jesus.

After the academic challenges posed by Wrede and Schweitzer, the third nail in the Liberal Lives' coffin was the First World War (1914–1918). The widespread evidence of human brutality and depravity shattered both the Romantic movement's optimistic belief in the goodness of humankind and late-nineteenth-century notions of moral evolution. In the face of utter social chaos, particularly in post-war Germany, the moral teacher of the Lives sounded rather hollow. It was only in the 1950s, well after the Second World War (1939–1945), that the quest was taken up again in Germany with any kind of intensity. The intervening period is often known as the period of 'No Quest,' though as we shall see, the title is rather misleading. The historical Jesus may not have been at the top of the scholarly agenda, but books and studies continued to be produced and to a large extent prepared the groundwork for the renewed quest in the 1950s.

## 'No quest'

The powerful critiques of Schweitzer and Wrede led many German scholars to question whether it was possible to reconstruct the historical Jesus. And even if it was, the theological landscape had changed considerably, so that it was now the Christ of faith rather than the historical Jesus who was seen as central.

The most influential thinker at this period was the distinguished Marburg professor, Rudolf Bultmann. Writing in post-war Germany and drawing on his existentialist outlook, Bultmann stressed that humans stand in a crisis of decision before their God, authentic existence depended on a person's repeated belief in God's saving act through Jesus. It was not that Bultmann had no interest in the historical Jesus. His oft-repeated quotation – 'I do indeed think that we can know almost nothing concerning the life and personality of Jesus'[8] – was an objection to the psychologizing accounts of his late-nineteenth-century predecessors. He stressed that Jesus had been a real historical person whose life was open to scholarly enquiry, and his own book on Jesus (*Jesus*, 1926; ET *Jesus and the Word*, 1934) sketched out a basic outline of his life and teaching. The important point, however, was that faith could not be dependent on the shifting sands of historical enquiry. It was not the historical Jesus but the kerygmatic Christ, the risen Lord of Christian proclamation, who was all-important.

Bultmann was one of the great pioneers of 'form criticism', which analysed the formation of the Gospels. He and his German colleagues argued that stories about Jesus had circulated orally for some time, quickly assuming a number of clearly defined 'forms' – sayings, miracles, conflict stories, legends and so on – which had been worked over by the early church and finally edited and placed randomly within the gospel framework by the evangelists. Some of these units of tradition, when stripped of later accretions, might well go back to the historical Jesus, but many had been made up by the church. They reflected the particular *Sitz im Leben* (or life situation) of early Christian communities, and displayed their earliest *kerygma* (or proclamation). The Gospels were, thus, expressions of the faith of the earliest Christian communities rather than historical accounts of the life of Jesus. They showed how the 'proclaimer' (the historical Jesus) became the 'proclaimed' (the risen Lord). It is this proclaimed Jesus, shaped by theological geniuses such as Paul and John and demythologized (that is, with their outdated worldview stripped away), who is the proper focus of Christian faith.

Such was Bultmann's influence, particularly in Germany, that the following decades saw little serious work on the historical Jesus. Following his lead, New Testament scholars turned to the study of the Gospels and the development of early Christian faith. Of course, not everyone gave up the quest, and scholars outside Germany were less inhibited. Writing in the *Harvard Theological Review* in 1940, E. F. Scott could still refer to 'the endless procession of Lives of Jesus,' and reviewed a number of contributions.[9] But, in general, there was a more chastened attitude towards the historical Jesus. Rather than attempt to reconstruct a 'life,' scholars tended to study discreet elements of the tradition: C. H. Dodd investigated the parables, T. W. Manson the teaching of Jesus, and in Germany, J. Jeremias wrote books on the parables, the words spoken at the Eucharist, and Jerusalem in the time of Jesus.[10] These scholars took the historical problems exposed by the form critics seriously and resisted the temptation to integrate their work into larger reconstructions of the historical Jesus.

Some of the more interesting attempts to write accounts of Jesus' life at this period came from Jewish scholars. Claude Montefiore, in a number of publications, regarded him as a prophet; Joseph Klausner, in the first scholarly work on Jesus in Hebrew, saw him as a broadly Law-observant Jew distinguished particularly by his ethical teaching (most of which however was already found in the Hebrew Scriptures); and Robert Eisler, drawing largely on recently found accounts of Jesus preserved in an Old Russian (Slavonic) version of Josephus, saw him as a revolutionary.[11]

An extreme inference from Bultmann's stress on the proclaimed Christ (and one which he strenuously opposed) was a proliferation of studies arguing that Jesus had never existed. The major proponent of this view was Arthur Drews, a German philosopher, who argued that the whole Jesus story was a myth. His views caused considerable controversy, to the extent that Schweitzer devoted a whole chapter to countering them in his 1913 revision of the *Quest*.[12] More disturbingly, this period witnessed a body of highly dubious scholarship influenced by Nazi ideology. An early example of this was the work of H. S. Chamberlain, whose popular book argued that Jesus belonged to a mixed ethnic group brought into Galilee after the Assyrian deportation and was possibly of Aryan stock. The work was a bestseller and was in its 29th German impression by 1944. More academically, Walter Grundmann argued that while Jesus' family belonged to the Jewish 'confession', they were not ethnically Jewish, and Jesus himself strongly opposed the Judaism of his day.[13] While these works are completely discredited today, they serve as a grim reminder of the extent to which one's own situation can influence one's portrait of the historical Jesus, and the extent to which historical enquiry is always open to the influence of contemporary ideas. It was partly as a reaction to these accounts that the Quest was taken up again – ironically enough by students of Bultmann.

## The New Quest (1953 – the mid-1980s)

The impetus for the renewed Quest is generally held to be a lecture given by Ernst Käsemann to a gathering of Bultmann's former students in 1953, entitled 'The Problem of the Historical Jesus'.[14] Käsemann pointed out that too clear a distinction between the Jesus of history and the Christ of faith was inadvisable. If Jesus' historical moorings were allowed to come adrift, it left the way open for his appropriation by anyone in the service of any agenda, however spurious (the Nazi appropriation of Jesus was a case in point). Furthermore, failure to appreciate the particularity of Jesus ran the risk of Docetism – the belief that Jesus was not fully human (a belief taken to its extremes in the work of the Jesus-deniers). The very format of the Gospels showed quite clearly that the earliest Christians regarded the life story of Jesus as important for faith. Käsemann was not calling for a return to the biographical approach of the nineteenth century, and was still deeply sceptical of the historical worth of the Gospels, but he did believe that it was methodologically possible to establish a few undeniable facts about Jesus. The 'New Quest,' as it came to be known, followed on from this call to action. If the Old Quest often displayed a distinct anti-dogmatic motivation, the New Quest had a much more theological agenda, attempting to establish continuity between the Christ of faith and the specific historical man at its origins.

The New Quest was carried out almost entirely by Protestants, with a preponderance of contributions from those associated with German theological faculties. Scholars continued to work within the confines of form criticism, which assumed that most of the Gospel record was the work of the early church and offered little help in finding the historical Jesus. Within four years of Käsemann's lecture, another of Bultmann's students, Gunter Bornkamm, published his now classic *Jesus of Nazareth*.[15] The book starts with a less than promising opening sentence: 'No one is any longer in the position to write a life of Jesus.' Again, Bornkamm was resisting a return to the earlier lives of Jesus, but his book did manage to assemble a reasonable collection of data – that he was a Jew from Nazareth, that he spoke Aramaic, that he was baptized by John, and so on. The form critics had categorized many of the *events* in Jesus' life as 'legendary additions' and had been highly sceptical about the chronology of Jesus' life as it now appeared in the Gospels; consequently, Bornkamm placed most emphasis on Jesus' *sayings*. Jesus, he suggested, was a man of great authority who had preached the Kingdom of God, a kingdom which was both present and imminent. He challenged the Law in a radical way, was seen as a threat by the leading Jews and was crucified after his action in the

Temple. What Jesus might have thought about his own role, or even his impending death, is for Bornkamm impossible to know. There was nothing particularly new in any of this, but Bornkamm's work became the standard work on Jesus for several decades to come.

The most striking feature of the New Quest was its attention to methodology. Participants wanted to get back to the words of Jesus, the *ipsissima verba*. But how was this to be done? Form critical analysis of the synoptic Gospels could identify a primitive form of a tradition, but that was not necessarily any guarantee that the tradition went back to Jesus. In an attempt to put such judgements on a firmer scientific level, scholars developed a number of criteria for determining which sayings went back to Jesus. The most important, and perhaps infamous, of these was the *criterion of dissimilarity*. Bultmann had already used this, but it was formulated most clearly by Nicholas Perrin:

> the earliest form of a saying we can reach may be regarded as authentic if it can be shown to be dissimilar to characteristic emphases both of ancient Judaism and of the early Church.[16]

What is most characteristic of Jesus, then, is material which has no parallel in Jesus' Jewish background, particularly when this material does not match the major theological emphases of the emerging church. Examples might be Jesus' command to 'Let the dead bury the dead' (Lk 9.60a), or the need to receive the Kingdom of God as a child (Mk 10.15 and pars.). Behind the criterion of dissimilarity are two assumptions. First, that Jesus stood out against his Jewish background and heritage, and that what was genuinely from him must have set him apart from his Jewish contemporaries. Second, that the creativity of the early church meant that we cannot simply assume a high degree of continuity between Jesus and the Gospels. While both of these would be challenged today, both were central assumptions of critical scholarship at the time.

To the criterion of dissimilarity, Perrin added two more. The *criterion of coherence* suggests that 'material from the earliest strata of the tradition may be accepted as authentic if it can be shown to cohere with material established as authentic by means of the criterion of dissimilarity'. That is, material which may not pass the strict hurdles of the criterion of dissimilarity may still be judged authentic if it is in broad agreement with material already judged to be from Jesus. And the *criterion of multiple attestation* ascribes material to Jesus if it can be found in various independent sources and in a variety of forms. In practice, this works better for motifs than for specific sayings, few of which are reproduced in more than one strand of the tradition. So, for example, Jesus' concern for tax collectors and sinners can be found throughout the Gospel tradition and occurs in a number of different forms (parables, sayings, conflict stories and so on). We may also be on reasonably good ground in accepting the fact that Jesus preached the Kingdom of God (in Mark and Q), that he spoke in parables (in Mark and Q), and that twelve disciples were especially prominent (attested in Paul, Mark and Q). A further criterion, utilized by Joachim Jeremias, placed particular confidence in the 'Aramaisms' contained within the Gospel tradition. Terms such as *abba*, *amen* and *rabbi* likely went back to Jesus himself, along with those sayings which more easily could be retranslated from the Greek back into Aramaic.[17]

Nowadays, these criteria have attracted a great deal of criticism, particularly the criterion of dissimilarity, which seems almost engineered to produce a Jesus strangely dislocated from both his Jewish environment and the church which followed him. Furthermore, it assumes that we know enough about first-century Judaism to be able to say what was distinctive.[18] The criterion of coherence, too, is problematic. Given that it builds on material declared genuine by the earlier criterion, coherence might only perpetuate a distorted picture of Jesus. More fundamentally, as Luke Timothy Johnson observes, just because 'one of Jesus' sayings spoke of a future kingdom of God, we cannot *on that basis* conclude that other future-kingdom-of-God sayings are more probable. It is theoretically possible that other such sayings were added by the tradition *on the basis* of that one authentic saying'.[19] Even multiple attestation, though still popular today, cannot guarantee historicity; all it can really suggest is that something is a very old tradition with a certain amount of popularity. And appeal to an Aramaic background only indicates that a saying originated in an Aramaic-speaking setting – which would include most of the eastern Roman Empire!

It is only fair to point out that many scholars operating within the New Quest were very much aware of the difficulty of using these criteria, but felt that it was the only way to proceed. After painstakingly separating authentic Jesus material from that which reflects the theology of the early church, Perrin was left with only 30 to 40 sayings which he believed to be genuinely from Jesus. These broadly formed three groups: the parables, preaching regarding the Kingdom of God, and the Lord's Prayer. The New Quest had restored credibility to Jesus studies, but its findings were rather limited, to say the least.

## The Third Quest (mid-1980s – present)

Since around the mid-1980s, observers have detected a new and exciting phase in Jesus studies. Perhaps the most important reasons for this are advances in 'Second Temple Judaism', the Jewish world in which Jesus lived and died. New documents have been published (the Dead Sea Scrolls and the Nag Hammadi library being the most prominent); well-known texts have been subjected to increasingly sophisticated study (Josephus, rabbinic writings, and apocryphal and pseudepigraphical literature); and archaeology has shed light on the places encountered in the Jesus tradition (particularly Jerusalem and various towns and villages in Galilee). The Jewish world in which Jesus lived is now seen to have been extremely diverse, with a variety of different ways of living out the Jewish faith, and an openness on many levels to the prevailing Hellenistic culture. E. P. Sanders's pioneering work on Paul rejected the dominant view of a legalistic Judaism, a faith characterized by works righteousness, and stressed instead the prior importance of grace within Jewish belief.[20] A better appreciation of first-century Judaism meant that a reappraisal of the most famous Jew from those times was in order.

It is difficult to date the precise beginnings of the Third Quest. Some might hold up the immensely influential work of Geza Vermes, whose works on Jesus from the 1970s onwards solidly grounded him in a first-century Jewish setting. Others might point to E. P. Sanders's groundbreaking *Jesus and Judaism* (1985). In

either case, something new has happened to Jesus studies in the last
30 years. The following are some of its distinctive elements:

1   Recent Jesus work has seen a shift of geographical location
    out of German theological faculties and into the English-
    speaking world, particularly the United States and the British
    Isles. Most striking in all this is the *diversity* of modern Jesus
    scholars. Participants are drawn not only from the ranks of
    Protestants (though they are still in the majority), but also
    include large numbers of Catholics, Jews and secularists.
    Significantly, this means that a Christian agenda can no
    longer set the questions, let alone the outcomes. In theory,
    the varying backgrounds of the participants means that
    common (and often unnoticed) presuppositions cannot
    remain unchallenged. What all modern Jesus scholars share
    is a commitment to historical reconstruction and the view
    that Jesus is to be studied like any other great figure from the
    past.

2   Perhaps the most important development in modern Jesus
    studies is the fact that the *Jewishness* of Jesus is now central.
    In many respects, that may seem like an odd claim: what else
    was the Jesus of Reimarus, Schweitzer or Bornkamm? What
    is distinctive about the recent work on Jesus is that it does not
    position Jesus *against* his Jewish environment, highlighting
    the ways in which he differed from his contemporaries.
    Rather, it sees him as very much *part* of the first-century
    Jewish world and its structures, sharing his contemporaries'
    hopes and aspirations. The Dead Sea Scrolls, along with
    the Old Testament Apocrypha and Pseudepigrapha, have
    been important in attesting to the diversity of contemporary
    Jewish belief. Second Temple Judaism is now seen to have
    been extremely complex and diverse; no longer can scholars
    imagine a 'normative', monolithic Judaism of works
    righteousness against which Jesus stood out. The question
    now is not so much 'Was Jesus a Jew?' (the affirmative is
    assumed), but *what kind of a Jew* was Jesus? An Essene, a
    Pharisee, a nationalist, a prophet?
       A corollary of this is that historical Jesus scholars now take
    time to reconstruct the Jewish world of the first century. Their

interest encompasses not only people's religious outlook, but also the social, cultural, economic and political strands of life so intertwined in an ancient setting. Studies of Galilee, in particular, have proliferated, investigating a number of areas which may well have informed Jesus' social critique: the degree to which Galilee was influenced by Hellenistic culture, the extent and effect of Antipas's building works, village/city relations, settlement patterns, taxation, trade, links with Jerusalem and so on.

3 A third feature of modern Jesus researchers is that, with a few exceptions, most have abandoned the process of sifting through the sayings of Jesus in favour of constructing a *larger picture* which incorporates most of the data. Rather than searching for *ipsissima verba*, scholars ask broader questions: what were Jesus' aims? Where do we locate him within Second Temple Judaism? How did he relate to his contemporaries? Why did he die? And how can we explain the movement which followed him? The emphasis tends to be on major trajectories and important overarching themes, rather than the minutiae of the tradition. Interdisciplinary approaches have also become popular in an attempt to flesh out our meagre facts, especially those drawing on the social sciences, such as cultural anthropology or sociology.

Beyond these three features, however, there is little unanimity in Third Quest studies. In fact, different methods can lead to a rather bewildering array of competing portraits of Jesus. Some stress his healing activity and characterize him as a magician (so Morton Smith), or as a charismatic healer and exorcist in the manner of other Jewish figures at the time (so Geza Vermes). Others stress the centrality of Jesus' apocalyptic eschatology, presenting him as an eschatological prophet of restoration (so E. P. Sanders, J. P. Meier, Dale Allison). Where teaching is central, Jesus becomes a sage or rabbi (David Flusser), a Pharisee (Hyam Maccoby), a wisdom teacher preaching a radical egalitarianism (Elisabeth Schüssler Fiorenza), a subversive sage (Marcus Borg) or a social revolution-ary (Richard Horsley). And some of those who see a high degree of Hellenism within Galilee detect similarities between Jesus and Cynic philosophers (Gerald Downing, J. D. Crossan). All these studies are trying to situate Jesus firmly within his Jewish environment and to show his significance within that setting. Yet the differences between them are considerable.

This very diversity has led some to question the whole attempt to uncover the historical Jesus. The Quest is criticized as too hopelessly subjective, with modern scholars (just like the authors of the Liberal Lives) quick to project their own priorities onto Jesus, to use him as a spokesman for their own concerns. Despite its superficial diversity, critics have often pointed out that it is still largely a white, Western (and often male) enterprise, marginalizing works on Jesus by liberation theologians and feminists (largely because they do not tend to work within historical-critical paradigms). Historical Jesus scholars are acutely aware of these problems, but remain committed to the fundamental belief that it is both possible and important to reconstruct something of the man from Nazareth.

The best way to appreciate the range of Jesuses constructed by the Third Quest is to take a handful of studies as examples. This will allow us to see a number of different methods as well as a number of different conclusions. It will also allow us to understand the complexity and coherence of each study. I have chosen to focus on the work of ten influential scholars or groups of scholars: Geza Vermes, E. P. Sanders, Richard Horsley, the Jesus Seminar, J. D. Crossan, David Flusser, J. P. Meier, N. T. Wright, J. D. G. Dunn, and Dale Allison. These scholars are drawn from a range of geographical backgrounds (the United States, Britain, Ireland and Israel) and hold a variety of confessional positions (Protestants, Catholics and Jews). It would be wrong to see them as *representative* of any particular position, however; there is clearly no 'Jewish view' of Jesus any more than there could be a 'Protestant view'. I have chosen these scholars rather because they exhibit different approaches and come up with different reconstructions of the historical Jesus. (Details of representative publications for each scholar are provided in the bibliography at the end of this book.)

## Geza Vermes

Raised a Catholic in Hungary during the Second World War, Vermes discovered that his family were of Jewish origin and converted in later life. He was Professor of Jewish Studies at Oxford University for many years (now Emeritus), and is the author of several books on Jesus. Vermes's first work, *Jesus the Jew* (1973), illustrates his desire to approach Jesus in the same manner as any other historical subject and his concern to place him within his first-century Jewish context.

Vermes's major contribution is his claim that Jesus is to be seen alongside other roughly contemporary charismatic holy men, or *Hasidim*. These men, he claims, were well known and revered within Galilean society. Heirs to the ancient prophetic tradition exemplified by Elijah and Elisha, their close relationship with God manifested itself in miraculous powers and often exposed them to criticism from the more mainstream channels of religious authority. Particularly good examples are Honi the Circle Drawer and Hanina ben Dosa, whose exploits are recounted in the Talmud (for further discussion, see Chapter 8 ). Jesus, for Vermes, was a pious, Law-observant Jew, who is best understood as one in a series – perhaps even the paramount example – of such holy men. While Vermes's construction of a charismatic 'type' in rural Galilee has been criticized,[21] his focus on Jesus' Jewish context set the agenda for much later study.

## E. P. Sanders

A Texan who taught at the universities of McMaster, Oxford and Duke until his retirement in 2005, Sanders stands very much in the tradition of Albert Schweitzer. His two major publications, *Jesus and Judaism* (1985) and the more popular *The Historical Figure of Jesus* (1993), present Jesus as a Jewish apocalyptic prophet, announcing the establishment of a new Temple and the restoration of the twelve tribes of Israel. Sanders is a respected authority on first-century Judaism and, like Vermes, strives hard to situate Jesus within a credible Jewish environment.

Rather than beginning with an analysis of Jesus' sayings, Sanders starts both his books with a list of 'almost indisputable facts' about Jesus: his baptism by John, his calling of twelve disciples, and so on. From these, he constructs a general framework which makes sense of as much of the data as possible, and finally turns to the words of Jesus once this larger view is in place. The most important 'fact' about Jesus is his demonstration in the Temple, and

Sanders makes this central in his reconstruction. Situating Jesus within an apocalyptic strand of contemporary Judaism, he argues that Jesus' actions were a symbolic prophecy of the Temple's imminent destruction and its replacement by an eschatological one in the coming Kingdom of God. Jesus saw himself as God's viceroy, divinely authorized to announce the imminent coming of a Son of man (probably not Jesus himself) who would usher in a time of tribulation, followed by the establishment of God's reign of peace and justice, and a transformed and ideal world. None of this happened, of course, and Jesus was, in the end, mistaken.

Like Vermes, Sanders finds no indication that Jesus broke the Law or that he taught his disciples to question Sabbath, food or purity regulations. Disputes over the Law, he argues, entered the tradition later as a result of early Christian disputes with synagogue authorities once the Law-free Gentile mission was underway. Similarly, heated discussions with the Pharisees reflect later Christian animosity towards Jewish leaders. What finally led to Jesus' death, Sanders argues, was not Pharisaic hostility but Sadducean outrage following the incident in the Temple.

Sanders's portrait of Jesus has been tremendously influential. Like Schweitzer's before him, it is built solidly on the Gospel of Mark; there is very little use of John or any non-canonical literature. He is familiar with Josephus and modern archaeology, and his sketch of Galilee as deeply Jewish, reasonably peaceful and largely free from Hellenistic influence is credible and convincing. Perhaps his most controversial claim is that Jesus did not require repentance from those who would enter the Kingdom. The 'sinners' who joined Jesus in table fellowship were, for Sanders, quite literally the 'wicked,' those blatantly living outside the Law. More radically than John the Baptist, Jesus' message was 'God loves you' rather than 'Change now or be destroyed.' Other criticisms are that he minimizes conflict with the Pharisees too much, and that he underplays both the present aspect of the Kingdom of God and the social dimension in Jesus' preaching.[22]

## *Richard A. Horsley*

In a number of publications from the late 1980s, Horsley, who is Professor of Liberal Arts and the Study of Religion at the

University of Massachusetts, Boston, argued that Jesus is best understood as a social revolutionary. Drawing heavily on the social sciences, he paints a bleak picture of first-century Galilee, a society ravaged by class struggle, economic inequalities, and a downward spiral of violence, repression and disenfranchisement. Jesus appeared as one in a long line of contemporary prophets, preaching a Kingdom which was not other-worldly and remote, but a concrete transformation of everyday life. He set himself against the rich and powerful, the ruling elite and even the Temple (which Horsley sees as a symbol of imperial legitimation and control), and sided with the poor and oppressed, the marginalized and downtrodden. Jesus' message was not *political* because it was not addressed to the rulers and was not concerned with a change of government (that aspect was left to God). Instead, it was a *social* revolution, primarily directed at the Galilean villagers who were called upon to renew society and abolish all forms of hierarchy, patriarchy and repression. Jesus rejected Rome and all it stood for; thus, when he commanded his followers to turn the other cheek, or to love their neighbours, it was relationships within the Galilean villages that he had in mind, not a wider landscape. Similarly, Horsley cannot believe that Jesus associated with tax collectors, people widely regarded as traitors and collaborators. In the end, Rome regarded Jesus (rightly) as a threat, and crucified him as a rebel against imperial order.

Horsley's work has had its critics. His heavy reliance on models drawn from sociology and cultural anthropology has been widely challenged, as has the resulting depiction of Galilee. Many have struggled with the retreat of any kind of 'religious' dimension in Jesus' preaching, and others have queried many of his interpretations.[23] His work is important, though, for bringing conditions in Galilee into the spotlight, and for its stress on the social dimension and political implications of Jesus' message.

## The Jesus seminar

This group of largely U.S. academics was founded in 1985 by Robert Funk under the auspices of the Westar Institute in Sonoma, California, and was co-chaired by Funk and John Dominic Crossan until the former's death in 2005. In a methodology reminiscent of the New Quest, the seminar looked first at Jesus' sayings, debating the historicity of a vast number of individual units of tradition before turning to evaluate his actions. One of their more controversial features is the seminar's manner of voting on the authenticity of traditions by means of coloured beads: *red* indicates that a tradition is from Jesus, *pink* that Jesus probably said or did something very similar, *grey* that there may possibly be some authentic material and *black* that the tradition does not go back to Jesus. Their findings have been characterized both by a high degree of scepticism regarding the canonical Gospels and an openness to the authenticity of material preserved in other, non-canonical sources, pre-eminently the *Gospel of Thomas*. Some of the seminar's findings were published in *The Five Gospels* (1993), a colloquial translation of the four canonical Gospels along with the *Gos.Th.* in which Jesus' sayings were colour-coded to reflect the seminar's estimation of their historicity. Overall, 18 per cent of the sayings tradition was thought to go back to Jesus, of which John's gospel could lay claim to only one saying in the red/pink category, Mark could muster 19 and the *Gos.Th* could boast 43.

The Jesus who emerges from all of this is an unconventional one. An illiterate peasant, he began as a supporter of John the Baptist but rejected both his ascetic lifestyle and apocalyptic preaching of imminent judgement. Instead, he became an itinerant sage, using pithy sayings to announce that the Kingdom of God had already arrived, and shamelessly celebrating its presence by eating and drinking with outcasts. Jesus' message was essentially a call to social justice; he enjoyed attacking the pomposity of Israel's religious leaders but showed little interest himself in the religious underpinnings of his Jewish faith – its Scriptures, its Law, or any hope of restoration. He made no exalted claims on his own behalf and was eventually arrested and summarily executed in Jerusalem after the incident in the Temple.

There is something very modern (and Californian!) about this Jesus, with his popular following and distaste for 'organized religion'.[24] At the same time, the seminar is rather old fashioned: noting their general rejection of church dogma along with an insistence that reconstructions of the historical Jesus should matter to faith, J. D. G. Dunn sees them as standing in the tradition of the nineteenth-century Liberal Lives. Reconstuctions by individual members of the seminar (such as J. D. Crossan and M. Borg) are much more nuanced and sophisticated than is the composite view of the seminar. What this perhaps shows is that committees are rarely the best way to engage in biographical reconstruction.

## J. D. Crossan

An Irish/American Catholic, Crossan's reconstruction of Jesus can be found in a number of publications, with the fullest study in *The Historical Jesus: The Life of a Mediterranean Jewish Peasant* (1991) and an abbreviated version in *Jesus: A Revolutionary Biography* (1994). His work builds on earlier studies of the parables, the passion narratives and non-canonical gospels.

As a prominent member of the Jesus Seminar, Crossan has clearly spent much time analysing the sayings of Jesus and his larger work opens with a list of about a hundred authentic words of Jesus, mainly consisting of parables and aphorisms (short pithy sayings). He compares his work to an archaeologist, sifting through various layers of tradition in an attempt to uncover the oldest deposit. He pays particular attention to the earliest sources, and uses only material multiply-attested in working out the earliest layer of tradition. Equally important is a reconstruction of society in Jesus' day. In a similar vein to Horsley, Crossan's reading of ancient sources is strongly informed by cross-cultural anthropology; he envisages Jesus as an illiterate peasant within an agrarian society dominated by patronage and exploitation.

Again in common with others in the Jesus Seminar, Crossan argues that Jesus was baptized by John the Baptist but later broke with him on two issues. First, Jesus proclaimed a *present* kingdom full of 'nobodies' – the destitute, beggars and expendables. Second, Jesus rejected the asceticism of his mentor, celebrating the kingdom through all-inclusive meals which, in their flagrant rejection of ordinary social conventions, underlined the openness and diversity of the new age which was beginning to dawn. Jesus was a sage, a wisdom teacher who offered an alternative to the patronal, non-egalitarian culture of his day. His miracles established him as a 'magician', a charismatic individual who challenged the exclusivity and even validity of official religion. The kingdom he proclaimed was not to be mediated by brokers (priests) or fixed locations (the Temple), but was one in which humans were directly in communion with God; Jesus' radically itinerant programme, with its refusal to make any one place central, was a powerful illustration of this.

Two aspects of Crossan's reconstruction are particularly noteworthy. First is his connection between Jesus and the Cynics, a group of Hellenistic philosophers who advocated a simple, itinerant life, with little time for ordinary social conventions or authority structures. Like other members of the Jesus Seminar, he imagines a strongly Hellenized Galilee and, even though there is no concrete evidence for the presence of Cynics in the region, he thinks it quite likely, especially in the larger cities. However, while Jesus' words might occasionally have been reminiscent of the Cynics (for example Mk 6.7-10 and pars.), his stress on complete dependence on God and the immediacy of a new age mark out his message as very different from theirs (and Crossan has withdrawn from this position to a large extent in his most recent writings). The second notable aspect of Crossan's work concerns his treatment of the passion narratives. Drawing on non-canonical texts, particularly the *Gospel of Peter*, he argues that the accounts of Jesus' last few hours contain virtually no historical details (see Chapter 2 for a fuller discussion). The only secure fact is Jesus' crucifixion, which followed swiftly on from his indignant outburst in the Temple. Although Jesus certainly challenged the Jewish Temple leadership, the Jewish trials in the Gospel reflect later church-synagogue antagonism and his execution was a purely Roman affair. Finally, like other victims of crucifixion, Jesus had no formal burial; the tomb traditions in the Gospels, then, are due to early Christian creativity.

Crossan has provided a rich and challenging portrait of Jesus, and a few short paragraphs cannot hope adequately to do justice to his many insights (or his sparkling prose). He has, of course, had his detractors:[25] while few would challenge the principle that older sources are usually the most historical, many are dubious about the particular ones that Crossan assigns to this early layer (particularly his arguments for earlier versions of the Gospels of *Thomas* and *Peter* and the decision to prioritize these above the Synoptics). His heavy-handed use of the criterion of multiple attestation has seemed unduly rigid to many, and not always consistent. Most do not see evidence of radical egalitarianism in Jesus' message; the appointment of twelve male disciples seems to run counter to such a proposal (not surprisingly, perhaps, Crossan doubts their historicity). And the removal of Jewish involvement in Jesus' death seems to many to be borne out of wishful thinking in a post-Holocaust world, rather than sound historical argument. Nonetheless, Crossan's work has posed important questions over sources and methods which those who follow after him are bound to address.

## David Flusser

A practicing Jew from Bohemia in the former Czech Republic, Flusser was Professor of Early Christianity and Judaism of the Second Temple Period at the Hebrew University of Jerusalem until his death in 2000. His work on Jesus was published in German in 1968, updated and translated into English in 1997, and rewritten and published in 2001 as *The Sage from Galilee: Rediscovering Jesus' Genius* (with help from his student and colleague, R. Steven Notley).

Flusser's Jesus was a well-educated Jewish carpenter. Although he was not an official scribe, it is quite possible that people called him *rabbi* (my teacher/master) to indicate his great learning in the Law. An ecstatic experience at his baptism by John convinced him that he had been set apart by God, chosen to proclaim salvation to the disadvantaged and the arrival of God's Kingdom. Throughout his ministry, Jesus preached only to Jews and remained thoroughly Law-observant. Most of his teaching, particularly concerning purity, morality and love, was shared by other moderate scribes. He had much in common with the Pharisees, his disputes with them demonstrating a typical clash between the charismatic holy man and more institutional religious leaders (the extreme hostilities reflected in the Gospels, Flusser argues, reflect Christian-synagogue controversies of a later period). Jesus had a strong messianic awareness, he argues, and saw himself as the prophet of the End Times, the superhuman Son of man, even God's Messiah. The Kingdom he preached would be fully consummated in the future, but was already being realized among his followers. In the end, it was the despised Sadducean leadership in Jerusalem who had Jesus executed. The night-time Jewish trial of Mark's gospel is a product of the evangelist's literary art; in reality, a 'temple committee' met to formulate the charges and a cruel but weak Pilate sent him to the cross as an agitator of the people and a messianic pretender.

Flusser treats the Gospels as broadly trustworthy. Aside from disputes with the Pharisees and the trial narratives, he makes little attempt to discern differing layers within the tradition. He regards the Synoptics, John and even rabbinic texts as useful sources (most Jesus scholars are wary of using the latter as they are notoriously difficult to date). Perhaps most problematic is Flusser's heavy use of Luke's gospel. He favours an unconventional solution to the Synoptic Problem in which Luke wrote first and was abbreviated by Mark, and Matthew subsequently drew on both works (there is, thus, no need for Q). Most scholars, however, regard Luke's gospel as relatively late and argue that the realized nature of much of the evangelist's kingdom language is due to the failure of the kingdom to materialize rather than the presence of authentic Jesus material. The real value of Flusser's work, though, is his attempt to ground Jesus' thinking within contemporary Jewish ideas of morality, God and love.

# J. P. Meier

Professor of New Testament at the University of Notre Dame and a Catholic priest, Meier's four-volume *Jesus: A Marginal Jew* is perhaps the lengthiest modern treatment of our subject. He sets himself the task of providing a consensus view of Jesus, accepting as authentic only material that an imaginary 'unpapal conclave' of scholars – a Catholic, a Protestant, a Jew and an agnostic – would agree upon. Reviews of Meier's work are peppered with terms such as 'judicious', 'meticulous' and 'cautious'. He delights in details, and has provided probably the most thorough analysis of the chronology of Jesus' life (he argues that Jesus was born some time between 7–4 BCE, and that his ministry lasted from 28–30 CE). He is sceptical of the value of most non-canonical texts and largely bases his reconstruction on the Synoptics, though appeal is often made to John (including some of the latter's miracles).

Meier's Jesus has much in common with Sanders's Jesus. The Galilean prophet moved away from John the Baptist's announcement of God's imminent fiery judgement to God's offer of mercy and forgiveness (demonstrated by healings and open table-fellowship with sinners). Yet he never abandoned the message of a coming day of reckoning; he proclaimed the restoration of Israel and he acted as an apocalyptic prophet rather than a social revolutionary. Unlike Sanders, however, Meier's Jesus did assume the right to rescind and change parts of the Law on his own authority, an activity which led to controversies with Pharisees and religious leaders of his day. In the end, it was his staged entry into Jerusalem and the Temple demonstration which led to Jesus' death. Jesus was 'marginal' for Meier in the sense that he was insignificant in the estimation of his contemporaries, in following his prophetic commission rather than his carpenter's trade, and in his lifestyle and preaching, which caused others to regard him as dangerous.

Most critiques of Meier's work have centred on his method.[26] Rather like the Jesus Seminar, he works from the ground up, establishing a core of reliable tradition rather than starting with a broader working hypothesis. Authentic material is discerned through a number of criteria, many of which are familiar from the New Quest: dissimilarity, multiple attestation and coherence. To this he adds the criterion of embarrassment (which accepts material which the early Christians might have preferred not to be there, such as Jesus' baptism 'for the forgiveness of sins', his association with sinners or his difficult relations with his family) and the criterion of rejection and execution (which allows as genuine traditions which explain the ways in which Jesus alienated powerful people). In all of this, Meier's work is open to the challenges that are levelled against any such use of criteria (see the earlier discussion of the New Quest). Some, too, question whether the historical–critical method can ever provide a reliable 'scientific' and 'objective' body of material. To most, though, Meier's work stands as a testament to careful and detailed scholarship.

## N. T. Wright

A former bishop of Durham, British New Testament scholar Tom Wright is currently Professor of New Testament and Early Christianity at the University of St Andrews. His fullest portrait of Jesus can be found in *Jesus and the Victory of God* (1996; the second in a five-volume series on Christian origins), along with a number of more popular studies.

Like others, Wright sees Jesus as a Jewish prophet, announcing and inaugurating the Kingdom of God. Most first-century Jews, he claims, saw themselves as still living in exile. Jesus proclaimed that God would defeat Israel's enemies, return to Jerusalem and bring the exile to an end. He challenged his hearers to repent, to join him in a new covenant and to become the new people of God. In exchange for the old symbols of death and exile (fasting and purity codes), Jesus proposed new ones celebrating the reign of God (forgiveness, blessing and love). Wright's Jesus saw himself as the Messiah (albeit in a rather new way), replaced adherence to the Temple and Torah with allegiance to himself, and understood himself as the embodiment of Israel's God. Not surprisingly, perhaps, Jesus' message got him into trouble with the Pharisees who, Wright claims, were particularly concerned with guaranteeing Israel's distinctive identity in the face of Gentile rule. In the end, though, it was the Jerusalem authorities who persuaded a reluctant Pilate to send him to the cross. Jesus died as Israel's representative – by taking God's wrath on himself he broke the power of Satan and brought the exile to an end.

A number of features distinguish Wright's work. First, like most other Third Quest historians, he eschews microscopic study of individual sayings in favour of the bigger picture, a grand narrative. He first produces his hypothesis, then proceeds to attempt to verify it. He aims to include as much of the data as possible, with little attempt to unpick the differing layers within the tradition. The result, unsurprisingly, is a portrait of Jesus very close to the synoptic Gospels on which it is based. Second, Wright offers a novel understanding of Jesus' eschatology. What Jesus predicted, Wright asserts, was not a cataclysmic, cosmic upheaval but the national disaster of 70 CE, in which the Romans destroyed Jerusalem and its Temple. Furthermore, certain 'Son of man' sayings foretell not Jesus' Second Coming at an unspecified future date but his *ascent* to heaven, where he now shares the throne of God. Jesus, then, was correct in his predictions; everything he foretold did, in fact, come true. Finally, Wright is much more concerned with the Resurrection than most historical Jesus scholars, and has recently devoted an 800-page book to arguing that Jesus was raised bodily from the grave.

In certain respects, Wright's methodology signals an advance in historical Jesus work. He develops what he calls the 'criteria of double dissimilarity and similarity', by which he means that elements within his reconstruction need to be credible both within first-century Judaism and also to have a connection (albeit in an undeveloped form) with later developments in the early church. Thus, he avoids the 'disembodied' or 'de-contextualized' Jesus of the New Quest, and ensures that the movement following Jesus has some connection with its leader. Other aspects of his method, however, have been criticized. His 'maximal' approach to the sources has led some to see his reconstruction as an exercise in biblical Christology rather than history. Others have challenged his portrait of first-century Judaism, particularly his contention that Jews in Palestine regarded themselves as still in exile, and his characterization of the Pharisees as nationalists. Furthermore, it is difficult to see why Jerusalem needed to fall if Jesus had already taken the nation's sin on himself, and many would dispute Wright's reading of the Son of man passages.[27] Still, Wright's erudite prose is a delight to read, he does not shy away from difficult theological or philosophical matters, and his portrait of Jesus provides a welcome alternative – particularly for his fellow evangelical Christians – to the more sceptical Jesus books currently on the market.

# J. D. G. Dunn

Jimmy Dunn was Lightfoot Professor of Divinity at the University of Durham until his retirement in 2003. Although the historical Jesus features in many of his publications, the fullest account can be found in *Jesus Remembered* (2003), the first of his three-volume *Christianity in the Making*.

The most distinctive aspect of Dunn's work is his stress on *oral traditions*. The material preserved in the Gospels, he argues, broadly reflects the impact Jesus made on his *first disciples* (not just after the Resurrection), and was given its essential shape through oral performance and retelling within the earliest Christian communities, an oral transmission which combined both stability (regarding the main points) and flexibility (regarding details). Rather than analysing the historicity of individual sayings and events, he constructs his portrait of the historical Jesus from regular emphases and motifs within the (largely Synoptic) tradition. His Jesus emerged from the Baptist's movement, preaching the arrival of an imminent Kingdom/Kingship of God, the renewal of Israel, and a return to the nation's covenant loyalties. He called on his listeners to repent and to live already as subjects of the Kingdom – to practice forgiveness, acceptance and gratitude to their heavenly father. All unnecessary boundaries were to be swept away, including those set up by over-scrupulous religious groups, and the reign of God found concrete expression through images of a new family and an open table. Jesus' activities had already marked him out as a troublemaker, but it was during his last visit to Jerusalem that the chief priests, regarding him as a threat to the Temple, the cult and themselves, passed him to Pilate for summary execution. Although some of his disciples questioned whether he was the royal messiah of Jewish expectation during his lifetime, this was a title Jesus rejected. Instead, he creatively reinterpreted the category of messiah in his own terms through Scriptural images and the more intimate language of sonship.

Dunn's portrait is largely a traditional one. Where he has been criticized most often is in his use of orality. While all accept the presence of an oral period, questions emerge over how we understand the flow of tradition, how fixed or stable it might have been within the earliest communities, and the relationship between individual and collective memories. Dunn bases himself largely on Kenneth Bailey's work drawn from Middle Eastern societies, though the latter's findings have been challenged by some. Others point out that, while Dunn argues that we cannot go beyond the remembered Jesus, he spends a great deal of time on the historical man behind the memories.[28] Nevertheless, Dunn has provided a credible account and his stress on the impact made by Jesus and the role of memory within the tradition is certainly significant.

## *Dale Allison*

The Professor of New Testament Exegesis and Early Christianity at Pittsburgh Theological Seminary has made significant contributions to Jesus research in a number of important areas. First, his most recent book, *Constructing Jesus: Memory, Imagination and History* (2010), includes a fascinating study of human memory. Drawing on a wealth of social–scientific analyses, he argues that observers tend to retain the gist of what was said or done but not the specifics. We are programmed to fill in the gaps, to make sense of what we see in light of later information, to blur several events into one, and to retell our memories differently according to diverging situations. Thus, we are on better grounds when we appeal to the *general storyline* of the Gospels – motifs, recurring themes and broad contours – rather than precise details. He goes further than Dunn, then, in worrying not only about the process of transmission but the memories of the eyewitnesses themselves. The implication of this is that the standard 'criteria of authenticity' are unlikely to be able to determine with any accuracy whether a saying does, in fact, go back to Jesus; most of the time, we simply cannot tell. Rather like Dunn, Allison prefers to follow the general impressions left in the records rather than analyse individual units. His approach is to start with a catalogue of everything relating to a particular topic; even if some elements are very likely to be secondary, he argues, the general gist of the tradition may well preserve an accurate memory of what the historical Jesus said and did. In common with a number of other Third Quest scholars, then, he starts with a broad reconstruction of the 'big picture', then goes on to test whether that offers the best explanation for specific details.

The broader picture that Allison finds most plausible is one in which Jesus emerges as an apocalyptic prophet. His *Jesus of Nazareth: Millenarian Prophet* (1998) draws on comparative religions and millenarian movements, arguing that even apparently contradictory elements within the tradition (such as a concern for society and ethics) are frequently found within apocalyptic groups. Allison's Jesus saw himself as the Herald of Is 63.1–3, as the expected prophet like Moses (Deut 18.15–18) and as the Baptist's Coming One. He expected to rule the Kingdom on God's behalf and was executed by Pilate for his kingly pretensions. Once again, Allison's portrait has its detractors, particularly those who argue for a non-apocalyptic Jesus.[29] His work on memory, though, is both commonsensical and compelling, and may well have sounded the death-knell for reconstructions based on a handful of details selected through criteria of authenticity.

The above reconstructions have revealed a number of unresolved tensions within modern Jesus scholarship.

1   Most basic, perhaps, is the question of *sources*. What sources a scholar relies on fundamentally affects the picture of Jesus which emerges. The Jesus of Sanders, Wright, Dunn and

Allison looks rather like the Synoptic portrait on which it is based. Adding John produces some differences (a lengthier ministry, a longer period of contact with John the Baptist), but a Jesus still recognizable within ecclesiastical circles. Once the *Gos.Th* is added, Jesus' death becomes less important, his teaching begins to acquire a decidedly 'gnostic' tone and the resultant portrait becomes less immediately recognizable.

2  What was Galilee like in the time of Jesus? Were the inhabitants economically drained and disenfranchised by their local rulers, or was reality less oppressive? Was the region Hellenized enough for Cynic ideas to be well known, or had Greek thought barely penetrated the largely rural region? And did Galileans, like their Judaean neighbours, privilege Torah and Temple, or did they cultivate their own distinctive ways of being Jewish?

3  How did Jesus fit in with other contemporary charismatic holy men and popular prophets? Did he correspond to a known 'type', or was his ministry more distinctive? And did Jesus see himself as Messiah in any way?

4  Did Jesus hold an *apocalyptic* outlook? Put differently, did he announce the cataclysmic end of this age, the imminent arrival of God as judge and the establishment of the Kingdom of God? Or is he better categorized as a prophet of social change, offering his own vision of society transformed in the present? And are the two mutually exclusive?

5  How historically reliable are the Gospel passion narratives? Do they rest on dependable memories, or are they largely post-Easter fabrications? To what extent were Jewish authorities involved in the death of Jesus? And why, in the end, was Jesus executed on a Roman cross?

These tensions will all be explored in subsequent chapters of this book, beginning in the next chapter with the all-important question of sources. Do any contemporary writers mention Jesus? And how valuable is their testimony?

# CHAPTER TWO

# Sources for the historical Jesus

As far as we are aware, Jesus left no first-hand trace in the historical record: no letters, no diaries, no inscriptions. All reconstructions, therefore, have to depend on literary sources written by others. But which ones? We saw in the last chapter that Jesus scholars have traditionally relied on the synoptic Gospels (Matthew, Mark and Luke), where the shared outlook between these accounts makes producing a coherent narrative reasonably straightforward. Recent scholarship, however, has seen an increasing openness to other sources. Least controversial perhaps is John's gospel, while a number of (often North American) reconstructions have drawn on more contentious works: Q, the *Gospel of Thomas* and the *Gospel of Peter*. Appeal to these sources, particularly as *major* components of the tradition, inevitably produces a radically different picture of Jesus. The question is: what claim to historicity do these texts have? And is their claim any greater than that of the Synoptics?

In this chapter, I shall start by looking briefly at what *outsiders* (Romans and Jews) said about Jesus, before turning to accounts by *insiders* (Christian writers both inside and outside the New Testament). Throughout our enquiry, questions of date and bias will be crucial.

## Roman authors on Jesus

It can come as something of a surprise to realise that no Roman author seems to have taken much notice of Jesus until the early

second century. Our earliest reference comes from the pen of the
Roman provincial governor and historian Tacitus. Describing
Nero's brutal persecution of Christians after the great fire of
Rome in the mid-60s CE, he explains that the victims 'took their
name from *Christus* [i.e. Christ] who was executed in the reign
of Tiberius by the procurator Pontius Pilate' (*Annals* 15.44.3).
Quite possibly, Tacitus learnt about Christians from his close
friend Pliny the Younger, who had cause to investigate Christian
activity as governor of Bithynia (*Epistles* 10.96), or maybe he
picked up this rather basic piece of information from Christian
preachers in Rome. In either case, however, while Tacitus's comment reinforces what we know from the Gospels, he adds no new
information.

Of even less use is our second Roman writer, the lawyer Suetonius,
who appears to have referred to Jesus in his *Lives of the Caesars*
(c. 120 CE). Explaining the reasons for an expulsion of Jews from
Rome in the 40s, Suetonius wrote: 'Since the Jews constantly made
disturbances at the instigation of Chrestus, he [Claudius] expelled
them from Rome.'[1] Suetonius seems to have been under the impression that a series of synagogue riots were caused by a troublemaker
with the common name Chrestus. More likely, however, the trou-
bles arose in synagogues where Christian missionaries preached
about the similar sounding 'Christus' and were met with opposition and hostility by their hosts. If so, Suetonius's information witnesses to Christian activity in Rome in the 40s, but does not help
to reconstruct the man in whose name they preached.

Roman authors, then, do not prove particularly useful in our
quest. This, though, is not surprising. We should hardly expect
a provincial of Jesus' status to have made much of an impact on
elite circles in Rome. As Robert Van Voorst notes, these writers
only started to take an interest once Christianity was beginning
to make reasonable numbers of converts and when it started to be
in a position to threaten the peace and stability of Rome and its
provinces. Even then, the historians of the Empire were much more
concerned with Christianity as it was in their own day, rather than
in the founder of the movement. Pliny the Younger, for example,
while supplying a number of interesting details about Christians
in Bithynia, is completely silent regarding Jesus. To most elite
Romans, Christianity was nothing but a foreign, depraved superstition; it was important to monitor the activities of its adherents,

but genuine inquiry into its origins would have been considered inappropriate or even suspicious.[2]

## Jewish authors on Jesus

Strangely, perhaps, non-Christian Jewish sources also turn out to have little to say about Jesus. Contrary to much popular belief, there are no references to him in the Dead Sea Scrolls. Rabbinic writings, too, contain only a handful of highly negative references to Jesus and his family, most dating to the fourth century or later. Quite clearly, there were a number of (possibly oral) stories in circulation which aimed at discrediting Jesus. Some of these were used by the pagan writer Celsus (whose claims we will look at in Chapter 3) but, in general, Jewish writers – like Romans – had other matters to occupy their interests and only took notice of Jesus once Christianity became a threat. Two Jewish references, though, are worth pausing to consider.

The most famous rabbinic reference to Jesus is found in a passage possibly dating to the third century CE and now part of the Babylonian Talmud. Known as b.sanh 43a it reads:

> It was taught: On the day before Passover they hanged Jesus. A herald went before him for forty days [proclaiming], 'He will be stoned, because he practiced magic and enticed Israel to go astray. Let anyone who knows anything in his favour come forward and plead for him.' But nothing was found in his favour, and they hanged him on the day before the Passover.

The striking element in this paragraph is the insistence that there was a long and exhaustive search for witnesses between Jesus' arrest and execution. There is no attempt to deny Jewish involvement in Jesus' death, in fact quite the reverse – the Jewish leaders seem to be in charge of the whole process, right down to the eventual 'hanging' (a common euphemism in Jewish texts for crucifixion). This contrasts strongly with the Markan–Matthean trial narratives, which describe an illegal and secretive night-time meeting at which 'false-witnesses' were prevailed upon to secure a conviction. As Van Voorst notes: 'this short narrative seems to be an inner-Jewish explanation and justification of how one famous criminal, Jesus of Nazareth, was put to death, and implicitly a warning to stay away from his movement'.[3] Interestingly, too, the passage shows that Jesus was widely regarded as a miracle worker, though in the eyes of his opponents this is seen as 'practicing magic'. There may be no new information here, but the text does seem to reinforce the Gospels' insistence that leading Jews were influential in Jesus' arrest, that he was believed to have miraculous abilities and that he was accused of enticing Israel to go astray (see Lk 23.2, 5, 14).

More revealing still is the famous paragraph known as the *Testimonium Flavianum*, written by Flavius Josephus (born 37 CE), a Palestinian Jew who defected to the Roman side during the war with Rome (66–70 CE) and spent his later years recording the great and glorious history of his native people. In the latter part of his *Antiquities of the Jews* (written around 95 CE), he gives a brief summary of the life, death and Resurrection of Jesus, though nearly all commentators are agreed that the present text cannot be what Josephus actually wrote:

> About this time there lived Jesus, a wise man, *if indeed one ought to call him a man*. For he was one who wrought surprising feats and was a teacher of such people as accept the truth gladly. He won over many Jews and many of the Greeks. *He was the Messiah*. When Pilate, upon hearing him accused by men of the highest standing amongst us, had condemned him to be crucified, those who had in the first place come to love him did not give up their affection for him. *On the third day he appeared to them restored to life, for the prophets of God had prophesied these and countless other marvellous things about him.* And the tribe of the Christians, so called after him, has still to this day not disappeared [Italics added]. (*Antiquities* 18.63–64)[4]

Josephus was not a Christian and it is highly unlikely that he could have written the sentences in italics. While some have argued that the whole paragraph is an insertion, it seems more likely that it has simply been altered by Christian copyists. Later on in the same work, Josephus refers to 'the brother of Jesus who is called the Christ' (*Ant.* 20.20), a phrase which seems to suggest either that Jesus was well known to Josephus' readers or, more probably, that he had referred to him earlier in the work. Origen, writing about 280 CE, stated quite explicitly that Josephus did not believe Jesus to be the Christ (a view he surely could not have held had he known the above paragraph in its present form). By about 324 CE, however, Eusebius knew the passage as we have it, suggesting that it was altered sometime around 300 CE. Unfortunately, our earliest manuscripts of Josephus date to the eleventh century, and since his works were preserved exclusively by Christians (Jews regarded him as a traitor), there is little chance of ever finding an 'untampered' manuscript.[5]

But how far did the scribes go in their rewriting of this paragraph? A widely held view nowadays is that Christian alterations may have been fairly minimal. Once the more explicitly Christian passages are omitted (the ones in italics above), the remainder of the text may well go back to Josephus. The language generally is Josephan and there are some features which would seem unlikely to have come from a Christian scribe (for example the reference to Jesus winning over both Jews and Gentiles during his lifetime – would a Christian make such a mistake? – and the reference to Christians as a 'tribe'). It is also possible, of course, that later editors have *omitted* sections. The context of the paragraph is a series of tumults in the time of Pontius Pilate; Josephus' larger point is to show that upheaval beset both Palestine and even Rome itself at this period. It is quite possible that the original version included an account of a riot (perhaps the incident in the Temple?) which was quietly deleted. The description, however, could not have been too hostile towards Jesus, otherwise it is difficult to account for Josephus's popularity amongst early Christians. In all probability, Josephus's attitude was fairly neutral, not dissimilar perhaps to his assessment of John the Baptist, which is broadly neutral to positive (*Ant.* 18.116-9; see Chapter 6 below).

Once again, Josephus adds no new information, but does confirm what we have in the Gospels: that Jesus belonged to a Palestinian context, that he was widely regarded as a miracle worker and teacher, that he was handed over by Jewish leaders and crucified by Pontius Pilate, and that his followers continued to support him after his death. The fact that some of the language is not what we would associate with Christians may suggest that Josephus's information derives from Jewish sources, possibly in Jerusalem. It would have been extremely useful to have had an 'untampered' first-century Jewish account of Jesus, though, of course, this would have required equally critical handling as Christian testimony. In the end, then, Jewish sources do not really get us very far;

reconstructions of the life of Jesus are almost entirely dependent on literature written by his followers. In the following discussion, I shall begin with Christian texts outside the New Testament.

# Christian authors on Jesus

## Non-canonical texts

The label 'non-canonical' refers to a wide body of literature. Some sayings of Jesus are preserved in the writings of the church fathers (usually referred to as 'agrapha'[6]), though it is not always easy to judge their historical reliability. Manuscript variants, too, which did not make it into the final canon of the New Testament might also come under this heading.[7] Of most potential interest, however, are the so-called 'apocryphal gospels'.

Christian apocryphal literature includes a wide variety of gospels, mainly dating to the second century or later. In theory, of course, even later texts may contain older traditions, but closer inspection shows that, in the main, this is not the case. There are infancy gospels, such as the *Infancy Gospel of James*, which supplies many legendary details relating to Jesus' birth, or the *Infancy Gospel of Thomas*, where Jesus as an infant exhibits superhuman knowledge and power. At the other end of Jesus' life there are several letters from Pilate to various emperors outlining Jesus' trial and death. Justin Martyr in the second century referred to the 'Acts of Pilate', presumably an account of Jesus' trial before the Roman prefect (*Apol.* 1.35.8–9, 48.2–3). Whether such a document was ever produced is highly unlikely – Roman governors were not in the habit of sending reports to Rome on every provincial crucifixion. The extant *Acts of Pilate* (now part of the *Gospel of Nicodemus*) is a fictitious document, dating to the fourth or fifth centuries and exhibiting a later Christian desire to place responsibility for the death of Jesus on a variety of Jews and to exonerate Pilate. While these texts are a fascinating window onto Christian piety in the first few centuries, they are generally no help in our search for the founder of their faith.[8]

Two of these texts, however, have come to some prominence lately, particularly in the work of the Jesus Seminar and J. D. Crossan, and deserve greater attention: the *Gospel of Peter* and the

*Gospel of Thomas.* I have also included discussion of the sayings source Q at this point. Not that Q is non-canonical – by definition it is the body of material common to both Matthew and Luke but not in Mark – but the study of Q raises similar issues to non-canonical texts and so is best treated here.

## The Gospel of Peter

Only a fragment of *Gos.Pet* now remains. It describes the trial of Jesus from just after Pilate washed his hands (see Mt 27.24) through to a miraculous account of the Resurrection and its aftermath. Our sole surviving copy was found by French archaeologists excavating a Christian cemetery in Pannopolis (modern Akhmim, on the eastern bank of the Nile, 250 miles south of Cairo) in 1886–1887. The fragment was found in a monk's tomb, as part of a codex containing a number of other early Christian texts and has been dated, on the basis of its handwriting, to the eighth century, though it is clearly a copy of a much older work. As the narrator refers to himself as Peter (14.60), it has plausibly been suggested that it is part of the *Gos.Pet* which circulated in Syria in the late-second century. Eusebius of Caesarea (c. 260–340) refers to it twice, noting both that it was not accepted by Catholic tradition and that it was used by Docetists (those who thought that Jesus only *seemed* to be human), though it did not appear to have been Docetic itself (*Hist. Ecc.* 3.3.2, 6.12.1–6). In its present state, it is clearly a popularizing account: it has close affinities with the canonical Gospels, contains novelistic features (including a talking cross!), heightens the miraculous, is determinedly anti-Jewish, and exhibits a number of anachronistic and devotional touches. Like other apocryphal gospels, it is a work of popular piety with little in the way of theological sophistication.[9]

Why, then, has the *Gos.Pet* come to prominence in Jesus research? The reason is largely due to J. D. Crossan's suggestion that behind our *Gos.Pet* lies a much older gospel. Crossan argues that the earliest followers of Jesus knew only that their master had been arrested and later crucified. All the details of Jesus' last few hours rest not on historical recollections of what actually happened, but on 'prophecy historicized'. That is, details of Jesus' death were drawn not from historical memory but through the blending into a coherent narrative of scriptural themes and passages, particularly those from the Psalms,

Isaiah and the scapegoat ritual.[10] By the late 40s CE, this scripturally inspired account was written down in what Crossan calls the *Cross Gospel*, a narrative which formed the basis of the passion narratives in all four canonical Gospels, before itself being revised in the light of the canonical Gospels some time in the second century and producing what we now know as the *Gos.Pet*. There are two important points here. First, if Crossan is correct, it would mean that all four canonical Gospels depend on an account of Jesus' trial and death which itself has no historical value – a contention which allows Crossan to disregard the passion narratives in his historical reconstruction. Second, the major editorial change in the transformation of the *Cross Gospel* into the *Gos.Pet* was the fact that the original account had Jesus buried by enemies, while the *Gos.Pet* amended that (in line with the canonical Gospels) into burial by his friends – a contention which underscores Crossan's argument that the empty tomb and Resurrection traditions are late developments.

It is fair to say that Crossan's arguments have not won widespread scholarly approval. His decisions as to what to assign to the *Cross Gospel* seem in the end to be a little arbitrary. While it is undeniably the case that the canonical Gospels have been *influenced* by scriptural passages, it is quite a different matter to prove that the entire passion narrative has been *created* from allusions and themes. Furthermore, to assume that all four canonical passion narratives were inspired by one written text (however early) does not seem to give enough attention to what must have been a vast number of oral traditions and competing interpretations of Jesus' last few hours. The majority of scholars, then, continue to regard the *Gos.Pet* as a later work, largely inspired by the canonical Gospels, with no historical significance.

## The Gospel of Thomas.

Rather like the *Gos.Pet*, the *Gos.Th* fell out of use in the early church, only to surface once again in modern times. A number of Greek fragments were found at Oxyrhynchus in Egypt around the turn of the twentieth century (P.Oxy 1, 654, 655), followed by a full text in Coptic (a late form of Egyptian) as part of the Nag Hammadi library in 1945. The work claims to be the work of Didymus Judas Thomas, or Thomas the Twin. Though it is called a gospel, the *Gos.Th* is very different from those contained in the

New Testament: there is no biographical information, no passion narrative, no Christological titles and much less apocalyptic material. Instead, the Coptic version (which is presumably a translation from the Greek) contains 114 unconnected sayings of Jesus, arranged seemingly by catchword. Most are wisdom sayings, parables and short dialogues. Roughly a quarter of these sayings are almost identical to ones in the synoptic Gospels (the Greek of *Gos.Th* 5, for example, parallels Lk 8.17 precisely), half have some similarities, and the remainder have what has seemed to many to be gnostic overtones (a particular preoccupation with knowledge, inner transformation and secret teachings; *Gos.Th* 28 is a particularly striking example). In its present form, the *Gos.Th* is probably a second-century work, often linked to Syria (a region with particular connections to Thomas). The question is: does it contain older traditions? And if so, which are the most authentic – those in the synoptic Gospels, or those in Thomas?

The *Gos.Th* has come to the forefront of Jesus research in recent decades largely due to the work of H. Koester and those associated with the Jesus Seminar, who have elevated the work to the status of a 'fifth gospel' (see chapter 1).[11] Basing his study on the *genre* of *Gos. Th*, Koester argued that the work belongs to the very earliest type of Christian literature, the 'wisdom book', with affinities to Jewish works such as Proverbs, Ben Sira, the Wisdom of Solomon and gospel sources such as Q (see below). Jesus is presented as a sage, speaking with the wisdom of heavenly Sophia. Those who compiled *Gos.Th* imagined that salvation was through hearing Jesus' words and taking them to heart rather than through his atoning death (which Koester sees as a later Pauline development). Much of the gospel is said to be very old, some of it possibly going back to the 50s, and possibly originating in Palestine amongst itinerant groups of Christian radicals who, like their master, rejected wealth and a conventional lifestyle.

Two important points emerge from this position. First, if many of the sayings in the *G.Th* predate the synoptic Gospels, perhaps even their sources, then the work may well contain more authentic sayings than those in the canonical Gospels.[12] Second, if we assume that the theological outlook of the earliest compilers was broadly in line with that of their master, then a very different picture of the historical Jesus begins to emerge, one in which he is seen primarily as a wisdom teacher rather than a prophet or apocalyptic visionary. This, in fact, lies at the basis of the reconstructions of both the

Jesus Seminar and Crossan, and their insistence that apocalyptic elements are a later addition to the tradition.

These views, however, have not won universal acceptance. The majority of scholars still regard *Gos.Th* as a late composition, often reflecting later strands of canonical material, such as John's gospel or Matthean and Lukan redaction of Mark. Even where the gospel appears to represent a more original form of a saying or tradition than does the canonical version (such as the parable of the wicked tenants in the vineyard in *Gos.Th* 65, which lacks the allegorical interpretation of Mk 12.1–9), it is difficult to know how to develop criteria to test this with any degree of accuracy. Most argue that the relative scarcity of apocalyptic sayings in *Gos.Th* is better explained by the delay of the kingdom and the later rewriting of the tradition, rather than as a reflection of an early sage-like Jesus. The second-century compilers of *Gos.Th*, facing the lack of fulfilment of these sayings, readily de-eschatologized Jesus' teaching, focussing on the present reality of the Kingdom, and moving in a gnostic or mystical direction.[13] The *Gos.Th*, then, though possibly containing one or two older forms of Jesus' sayings, is not to be regarded as a major source for the life of Jesus, still less a Jesus radically different from that of the synoptic Gospels.

## The sayings source Q

As we saw in Chapter 1, Q is a central element in the 'Two Document Hypothesis', the theory seeking to explain the verbal similarities within the synoptic Gospels. The theory suggests that Matthew and Luke drew on Mark's gospel and another source, Q. The high degree of verbal similarities and order within Matthew and Luke's shared material suggests that Q was a *written* document rather than a collection of oral material. No copy of Q has ever been found, but the hypothesis is a strong one, and for the majority of New Testament scholars provides the best explanation of the literary parallels within the synoptic Gospels.

Recent decades have seen an explosion of interest in Q. Clearly, the document predates both Matthew and Luke (both written perhaps in the 80s) and may well be as old or even older than Mark. Although there is much room for uncertainty, there is a reasonable degree of agreement among scholars in terms of the extent, content and order of the document. A critical edition of Q was published in 2000 under the auspices of the Society of Biblical Literature's International Q Project.[14] The reconstructed document has similarities with *Gos.Th* in that both are collections of sayings with no passion narrative (both Matthew and Luke appear to follow Mark at this point). The most influential analyses of Q are the detailed studies by John Kloppenborg. He argues, on literary grounds, that the earliest layer of Q contains wisdom material, dealing with a range of human interactions. Later on, material containing woes and judgement was added (perhaps in response to opponents who failed to join the Q group). A third, redactional layer, in which the Temple and Torah appear in a positive light, completed the document shortly after 70 CE.[15]

What help, then, is Q in reconstructing the historical Jesus? J. D. Crossan and the Jesus Seminar have dated the earliest wisdom layer to the 50s CE, and assumed on that basis that Jesus is best characterized as a wisdom teacher or sage.[16] The fact that there is no passion narrative in Q persuades them that this was a Christian group with no interest in Jesus' death (on both of these points there are similarities between their use of Q and *Gos.Th*). But few have been convinced by these arguments. Kloppenborg has emphasized that his study was a *literary* investigation, and that the presence of an early document which presents Jesus as a wisdom teacher should not necessarily be privileged over other portraits. There is no reason to assume that material from the secondary layer (specifically apocalyptic elements) are later developments; they simply did not fit into the argument of Q's first stage. Similarly, he notes that 'it would be absurd to suppose that those who framed Q were unaware of Jesus' death'; they may have understood his death differently, but it is difficult to imagine any early Christian group which was not focussed primarily on Jesus' death and Resurrection.[17] At a more basic level, others have expressed doubts as to whether detailed redactional work is possible on a document which is no longer extant, and a significant minority of scholars doubt the existence of Q, preferring to explain the literary relationship between the gospels without recourse to a hypothetical document (Sanders and Wright, for example, do not privilege material commonly assigned to Q).[18]

What then is Q's significance? Clearly, the document is early and, so, of comparable historical value to Mark's gospel. Both what is contained in, and omitted from, Q needs to be given particular attention. In the end, though, precise decisions over Q do not need to detain us long. Although I have grouped Q with non-canonical literature, all the material connected with it is scattered throughout Matthew and Luke, that is, firmly within the New Testament itself. To this body of literature we shall now turn, focussing first on the apostle Paul.

## New Testament Literature

### Paul

The earliest sections of the New Testament are the letters of Paul, dating to the 50s CE. The great apostle joined the new movement only a couple of years after Jesus' crucifixion, and although he does not seem to have met Jesus personally, he did meet the leading apostles and Jesus' brothers on more than one occasion (Gal 1.18–2.21). Despite this, Paul has little to say regarding Jesus' earthly life: he knew he was Jewish (Gal 4.4, Rom 1.3), that he had brothers (1Cor 9.5, Gal 1.19), that he was remembered for his 'meekness and gentleness' (2Cor 10.1), and that he was betrayed (1Cor 11.23–5). He frequently refers to Jesus' crucifixion (1Cor 1.23, 2.2, Gal 3.1 etc) and once (in a disputed passage) puts responsibility for his death on 'you Jews' (1Thess 2.15). Paul recounts the institution of the Lord's Supper (1Cor 11.23–5) and occasionally mentions aspects of Jesus' teaching: divorce (1Cor 7.10-11), the right of Christian missionaries to claim support (1Cor 9.14) and possibly on eschatology (1Thess 4.15-17). All this does not amount to a great deal. Quite possibly, Paul had outlined the life, ministry and teaching of Jesus to his new converts when he was with them, and his letters, arising out of pastoral or theological difficulties, did not need a further rehearsal of these particular details. But it is clear that, for Paul, the cross and Resurrection were what really mattered; such was his stress on the atoning significance of the cross that details of Jesus' life simply paled into insignificance.

It was left to the canonical Gospels, beginning with Mark around 70 CE, to provide a biographical account of Jesus' life and ministry. These remain our best sources for the historical Jesus. Mark's gospel is usually dated to around about 70 CE, Matthew and Luke to 80–90 CE, and John to some time before the close of the first century. Judged by the standards of ancient history

generally, documents written 40 to 70 years after the death of their
subject can be considered reasonably contemporary. After two centuries of critical biblical scholarship, however, the pitfalls in using
the gospels uncritically are only too clear.

## John's Gospel

Ever since D. F. Strauss and F. C. Baur argued against the historical reliability of John in the nineteenth century, the fourth Gospel
has tended to be sidelined in historical Jesus research. In many
respects, this is hardly surprising. John's miracles are greater than
anything in the Synoptics: the man at the pool of Bethesda, for
example, had been ill for 38 years (Jn 5.5), while Lazarus had
been in the tomb for four days (Jn 11.17)! The pithy sayings and
Kingdom parables familiar from the Synoptics have given way in
John to extended discourses on the person of Jesus articulated
in distinctive Johannine terms. Throughout, Jesus engages in
dialogue not with a range of Pharisees, Sadducees, scribes and
Herodians, but with an amorphous group known as 'the Jews',
who have become almost a cipher for unbelief and rejection. And
for John, Jesus is not simply a Galilean carpenter, but God himself, the divine Word who descends to the earth for a short time
to reveal the Father to those who live in darkness. Small wonder,
perhaps, that the form critics, the 'New Questers' and the majority of recent studies have almost completely ignored John. Indeed,
the Jesus Seminar see more of historical value in the *Gos.Th* than
in John!

Yet not everyone would dismiss John as historically worth-
less. C. H. Dodd in the 1960s argued for the presence of historical traditions in John, as has D. Moody Smith more recently.[19]
A current Society of Biblical Literature project on 'John, Jesus
and History' has addressed the question with renewed vigour,
and J. P. Meier and P. Fredriksen have produced books on Jesus
which do take certain Johannine traditions seriously.[20] Although
few scholars would want to argue for much historical material in
John's *discourses*, there are arguably solid traditions in the narrative sections. Some have favoured John's longer ministry, the
more complex involvement with John the Baptist and his dating
of the crucifixion. While I would not wish to place too great a
reliance on John, it does seem to me that John has a good grasp

of the realities of first-century Judaea and his account of Jesus' trial in front of the Jewish authorities, as we shall see, has a certain degree of historical plausibility. For the remaining elements of Jesus' life, however, we are largely dependent on the Synoptics. But how should we use them?

## Synoptic Gospels

Like John, the Synoptics were written at the end of the first century and clearly reflect the post-Easter reflections of the early church. They were not written by eye-witnesses, nor are they *primarily* historical accounts of the life of Jesus (though they are presented in biographical form).[21] Instead, they are declarations of the true identity of Jesus as Christ and Son of God, written with the intention of encouraging or strengthening the faith of their earliest readers. Each presents a subtly different portrait of Jesus. For Mark, Jesus is the suffering Messiah, the Son of man who is crucified and later vindicated by God. Matthew's Jesus is the Jewish Messiah, the Son of David and a new Moses. And Luke's Jesus is a prophet, like those of Israel's past, who dies as an innocent martyr. However, even if their details vary, the *broad contours* of the Synoptic portrait – Jesus' link to John the Baptist, his preaching the Kingdom of God, his healing ministry and his death on a Roman cross – seem to be historically grounded. When used with caution, the Synoptics provide our best sources for recovering the historical Jesus.

When we are sifting through traditions contained in these Gospels, three points must always be borne in mind:

1. The Synoptics give the impression of being three independent witnesses, but we need to remember that they are linked to one another by a close literary relationship. All follow the Markan pattern of a short Galilean ministry, followed by an extensive account of Jesus' passion in Jerusalem. Both Matthew and Luke draw on alternative traditions (most notably Q), but their broad structure is taken from Mark.

2. Sometimes, of course, Matthew and Luke alter their Markan source, often quite substantially. Not only do

these alterations tell us a great deal about these evangelists' particular theological interests and concerns, but they show just how fluid the tradition was, even at the end of the first century. It would be tempting to imagine that Mark, our earliest Gospel, written around 70 CE, might preserve a more historical account. Yet, as we saw in Chapter 1, Wrede showed beyond doubt that Mark also had theological concerns which shaped his narrative. Presumably, the evangelist worked with his sources (whether oral or written) in precisely the same way that Matthew and Luke worked with theirs, and just as thoroughly adapted his material to suit his theological outlook.

3) Besides being gifted storytellers and theologians, the evangelists were also pastors. Many of the alterations made by Matthew and Luke were in response to the needs of their communities: strengthening faith, perhaps in the face of persecution; coping with the delay in Jesus' return; showing that Jesus was innocent under Roman law, and so on. The Gospels (including John) were written at a time when relations between Christian churches and local Jewish synagogues were deteriorating and the two faiths were beginning to go their own separate ways. In some places, Christians were being expelled from the synagogues, and the levels of hurt, tension and loss of identity to which this led should not be underestimated. Much of this contemporary conflict is doubtless reflected in the Gospels. Jesus' debates with the scribes and Pharisees (though clearly based on genuine disagreements) have quite likely been preserved and enhanced to reflect the recent and traumatic debates between the evangelists' audiences and local synagogue leaders. Matthew, in particular, has Jesus distance himself from fellow Jews by speaking of 'their Law' or 'their synagogue'; he includes a series of vehement woes against the Pharisees and scribes in chapter 23, and has the Jewish people accept responsibility for Jesus' death in 27.25. All of this means that we have to be particularly vigilant in inquiring whether Gospel material really reflects the life of Jesus or perhaps more naturally derives from a later situation.

The New Questers, and still some today, see the historian's task as stripping back later accretions to uncover a 'pure' form of the tradition. The image is often one of an onion, where outer layers are peeled away, or a dirty oil painting, where the grime of the centuries can be removed to reveal the pristine colours of the original. But this approach is problematic. Not only is it clear that the Gospel material has gone through a process of translation (from Aramaic into Greek), but modern study of memory has shown how unreliable and fragile human recollection can be, and how dependent it is on unconscious inferences and wider assumptions. Dunn is surely correct in arguing that it is unrealistic to expect to sweep away the faith perspective of the Gospels and uncover a different historical Jesus behind them. The Gospels reflect the impact Jesus made on his earliest followers, and to a large extent this impact *is* the historical Jesus, or as close as we are ever likely to get to him. While we may be able to disentangle some of the clearly later elements in the Gospels (post-Easter theology, pastoral concerns reflecting the later church and so on), we will never be able to present an uninterpreted Jesus, completely cut free from the hopes and dreams of those who followed him. The Synoptics, then, are an extremely good source for the life of Jesus, but we should not ask more of them than they can possibly give.

## The way ahead

We have now spent some time surveying the range of sources utilized in modern Jesus study. Of the non-Christian sources, only Josephus and *b.Sanh* 43a appear to be of any help, and their contribution is largely one of substantiating the Gospel record rather than adding anything new. Non-canonical material offers little of value, particularly the gospels of *Peter* and *Thomas*. The material assigned to Q is clearly relatively old and deserves to be taken seriously. But Q, as we have it now, is woven into the canonical Gospels and, in the end, a cautious and critical reading of these texts provides our best source for reconstructing the life of Jesus.

In Part II of this book, I shall present an overview of Jesus' life, arranged as a series of snapshots covering key aspects or events. My main source will be the synoptic Gospels, with occasional elements drawn from John, Josephus and *b.Sanh* 43a. I shall draw on archaeology, too, where appropriate, particularly for the reconstructions of Galilee in Chapter 5. My focus in what follows will not be on reconstructing the words of Jesus, or a heavy-handed use of the so-called 'criteria of authenticity'. This is partly a matter of space, but, more fundamentally, it reflects my view that the actual words spoken by Jesus (even if they could be recovered) would not take us very far. In general, I shall assume that those who formulated the Gospel worked creatively with their traditions, that some sayings may have been originated within the church (perhaps under the inspiration of Christian prophets?), but that, in general, the Gospels are a broad indicator of the types of things Jesus' earliest followers remembered him doing and saying. Historical reconstruction, as Dale Allison argues, is fundamentally an art form, the 'task requires intuition, analogy, metaphor, and imagination'.[22] Although the words of Jesus will clearly play some role in what follows (particularly in Chapter 7), my more immediate concern will be with the broader picture of what Jesus stood for, how he saw his role, and why he died on a Roman cross. Our first task, though, is to situate Jesus in his historical context. Into what kind of a world was he born?

# PART TWO
# Snapshots of Jesus

# CHAPTER THREE

# The historical context

Jesus was born into a world which had recently known profound upheaval. In order to understand his story, we need to be aware of the historical, political and religious context of his day. This chapter will provide a brief sketch of these troubled times, before considering the messianic hopes they produced in Jesus' contemporaries and the way in which some took up the fight themselves.

## The historical context

In certain respects, the story of Jesus begins in the early second century BCE. Alexander the Great had swept through the east over a century earlier, incorporating the small territory of Judaea into the largest empire ever known. When Alexander died leaving no heirs, his lands were divided amongst his warring generals and Judaea came first under Ptolemaic (Egyptian) and then later Seleucid (Syrian) control.[1]

Alexander had built his empire not only on territorial gain, but equally on the dream of a shared language (his native Greek) and a shared culture (an eclectic mix of Greek and Eastern traditions known as Hellenism). Most Jews were reasonably happy to incorporate Hellenistic elements into all aspects of life, always assuming, of course, that such acculturation was their own choice and that the distinctive features of their religious beliefs were not compromised. In 167 BCE, however, the nation was plunged into

conflict. The Seleucid king Antiochus IV Epiphanes (for reasons
which are not entirely clear) directed a series of measures against
Judaea which culminated in the suppression of Jewish worship.
The Temple was desecrated, circumcision proscribed and absten-
tion from pork was outlawed. Opposition broke out all over the
country, but the most famous resistance came from a priest named
Mattathias and his five sons. Relying first on guerrilla tactics and
later commanding a well-trained army, Mattathias' son Judas won
a series of victories which earned him the title Maccabee, or ham-
mer. Antiochus, beset by dynastic squabbles at home, was forced
to rescind his decree in 164 BCE. The Temple was rededicated (an
event commemorated each year at Hanukkah) and Jews were once
again allowed to worship freely.

Having achieved their initial goal, the Maccabees set their
sights even higher, now dreaming of an independent Jewish state.
Underpinning their hopes was a powerful national mythology
harking back to the kingdom of Israel as it had been in the glorious days of David and Solomon. Religion and politics were closely
linked here, as they were in all aspects of first-century culture: the
stronger Judaea was politically, the more assured was its religious
freedom. And for many, the true leader of Israel was none other
than God himself. Taking full advantage of the dynastic rivalries
which continued to beset the Seleucids, the Maccabean brothers
finally succeeded in shaking off foreign control and establishing
themselves first as high priests and then as high priest-kings of
the Jewish nation. Their heirs, the Hasmonaeans, were to rule for
almost a century.

Not everyone supported the Hasmonaean bid for power, and
some left the fight once religious independence had been gained. As
far as they were concerned, their homeland had been overshadowed
by greater nations ever since the return from exile, and as long as
religious freedom was maintained they were content to accept this
state of affairs. More dramatically, the authors of the Dead Sea
Scrolls (generally believed to have been Essenes) took themselves
off to the wilderness at Qumran in protest at the Hasmonaean
usurpation of the high-priesthood: the family were priests, but
did not belong to the Zadokite line, which was believed to have
held the high priestly office for centuries. However, the majority of people were swept along by the tide of religious and political independence, and hailed the Hasmonaeans as great national

liberators. Under them the nation flourished, its borders were extended into Galilee and Samaria in the north and Idumaea in the south, Jerusalem prospered, and Hellenistic culture once again began to permeate all aspects of life. An indication of Hasmonaean popularity still visible in the New Testament is the popularity of their names: Mattathias, Judas, Simon, Mary and Salome.

By the 60s BCE, however, Hasmonaean power had begun to wane. Ironically perhaps for a dynasty which had emerged from Seleucid power struggles, the Hasmonaeans themselves were to disintegrate into dynastic wrangling and eventual civil war. Two rivals for the throne, Aristobulus II and Hyrcanus II both made advances to Rome, the emerging new superpower in the east. In 63 BCE, the Roman general Pompey installed the rather docile Hyrcanus as high priest, reduced Judaean territories considerably and demanded heavy tribute. It was clear that Rome was now in charge.

The following two decades saw a number of Hasmonaean attempts to regain the Judaean throne. Order was maintained, however, by an Idumaean Jew and loyal supporter of Hyrcanus named Antipater, along with his son Herod. The young Herod favourably impressed a number of Roman generals with his energy, bravery and intelligence, and when the powerful eastern empire of Parthia installed a Hasmonaean as king in 40 BCE, Mark Antony and Octavian (later to become the Emperor Augustus) offered Herod the throne of Judaea. Three years later, following a successful siege of Jerusalem, Herod claimed his crown, taking his place on Rome's eastern border as one of a series of 'friendly' (or client) kings. These kingdoms acted as buffer states between areas of direct Roman rule and outside territories. Their rulers enjoyed a certain amount of autonomy but were expected to offer loyal support and assistance to Rome when required.

Herod I (or 'the Great' as he is popularly known) enjoyed a long and, in many respects, successful reign (37–34 BCE). He presented himself as a major player on the world stage, a confident and generous Hellenistic monarch quite at ease with his Roman patrons. His loyalty to Rome was rewarded by increased territories, so that in the end, his realm could rival that of Solomon's. He was a great builder, gave generously to cities around the Mediterranean, and strove to protect Jewish rights in the diaspora. Under Herod, the city of Jerusalem was rebuilt and the Temple refurbished, transforming it into one of the wonders of the ancient world. Yet, as an absolute monarch, his reign was undoubtedly oppressive and there are hints of ongoing tension. Herod ascended the throne in the aftermath of a brutal and prolonged civil war and began by executing large sections of the Judaean nobility (particularly those who had supported his Hasmonaean opponents). Josephus also records the presence of bandits (*lēstai*) at this time; one of these, Hezekiah, attracted many supporters on the Syrian border until he was put down by Herod (*War* 1.204), and others continued their activities in Galilee several decades later (*War* 1.304–13, 314–16). Reading through Josephus's disapproving prose, it is difficult to know whether these men were simply robbers and raiders, taking advantage of the lawlessness of the times, or whether they were opposed to Herodian/Roman rule on ideological grounds. At all events, Herod built a series of desert fortresses, not to protect his borders, but to maintain order among his people.

Following Herod's death in 4 BCE, the country quickly descended into almost complete anarchy. Uprisings broke out throughout the land and a number of royal aspirants tried to seize the throne, perhaps inspired by stories of the young King David at the head of a band of brigands in 1Sam 21–30 (*War* 2.56-65). Rome responded swiftly and aggressively. Sending two legions under the Syrian governor Varus, they swept down through Galilee, crucifying protesters and stamping out insurrection. The city of Sepphoris, only an hour's walk from Jesus' home town of Nazareth, was burnt to the ground and its inhabitants taken into slavery. Further south, a bloody battle took place in the Temple in which many Jews lost their lives; the porticoes surrounding the outer courts were burned, and the treasury was plundered. Order was soon resumed but the memories of those difficult times and the sheer brutality of the Roman legions must have left their mark.

As a special honour, Herod had been granted the unusual privilege of selecting his own successor. The will, however, needed to be ratified by the emperor, and Herod's sons quickly left their troubled homeland and presented themselves in Rome. Augustus decided to uphold the old king's wishes and divided the realm among three of his sons. Archelaus was given almost half, incorporating Judaea, Idumaea and Samaria, with the title *ethnarch* (literally a 'national ruler'), and the promise that he would be made king if he proved himself worthy. Two other sons, Antipas and Philip, were to rule

Figure 3.1 Map of Israel at the Time of Jesus

as 'tetrarchs' (literally 'ruler of a quarter'): Antipas received Galilee and Peraea, while Philip was allotted largely Gentile territories to the north and east of the Sea of Galilee. Within a decade, however, Archelaus had been deposed for cruelty and Augustus decided to turn his lands into a Roman province under the supervision of a Roman governor sent out from Rome. And so it was that Galilee at the time of Jesus was ruled by a Jewish tetrarch, Herod Antipas, while the southern province of Judaea was under direct Roman control. (See Figure 3.1 for a map of Israel at the time of Jesus.)

## Messianic hopes

It would be only natural that such intense political upheaval would lead to a variety of religious and nationalistic hopes, associated both with the present and the future. It is important to recognize, though, that first-century Judaism was far from monolithic, and that Jews held a variety of aspirations and expectations. Most importantly, there was no universally agreed picture of what a messiah figure might look like, and still less any kind of blueprint for what he might do.[2]

The Hebrew 'messiah' corresponds to the Greek *christos* (Christ) and simply means 'anointed'. The term is never used on its own ('the Messiah') to refer to a future redeemer or saviour figure in the Hebrew Scriptures. It tends to be used of kings, high priests and prophets; that is, people who are given a special status or set apart by God for a particular task (even Cyrus the king of Persia can be said to be anointed by God in Is 45.1). The stress is generally on God's work in the present or imminent future, rather than on a clearly defined 'anointed figure' in the End Times. Similarly, it is perfectly possible for some texts to envisage a glorious future age with no reference to a messianic figure whatsoever (for example Deut 30.1–10, Sir 36.1–17, *Jubilees* 23, *Test.Moses* 10.1, 3); God, of course, was quite capable of bringing in a future age himself, with no need for any kind of an intermediary.

A number of texts, however, seem to envisage an *ideal anointed king*, an expectation which seems to have grown in the century before Jesus' birth. The so-called Royal Psalms (Pss 2, 18, 20, 21, 45, 72, 89, 101, 110, 132, 144) often speak of the king as the Lord's anointed. Originally, these simply referred to the reigning monarch, but gradually they began to be interpreted as referring to a future anointed king. Ps 45.6-7 declares:

> Your divine throne endures for ever and ever.
> Your royal sceptre is a sceptre of equity;
> You love righteousness and hate wickedness.
> Therefore God, your God, has anointed you
> With the oil of gladness above your fellows . . .

Ps 89.19–37 celebrates a permanent covenant with David and his line, and a number of prophetic texts continue to hope in broad terms for an ideal Davidic monarch (most notably Is 9.2–7, 11.1–9, Mic 5.2–4, and Ezek 34.23–4). Often, they imagine a future age inaugurated by God, a time of peace and prosperity, when the twelve tribes of Israel would be reunited under a Davidic king who would rule in God's name (a hope also expressed in Acts 1.6–7).

The only detailed description of a future Davidic monarch is found in the *Psalms of Solomon*. Writing in the late first century BCE in response to Pompey's capture of Jerusalem, the psalmist has little time for either usurping Rome or the non-Davidic Hasmonaeans. *PssSol* 17 looks forward to a day when an anointed Son of David will purify the nation from its enemies, restore Jerusalem to its proper place, and establish a just society. But the ideal king is not a military figure; he trusts in God, not his horse, rider or bow, and his strength is in his wisdom and the spoken word. Building on Ps 2, Is 11, Jer 23 and Ez 34, the author sees the anointed Davidic ruler as an ideal king, judge and shepherd, reigning under the ultimate authority of God himself.

Other texts put their hope in an ideal *priestly* figure. Given the role of the priests in general, and the high priest in particular, as mediators between God and humanity, the desire for a priestly ruler serving under God – a truly theocratic or perhaps hierocratic state – was perhaps not an unexpected development. Ps 110 had already combined messianic kingship with an ideal priesthood after the order of Melchizidek, the mysterious priest-king of Gen 14.17-24,[3] but it was in the first century BCE that the idea of a priestly messiah really flourished, perhaps as a reaction to the Hasmonaeans, who had illegitimately (in the view of some) seized the high priesthood and combined it with kingship. The *Testament of Levi* expected God to raise up a 'new priest' (17.2–11, 18.2–9).

And though messianic expectations do not seem to have been a particularly strong feature of the Dead Sea Scrolls, a number of texts speak of the 'messiah of Aaron' and the 'messiah of Israel'. While it is not always clear how many figures are imagined here, the priestly aspects seem to be dominant. Given the priestly background of these authors, this may not be surprising.

There was, thus, no clearly defined concept of 'the Messiah' by the time of Jesus, nor any clear idea of what such a figure might do. The desire for some kind of a kingly leader was probably most common among ordinary people, with an expectation of an ideal priest popular in other circles, but most seem to have left their expectations rather vague. Precisely how such a figure would function in the age to come, and how he would relate to God as King, are ideas which are often left unexplored. What we can assume, though, is that present political struggles led many Jews at the time of Jesus to dream of what the land would be like if God and not Rome were in control. Hopes for national restoration, which had been partially realized under the Hasmonaeans, continued to flourish. Most people were presumably content to dream their dreams, and to put their hope in God's deliverance. Others, however, took matters into their own hands, both violently and through prophetic announcements. It is to these that we must now turn.

## Revolutionaries and prophets

We have already seen that Herod's early years were plagued with bandits, and that kingly aspirants and rebels gathered supporters at his death. Ten years later in 6 CE, when Judaea was turned into a Roman province, a census was taken by Quirinius, the legate of Syria, to determine appropriate levels of taxation. According to Josephus, this prompted a Galilean named Judas to incite the Judaeans to revolt, declaring that God alone was their master (*War* 2.118, *Ant.* 18.23–5). The revolt was short lived, but indicates once more how volatile the situation had become. Josephus describes Judas as the founder of a 'fourth philosophy' (the Pharisees, Sadducees and Essenes being the other three) and an older generation of scholars took this to mean that the Galilean founded a nationalist movement, known as the Zealots, which was active throughout the first century until their actions culminated in the disintegration of society and the outbreak of the war with Rome in 66–70 CE. Modern scholars have challenged this, noting that the Zealots as a group are first attested only during the war itself (their name presumably derived from the zealousness of biblical heroes such as Phineas in Num 25, or Elijah in 1Kings 19). But even if there were no *organized* resistance, it is highly likely that sporadic riots and protests broke out against Rome, even in the relatively stable 20s and 30s CE. At the very least, the subjugated people of Judaea would have found their own, often minor, ways to oppose their foreign overlords.[4]

Josephus notes the emergence in the 50s of a group known as the 'assassins' or *sicarii*; their name comes from their hidden daggers (*sica*), which they plunged into unsuspecting victims (*War* 2.254-7). He contrasts these with a series of prophets who, he notes, had 'purer hands but more impious intentions' (*War* 2.258). One of these, a Samaritan, emerged shortly after Jesus in 36 CE. He gathered a large crowd and promised to lead them up the sacred Mount Gerizim, where he promised to show them certain holy vessels hidden by Moses. Armed followers assembled, but were quickly dispatched by Pontius Pilate before they could make their ascent (*Ant.* 18.85-7). Around 44–5 CE, a prophet named Theudas persuaded a large number of people to go to the River Jordan, where he would command the water to part and allow them to cross. Again, the Roman procurator acted swiftly, sent in the cavalry, and many were killed (*Ant.* 20.97-8, Acts 5.36). Later still, an Egyptian persuaded 30,000 people to follow him from the wilderness to the Mount of Olives, ready to break into Jerusalem by force, after which he planned to overthrow the Roman garrison and to take command of the city. Once more Rome intervened, though the Egyptian himself escaped (*War* 2.261, Acts 21.37-9). The 50s CE seem to have been characterized by the emergence of 'brigands,' 'deceivers' and 'imposters,' as the country moved ever closer to revolt.[5] Even in the final stages of the Roman siege of Jerusalem in 70 CE, as the Temple burned, a prophet proclaimed that God was about to come and deliver his people.[6]

Evaluating these prophets is made particularly difficult by the fact that our only source, the pro-Roman Josephus, clearly detests them. He routinely characterizes them as 'charlatans' or 'false prophets', and it is clear that, like other educated writers of his day, Josephus considered prophecy in its classical sense to have ceased.[7]

There is no reason, however, to doubt the sincerity of these men, or that of their followers who clearly took them to be prophets. What is interesting about them is that their choice of location harks back to Israel's past, particularly the River Jordan and the wilderness. Both of these were hugely symbolic, evoking an earlier idealized time when God's relations with his people were stronger and more direct. The prophets seem to have modelled themselves on great figures from Israel's history, specifically Moses and Joshua, and their 'signs' evoked the great acts associated with these men. While the Egyptian seems to have had kingly pretensions, the others seem to have seen themselves as God's prophets, announcing his imminent arrival and the establishment of God's new age. Presumably, they expected God to intervene very quickly after the 'sign' itself, or perhaps they hoped that the 'sign' in some way would force God's hand.

As we shall see in the following chapters, the ministries of both Jesus and John the Baptist can be dated to the late 20s or early 30s CE. Compared with later decades, which were characterized by escalating civil unrest and descent into revolt, we know of few riots or uprisings at this period. Indeed, from a Roman perspective, Tacitus could remark that under Tiberius (14-37 CE) Judaea was quiet (*Histories* 5.9.2). Yet tension was clearly brewing beneath the surface, and in many ways the two men can be seen as forerunners of the later 'sign prophets.' They, too, announced the imminent arrival of God's kingdom, saw themselves as God's prophetic ambassadors and expected the renewal of Israel.

By the time of Jesus, then, the land of Israel had experienced well over a century of political turmoil. While stories of past glories led some to hope for better conditions, a golden age, there was no consensus on what it might look like, or how it might be brought about. A range of kingly and prophetic figures emerged at various times throughout the first century, all claiming to herald this new age. Each one enjoyed a great deal of popular support, but each was swiftly dispatched by Rome. This was the world into which Jesus was born, but when exactly was his birth? And where did it take place?

# CHAPTER FOUR

# The birth of Jesus

The story of Jesus' birth is for many the best-known feature of his life. Every Christmas, Christians tell stories of Mary's unexpected pregnancy, the journey to Bethlehem, visiting shepherds, angels and magi, Herod's murder of the young boys, and the Holy Family's escape to Egypt. Yet, as we shall see, this is one of the most controversial aspects of the whole Jesus story, and for most scholars the area where the gospel record is most at variance with historical fact. We shall look first at the date of Jesus' birth before going on to consider the claim that Mary conceived Jesus while still a virgin, and the tradition that Jesus was born in Bethlehem.

## When was Jesus born?

The New Testament gives no clear date for Jesus' birth.

- Matthew puts it roughly two years before the end of Herod I's reign (Mt 2.1, 16, 19), giving a date of roughly 6 BCE.

- Luke sets his birth stories 'in the days of Herod, King of Judaea' (1.5), but later links the birth of Jesus with Quirinius' census of 6 CE (Lk 2.1–2). Unless King Herod here is to be equated with Archelaus the tetrarch, who ruled from 4 BCE – 6 CE, Luke's account is inconsistent. Later on, he dates the beginnings of John the Baptist's ministry to the fifteenth year of Tiberius' reign, giving a date of roughly 29 CE (Lk 3.1). Jesus, he says, was 30 at the start of his own ministry (3.23) which, depending on how long John's ministry lasted, takes his birth to 1 BCE at the earliest.

● John's gospel is even less helpful. In Jn 8.57, opponents remark that Jesus is not yet 50, placing Jesus' birth around 10 BCE at the latest.

This lack of agreement is hardly surprising; the first Chrisitans were interested primarily in Jesus' ministry and death, it was only in the late first century that 'lives of Jesus' began to be written and, by then, the precise year of Jesus' birth had been lost. Witnesses may have remembered Jesus as a man in his thirties, and perhaps it was also known that he was born around the end of Herod the Great's reign, but clearly little else of any historical value was known to the evangelists.

Only Matthew and Luke record the details of Jesus' birth, but the two accounts are very different. In Luke, the Holy Family live in Nazareth and the evangelist has to find a way to bring them down to Bethlehem for Jesus' birth (which he does through the census), while in Matthew the Holy Family already live in Bethlehem and this evangelist's task is to show how they relocated after Jesus' birth to Galilee (which he does through the story of Herod's massacre of the boys under two and Archelaus's brutality). It is impossible to harmonize the two accounts and almost certain that neither one rests on the kind of factual information that we would like today. Furthermore, there are historical problems with both accounts. The Roman census under Quirinius involved only those resident in the newly established province of Judaea, not those living in Antipas's Galilee; and despite Josephus's detailed account of the end of Herod's reign, there is no evidence for the so-called 'massacre of the innocents' in and around Bethlehem. Both Gospels do agree, however, on two things: (a) that Jesus was conceived while his mother was still a virgin, and (b) that he was born in Bethlehem. Thus, while Matthew and Luke are unlikely to have been written earlier than the 80s CE, these two traditions clearly predate this date. The fact that the traditions are used in such different ways in each account may well suggest a long period of development and, therefore, a relatively early tradition. Both, then, need investigating.

## The virginal conception

Although a central element in much modern Christian belief, it can come as a surprise to realize that large parts of the New Testament appear to know nothing about the virginal conception.[1] In fact, the documents offer three competing alternatives:

1   Large sections of the text appear simply to assume that Jesus was the *son of Joseph*. Paul nowhere discusses Jesus' conception, and his comment that Jesus was 'descended from David according to the flesh' seems to assume a 'normal' paternity (Rom 1.3). John openly refers to Jesus as the 'son of Joseph' (Jn 1.45, 6.42), as does Luke outside the birth narratives (Lk 4.22). The genealogies, too, clearly trace Jesus' descent back through Joseph; the awkward attempts to bring things back to Mary in both Matthew 1.16 and Luke 3.23 suggest that the genealogies were originally composed in a setting which simply assumed Joseph's paternity.

2   Matthew 1.18–25 and Luke 1.34–5 suggest that Mary was a *virgin* when she conceived Jesus. The story makes it quite clear that Jesus was, quite literally, the son of God. (Parallels to this exist in the Roman world, notably Suetonius's suggestion that the Emperor Augustus was conceived in the Temple of Apollo, *Augustus* 94.4). The story has clear theological importance, but the complete silence of the rest of the New Testament, including the earliest writers, Paul and Mark, has led most Jesus scholars to question its historicity. The second century *Infancy Gospel of James* goes even further than Matthew and Luke, suggesting that Mary continued to be a virgin *after* Jesus' birth. The work, which clearly paves the way for the Catholic doctrine of the perpetual virginity of Mary, reflects the growing interest in the second century with the sinlessness of Jesus' mother, expressed here through abstinence of sexual contact. Once again, theological interests have coloured the presentation of the story.

3   Certain texts raise the possibility that Jesus was *illegitimate*. Clearest is Mark 6.3, where Jesus is referred to by the people of Nazareth as the 'son of Mary'. Given the unusualness of linking a son to his mother in first-century society, scholars such as Jane Schaberg, Gerd Lüdemann, and Bruce Chilton have suggested that Jesus was indeed regarded as illegitimate.[2] Appeal is also sometimes made to the comment of Jesus'

opponents in Jn 8.41 ('we were not born of fornication') and to *Gos.Th.* 105 (Jesus said, 'Whoever knows the father and the mother will be called the child of a whore'), though neither of these offer clear support. Even the reference to Jesus as 'son of Mary', however, is ambiguous. The most obvious explanation for this odd identification is simply that Joseph had been dead for some time, making Jesus' identification through Mary more understandable.

The charge of illegitimacy was clearly one which was raised by opponents of Christianity. We find it first in the writings of a neo-Platonic philosopher named Celsus whose work, *True Doctrine*, is the earliest known attack on Christianity. The work itself is now lost, but large amounts are preserved in Origen's response, *Against Celsus*, written about 250 CE. Drawing on contemporary Jewish anti-Christian polemic, Celsus seems to have alleged that Jesus was conceived as a result of his mother's adultery and that his true father was a Roman soldier named Panthera. A number of later rabbinic traditions refer to Jesus as 'ben Panthera/Pandera' and Pandera is mentioned as Mary's adulterous lover.[3] The difficulty here lies in knowing whether the tradition of the virginal conception is a *Christian reworking* of the Panthera story, or whether the Panthera story is an *anti-Christian distortion* of the Christian claim that Jesus was born of a virgin (the word Panthera has some similarities with the Greek word for virgin, *parthenos*). Most historical Jesus scholars would argue for the latter. This does not mean that the virginal conception story was historical, only that it was in general circulation by the early second century and, as far as opponents were concerned, needed refuting.

The simplest way through the evidence is to go along with the assumption of the majority of the New Testament writers and to take it that Jesus was born quite naturally to his father Joseph. The story of the virginal conception, preserved by both Matthew and Luke, seems to have been an early attempt to show both that Jesus' miraculous birth signalled from the start that he would be a great man, and also an attempt symbolically to underline his divine paternity. But where did his birth take place?

## *Birth at Bethlehem?*

As we have seen, the tradition that Jesus was born in Bethlehem is probably earlier than both Matthew and Luke. Yet, like the virginal conception, the rest of the New Testament shows no knowledge of it. Paul never mentions Jesus' birthplace, and Mark simply links him with Nazareth (Mk 1.9), as does John (Jn 1.46). The latter's silence is particularly surprising, given that Nathanael shows a southerner's prejudices in demanding, 'Can anything good come from Nazareth?' If John knew a tradition that Jesus had actually been born in Bethlehem he surely would have mentioned it.

In all likelihood, however, the reference to Bethlehem is once again symbolic. Bethlehem was the city of David and a tradition in Micah 3.2 foretold that God's anointed one would be born there. Speculating on Jesus' birth several decades later, and with the full belief that Jesus truly was the Messiah, the kingly ruler who would inaugurate God's glorious reign, the tradition known to both Matthew and Luke had no qualms about placing his birth in Bethlehem. Jesus was now seen to be a true Son of David, none other than God's anointed one from birth. If Jesus' family were genuinely descendants of David (as Rom 1.3 suggests), the move would have been all the more obvious.[4]

That the tradition was not fully worked out at this early stage is illustrated, as we have seen, by the completely different ways that Matthew and Luke link their two geographical elements, the birth in Bethlehem and childhood in Nazareth. Furthermore, both narratives reflect each evangelist's particular theological interests. Matthew knows that in the future it will be Gentiles who come to the new faith (hence, the visit of the magi), and wants to show Jesus as a second Moses (Herod's massacre of the boys links him firmly to Pharaoh in Exodus 2, and draws unmistakeable parallels between Jesus and the Jewish lawgiver). Luke likes both to link Christian events with those on the world stage (hence, the census) and to show that Jesus came for the poor and marginalized (hence, the story of Mary and Joseph finding no room at the inn and the presence of the shepherds). The birth stories in both Gospels, then, are not so much attempts to give biographical information regarding Jesus' origins as theological overtures to the rest of the works.

To summarize the findings of this chapter, the probability is that Jesus was the son of Joseph and was born in Nazareth, the small Galilean village where he grew up. Such a conclusion is generally held by most historical Jesus critics, including all those detailed in Chapter 1 (except N. T. Wright). But what was Galilee like in the first century? To this we must now turn.

# CHAPTER FIVE

# Galilean origins

What was life like in Antipas's Galilee? And what was it like to grow up in a small village like Nazareth? The answers to these questions are important – the firmer grasp we have of Jesus' context, the better chance we have of understanding his message. This chapter will look at both the religious outlook and economy of Galilee, before turning to Nazareth more specifically and offering a tentative reconstruction of Jesus' early life.

## How Jewish was Galilee?

At first glance, this might seem like an odd question. Galilee had traditionally been part of Israel, where the national religion was Judaism. Yet the particular history of Galilee has led some to doubt this straight-forward identification.

One of the most prominent scholars in this debate is Richard Horsley, who pointed out that Galilee was part of the Northern Kingdom of Israel, which had split from the Southern Kingdom of Judah at the death of Solomon. When the Assyrians transported large numbers of people into exile in the eighth century BCE, they were replaced with Mesopotamians who brought their own culture with them (see 2Kgs 17.6, 23–4). The resulting group of northerners, Horsley argues, developed their own popular oral traditions, which were often at variance with the more literate scribal circles in Jerusalem. Even after the Hasmonaean rulers forcibly converted Galilee to Judaism in 104 BCE, they were never fully integrated into Judaean culture and few made the long trek down to Jerusalem for the pilgrimage festivals. Jewish ways were regarded as an imposition thrust upon them by their southern neighbours rather than

something to be welcomed or accepted, and the fiercely independent Galileans were never truly 'converted'.[1]

A completely different picture of first-century Galilee emerges,
however, from the work of Sean Freyne, who argues that Galileans
maintained close connections throughout their history with
Jerusalem and the Temple. Drawing largely on literary evidence,
Freyne argues that there were priests in Galilee, that people did
make the long journey to the capital city for festivals, and that they
paid their tithes to the priests and the Temple. Most revealing of
all, perhaps, is that when the Emperor Gaius threatened to des-
ecrate the Jerusalem Temple only a decade after Jesus' death, the
Galileans were quick to protest; and later, when Josephus sought to
establish his own authority in Galilee during the Jewish revolt, he
did so by stressing his Jerusalem and priestly connections, clearly
expecting that they would resonate with his northern audience. No
less significantly, Jesus' knowledge of the Torah suggests its wide
acceptance and centrality in Galilee.[2]

Recent archaeology has overwhelmingly reinforced Freyne's
portrait of a Jewish Galilee. The region seems to have been virtually depopulated prior to the Hasmonaean expansion, after which
a wave of Judaean settlers moved into the area, bringing their
distinctively Jewish culture with them. Jewish identity has been
confirmed by the absence of pig bones (which shows that the inhabitants kept the dietary laws), the abundance of stone vessels (which,
unlike pottery, could not become ritually unclean), the presence in
many places of *miqvaoth* (Jewish immersion pools used for ritual
purity), and evidence of Jewish burial customs. In addition, compared to its non-Jewish neighbours, there is little evidence of the
remains of pagan Temples or cultic objects in Galilee, even in the
larger cities.[3]

It is true that very few synagogues dating from the first century
have been found in Galilee, but the same is true of the rest of Israel.
The reason for their absence is probably because Jewish gatherings
at the time of Jesus were held in large buildings which served a
variety of purposes, not only religious ones (the word 'synagogue'
means a gathering of people, as well as the building itself). Quite
probably, such buildings, lacking indications of their purpose, simply have not been identified. Only a handful of synagogues in Israel
can be securely dated to the first century: Gamla (in Philip's ter-
rirory), Masada and Herodium (in Judaea), possibly Magdala (in

Galilee), and the Theodotus synagogue in Jerusalem. The evangelists, writing several decades later, simply assumed that Palestinian
'synagogues' were clearly identifiable buildings, as they were in
their own diaspora settings (see Lk 7.5, in particular).[4]

The overriding conclusion appears to be that Galileans at the
time of Jesus were thoroughly Jewish, that they shared the Judaean's
devotion both to the Law and the Jerusalem Temple, and that they
embraced their southern neighbours' hopes of future restoration.
Of course, they may well have maintained a strong sense of their
own history and distinctiveness, and may have particularly prized
northern prophets such as Elijah and Elisha, but we should not
push their religious distinctiveness too far. In all the ways that mattered, Galileans were Jewish.

## The Galilean economy

A further debate surrounds the Galilean economy, much of it connected to Antipas's building activities. Antipas's father, Herod
the Great, had been widely applauded both for his spectacular
buildings and magnificent cities. But despite Herod's munificence,
Galilee had been left rather bare. In an effort to address this defi-
ciency, and perhaps to establish himself as a true son of Herod,
Antipas began his own building programme. First to be rebuilt
was the city of Sepphoris, which had been completely destroyed
in the revolt of 4 BCE, and was turned by Antipas into the 'jewel
of all Galilee' (*Ant.* 18.27). Only four miles from Nazareth (and
visible from it), Sepphoris was now the largest and most important
city in the region, the location of Antipas's royal palace, and the
seat of government. In 19 CE, the tetrarch founded another city on
the Sea of Galilee, naming it Tiberias (in honour of the emperor),
and transferring his administration there. It would be a mistake,
however, to assume that Antipas's cities were major urban centres like Caesarea Maritima on the coast or even Jerusalem. Both
were relatively small (neither had a population of more than about
12,000 people), they were not on major trade routes, lacked the
typical amenities of Hellenistic cities (the much publicized theatre
at Sepphoris probably belongs to the second century at the earliest),
and do not seem to have incorporated any sizeable non-Jewish population. They might boast a thin veneer of cosmopolitan culture,

but were at best minor provincial centres. Antipas had nothing of his father's architectural vision; his building work gave a certain amount of dignity to his realm, but nothing more.

But what was the effect of this urbanization on the surrounding villages? And how might we categorize urban-rural relations at this time? Drawing largely on cross-cultural anthropology, some have described the relation between Antipas's cities and rural areas as 'parasitic'; building work required heavy taxation, draining local economies and imposing a heavy burden on the surrounding areas. Previously self-sufficient village communities would no longer be sustainable and their inhabitants would be quickly caught up in a spiral of hardship, destitution and social banditry.[5] These views have been influential (most notably in the reconstructions of Crossan and Horsley) but have been increasingly challenged from a number of angles.

First, it is debateable how far it is appropriate to apply cross-cultural models to the first century. The Lenski–Kautsky model employed by Horsley and Crossan is based on modern, Eurocentric assumptions (such as class consciousness) rather than on the values of Galilean villagers (where kinship was more important). In the absence of data, models *may* be able to fill in some of the gaps but should not be allowed too much influence.[6] Second, as we have seen, Antipas's cities were relatively modest, with few public amenities. Although there may have been some increase in taxation to pay for the work, the cities themselves probably had little impact on the surrounding districts. Third, archaeological excavations in Galilean rural settlements suggest thriving local economies, vigorous trade networks, and no major changes in population, inhabitation or economic activity at this time. In short, nothing to suggest that relations between cities and rural communities were particularly strained.[7]

Finally, Josephus provides no evidence for widespread banditry in the time of Antipas. There were certainly occasional protests, but most tended to be non-violent, for example those associated with Pilate's standards and Gaius's statue.[8] This does not mean, of course, that there were not occasional city–rural disputes or rivalries. The influx of new people and bureaucrats into the cities, along with the acquisition of the best land by Antipas's retainers, undoubtedly led to tensions. Jesus' parables reflect the presence of wealthy estate owners, absentee landlords and exploitative stewards. Yet, the picture of extreme social tension outlined by some seems to be an exaggeration.

In view of the above points, the picture that emerges of Antipas's Galilee is of a reasonably prosperous, stable realm, relatively at ease with its Jewish ruler. In many respects, Antipas's long reign acted as a buffer against direct Roman rule and exploitation. Mark Chancey points out that although Hellenistic and Roman culture became more visible during his reign, the tetrarch's innovations were relatively minor and do not amount to any serious attempt to 'Romanize' his land. Public bathhouses, pagan Temples and games do not seem to have been a feature of Galilean life, nor is there evidence for widespread use of Greek language. Antipas's army was drawn from the nearby pagan cities of Caesarea and Sebaste, and Roman troops would not have been used in the region (the 'centurion' in Mt 8.5–13//Lk 7.1–10 was probably one of Antipas's officers). The evidence suggests a certain insularity to Galilee, a self-contained region with little connection to the wider world, where village life continued much as it had done for decades. As for Antipas himself, Morten Jensen's recent study suggests a mediocre and unremarkable ruler, able to maintain peaceable and even prosperous conditions for his subjects.[9]

As an agrarian society, the vast majority of Galileans were engaged in working the land. The mild climate and fertile soil allowed for the cultivation of root crops and grains, and many people had a small flock of sheep or goats. The production of olive oil, pottery and wine added to the region's economic activities. Each town had its own small-scale industries; for example, Cana had dovecotes, an olive press, glass-blowing and, possibly, facilities for dying wool or leather. Of particular significance was the fishing industry around the Sea of Galilee, dried fish production in the thriving town of Magdala on the western shore and associated activities such as boat building.[10] There is evidence in both Josephus and the Gospels that people in Jerusalem thought of Galileans as rather backward (Jn 7.41, 52) – a common occurrence the world-over when city people meet country folk. They seem to have spoken Aramaic with a distinctive regional dialect (Mt 26.73) and were probably in general fairly conservative, with a strong sense of kin and family ties. It was among these small towns and villages that Jesus grew up and began his ministry, but can we say anything more about Nazareth and his early life?

# Jesus' early life

We know nothing about Jesus' early life with any degree of certainty. A number of apocryphal infancy gospels tried to fill in the gap with wild and fanciful tales of his boyhood exploits, but these clearly have no historical value. Luke includes a story of Jesus in the Temple at 12 years old, impressing the gathered teachers with his erudition (Lk 2.41-51). The similarity of this story to other tales of precocious lads who went on to become great leaders (including one told by Josephus of himself, *Life* 9!) suggests that here, too, the story owes its origins to Christian piety rather than historical recollection.

What we do know is that Jesus grew up in Nazareth, a fact attested by all the Gospels.[11] In the time of Jesus, Nazareth was a village with a population of no more than 400 or so. Both Josephus and the Talmud list a number of Galilean towns and settlements, but neither mention Nazareth, once again underlining its insignificance. Most people were presumably engaged in agriculture or minor industries. Mark 3.6 gives Jesus' occupation as a *tektōn*, a word which can mean carpenter, stonemason or builder. In a parallel passage, Matthew 13.55 refers to him as a '*tektōn*'s son.' While this may betray a certain embarrassment at linking Jesus with a trade, it seems reasonable enough to suppose that Joseph, too, was a *tektōn*. A small settlement like Nazareth may not have provided enough business for Joseph to support his family, and he may have moved around surrounding villages, perhaps even Sepphoris, looking for work.

Where would such a trade put Jesus' family socially? At one extreme, Crossan argues that carpenters are referred to disparagingly in ancient sources and that Jesus and his family belonged to what he calls the 'artisan class', a group of people drawn from the dispossessed peasantry. This group was poorer than peasants but just above beggars and 'expendable classes'. At the other extreme, Flusser argued that Jesus and his family were relatively well-to-do, and that carpenters were looked up to in society. Craig Evans, too, argued that Jesus' ministry indicates a certain measure of financial means (even if it was supplemented by the generosity of others), and that some of Jesus' disciples were also comparatively well-off (for example, the fishermen with their own boats and hired help in Mk

1.19–20, and the toll collectors of Mk 2.4). He suggests we should think of a 'family of modest but adequate means'.[12] In any assessment of Jesus' social standing, it must be remembered that wealth in Israel, as in all ancient societies, was unevenly distributed, with a small upper and middle class owning the bulk of the nation's resources, and the vast majority of people belonging to the lower classes. Perhaps Jesus and his family belonged somewhere between the two extremes outlined above and might broadly be classed as peasants. The family trade allowed them to be self-sufficient economically, but poverty was never far away.

Would a boy from such a family have been educated? Could he read and write? At first glance, two Gospels suggest that Jesus was literate. John describes his writing (or is it doodling?) in the sand (Jn 8.6, 8), and Luke has him read from the Torah scroll in the synagogue (Lk 4.16-30). Neither of these passages, however, is straight-forward. John 8 belongs to the story of the adulteress (7.53-8.11), which by common consent was a later addition to the Gospel. And Luke 4 is an elaboration of Jesus' visit to the Nazareth synagogue in Mk 6.1-6, an account which says nothing about Jesus reading from the scroll himself. Perhaps both John 8 and Luke 4 reflect a later Christian desire to enhance Jesus' prestige by suggesting that he was literate and, therefore, educated. It is true that both Philo and Josephus claimed that Jewish parents not only taught their children Torah but also how to read it,[13] but in this they may reflect the practice of more affluent Jews who would have had the time and leisure for such pursuits. Although Dunn, Flusser, Meier and Wright all agree that Jesus could at least read (writing required a higher level of literacy), the lack of formal schools and the universally low literary rates in ancient societies (usually put at 10 per cent, at best), suggest that any literacy Jesus may have achieved would have been extremely basic. This does not detract, of course, from the fact that Jesus was clearly a gifted communicator with a particular ability to tell stories and to hold people's attention. His native language would have been Aramaic (the language of Palestine and the surrounding area), though he may also have known some Hebrew (the language of the Hebrew Scriptures) and possibly a little Greek.

The question of whether Jesus was married has become prominent recently, particularly in popular treatments, with Mary Magdalene as prime contender for the position of Jesus' wife. It would certainly be unusual in Jewish society of the time for a man to remain unmarried into his thirties; the command to 'Be fruitful and multiply' (Gen 1.22) was taken seriously. But although we catch occasional glimpses of the families of Jesus' disciples (particularly Peter's mother-in-law, wife and children),[14] there is no indication that Jesus himself was married. The people who worry that Jesus is causing a scene in Mark 3.20–31 and come to take him home are his mother and siblings; there is no mention of a wife. And later, after his death, the women who anoint Jesus' body are friends and followers; once again there is no indication that one of them is his wife (Mk 16.1 and pars). Since the early church could have had no reason to suppress a reference to a wife if she had existed, the likeliest inference is that Jesus was unmarried. (We shall see in Chapter 7 that Jesus' lack of a wife and children fits with his apocalyptic sense that his was the last generation.)

# Jesus the Jew

We noted in Chapter 1 that modern Jesus research takes Jesus' Jewish heritage for granted. It is clear from the Gospels that Jesus attended the synagogue (Mk 1.12, 23, 3.1, 6.1–2, etc) where he would have heard the Hebrew Scriptures read out in Hebrew, translated into Aramaic, and expounded by a prominent member of the congregation. Luke, in particular, stresses the piety of Jesus' family, that he was circumcised on the eighth day and presented in the Temple (2.21–40), and that the family attended the Passover in Jerusalem every year (2.41–52). In all three Synoptic gospels, Jesus wears a garment with fringes (Mk 6.56, Mt 9.20, 14.36, Lk 8.44) as prescribed by the Law.[15] Whatever the historicity of these precise details, Jesus clearly grew up in a Jewish family, knew the story of Israel, and was familiar with the Hebrew Scriptures. His concerns in debates with opponents are clearly Jewish ones: the interpretation of Torah, Sabbath observance, what counts as clean and unclean, and the place of the Temple. Alhough the Gospels do not specifically tell us this, we can also presume that each day he recited the *shema*, the daily prayer based on Deuteronomy 6.4 which celebrated a person's love for God. This deep love, passionate commitment and total obedience to God accompanied him throughout his ministry and was doubtless a feature of Jesus' outlook from a young age.

Beyond this, however, it is difficult to go with any certainty. Post-Holocaust Christian scholarship is perhaps understandably anxious to present a Jesus who would be unmistakeably Jewish in modern times as much as his own. Yet, as we have seen, first-century Judaism was extremely diverse, with all kinds of different ways of being Jewish. As a profound religious thinker, Jesus would inevitably have had his own views on many aspects of his faith, views which – as we shall see – would lead to heated arguments with opponents. Perhaps at first, though, Jesus was not entirely sure where his path lay. It was presumably the search for greater spiritual understanding that led to his encounter with John the Baptist and a deeply religious experience at his baptism.

# CHAPTER SIX

# John the Baptist

All four evangelists begin their accounts of Jesus' ministry with events at the River Jordan, and in Acts 1.21–2 the qualification for those who sought to replace Judas as one of the twelve was that they had been with Jesus from 'the baptism of John', that is, from the very beginning. But what do we know about John? And why is his ministry so inextricably connected with that of Jesus?

Fortunately, we are not entirely dependent on the Gospels for our information here. The Baptist is mentioned in positive terms by Josephus, who provides the following relatively lengthy paragraph:

> But to some of the Jews the destruction of Herod's army seemed to be divine vengeance, and certainly a just vengeance, for his treatment of John, surnamed the Baptist. For Herod had put him to death though he was a good man and had exhorted the Jews to live righteous lives, to practice justice towards their fellows and piety towards God, and so doing to join in baptism. In his view, this was a necessary preliminary if baptism was to be acceptable to God. They must not employ it to gain pardon for whatever sins they committed, but as a consecration of the body implying that the soul was already thoroughly cleansed by right behaviour. When others too joined the crowds about him, because they were aroused to the highest degree by his sermons, Herod became alarmed. Eloquence that had so great an effect on mankind might lead to some form of sedition, for it looked as if they would be guided by John in everything that they did. Herod decided, therefore, that it would be much better to strike first and be rid of him before his work led to an uprising, than to wait for an upheaval, get involved in a difficult situation and see

his mistake. Though John, because of Herod's suspicions, was brought in chains to Machaerus, the stronghold that we have previously mentioned, and there put to death, yet the verdict of the Jews was that the destruction visited upon Herod's army was a vindication of John, since God saw fit to inflict such a blow on Herod. (*Ant.* 18.116-19)[1]

The most striking aspect of John's activity was clearly his baptizing, which was important and distinctive enough to earn him the nickname 'the Baptizer'. Ritual bathing and baptism were commonly used among first-century Jews as ways of effecting and maintaining purity; the large number of ritual baths, or *miqvaoth*, found in first-century settlements suggests a great concern for the purity laws outlined in Leviticus 11– 15.

A number of features, however, set John's baptism apart. First, John called for an inner cleansing, a repentance of immoral ways and a true turning to God *prior* to baptism; it was only when the heart was truly righteous that bodily purification could be effective before God.[2] As Joan Taylor notes, similar sentiments were expressed by the prophets of old, most notably Isaiah 1.12–17, 35.8, 52.1, 11.[3] Whether John's baptism actually atoned for sin in some way (as Mk 1.4//Lk 3.3 seem to imply) or whether the outward cleansing simply 'finished off' the person's preparation by adding outer to inner cleansing (as Josephus claims) is uncertain. Second, while most Jews would have carried out their own ritual immersions, John appears to have played an active role in the baptism of those who flocked to him, perhaps accompanying them down into the water. And third, unlike most Jewish immersions, John's seems to have been a one-off event; there is no evidence that he expected anyone to come to him for baptism more than once. Some have drawn parallels with Jewish proselyte baptism here, where the point of baptism was to signal a person's entry into the Jewish faith. Quite apart from the fact that evidence for this is late, however, the main reason for John's once-only baptism seems to have been linked to his conviction that he was living in the last days.

The Synoptics suggest that John's message had a strongly eschatological orientation, and that he preached a fiery apocalyptic message, foretelling imminent judgement and the arrival of a mightier one who would baptize with the Holy Spirit and fire (Mk 1.7–8 and pars.). Josephus says nothing of this, but his reticence is easily explained: writing for a Roman audience after the disastrous revolt of 66–70, he was anxious to suppress any hint of Jewish apocalyptic hopes. The Synoptic portrait is clearly more historical here. John and those who came out to him thought that they were living at the end of the age, that God was about to intervene in human affairs, and that the only appropriate response was to repent and to prepare themselves for the coming tribulations. Being descendants of Abraham was no guarantee of continuing security (Lk 3.8).

The apocalyptic fervour aroused by John was underscored all the more by the *location* of his ministry. The Synoptics make it clear that he based himself at the River Jordan, a place replete with symbolism from Israel's past. It was here that the Israelites entered into the Promised Land (Josh 3–4). As with the 'sign prophets' who would emerge later (see Chapter 3), the wilderness evoked a time when Israel was closer to its God, a place where God revealed himself to his people (Ex 3, 1Kgs 19), and which would 'rejoice and blossom like the crocus' on the Day of the Lord (Is 35). Those who went out to John and subjected themselves to his baptism knew all of this. Presumably they longed for national restoration in a cleansed and restored promised land and believed that, with God's help, it was about to become a reality.

But who was the 'coming one' who would inaugurate this new order? He is said to come in judgement, to wield an axe and a winnowing fork, and to baptize with the Holy Spirit and fire.[4] He is mightier than John, to the extent that John is not worthy even to untie his sandals (Mk 1.7 pars.). If the language here is metaphorical and anthropomorphic, the 'coming one' could be God himself, drawing near in judgement. More likely, perhaps, John imagined a heavenly agent such as Elijah, who was expected to come before the end and to purify the nation with fire.[5] John's question to Jesus from prison, if historical, only makes sense if it was conceivable that a human being could fulfil this role (Lk 7.18–23// Mt 11.2–6). Church tradition, of course, has always argued that *John* was Elijah. The link is already made explicit in the Synoptics, where the description of John's clothes and ascetic lifestyle mirror those of Elijah (Mk 1.6 and pars. echo 2Kgs 1.8), and where Jesus clearly identifies him as the great prophet (Mk 9.11–13 and pars.). This identification makes sense later on, when Christians saw Jesus as God's anointed one and cast John as his forerunner, but John himself might well have been much less clear about his own role, preferring simply to predict the imminent appearance of God's heavenly agent. Those who came out to John undoubtedly saw him as a great prophet like those from Israel's past, inspired by God and calling the nation to repentance and future deliverance. As Dunn notes, the evidence from Josephus suggests that the Baptist might well have been more important in his day than was Jesus.[6]

## Jesus' baptism

That Jesus was baptized by John is certain. The close connection between baptism and the removal of sin led to a certain embarrassment on the part of the earliest Christians in admitting that Jesus underwent the rite. Luke and John pass over the baptism very quickly (Lk 3.21–2, Jn 1.32–4), while Matthew adds a brief conversation in which John expresses his unworthiness to baptize Jesus (Mt 3.14–15). This very embarrassment, however, confirms the historicity of the event. As a man of strong religious convictions and yearnings, almost certainly from his youth, it is quite probable that Jesus would have sought out the Baptist (all the more so if there was a family connection between the two men, as Lk 1.36 suggests). Like many others, Jesus may have attached himself to the Baptist's circle of disciples; he would have heard John's ethical and apocalyptic teaching and, after an appropriate period of preparation, offered himself for baptism.

Mark describes the event: Jesus came out of the Jordan, saw the heavens opened and the Spirit descend on him like a dove, and heard the voice of God saying 'You are my beloved son, with you I am well pleased' (Mk 1.9–11). The descent of the Spirit clearly shows a sense of being anointed by God, set aside for a particular purpose (see Is 61.1), as, too, do the divine words drawn from Ps 2.7 and Is 42.1. The scene as we now have it, written in the third person, clearly goes back to the earliest Christians and their attempts to describe what happened. Yet behind it may be the recollection that Jesus experienced a profoundly moving religious experience at his baptism, and presumably a realization that his life was to move in a completely different direction. Perhaps the closest parallel to this in the Old Testament is the prophetic call: sometimes this is a visionary experience (so Is 6, Ezek 1.1–3.15, or Jer 1.13–19), sometimes a realization that God has a particular task for an individual (so Amos 7.14–15), and sometimes a sense that a person has been marked out since before his birth (so Jer 1.4–6; see also Paul in Gal 1.15–16).

Jesus' response to this overwhelming experience was to with-draw into the desert for a period of time ('forty days' in Mark 1.13 and pars. is simply a round number). This has an air of plausibil-ity: Paul, too, withdrew into Arabia and Damascus for three years after his vision of the risen Jesus (Gal 1.17) and Josephus spent time with an ascetic in the wilderness as a young man, exploring his spirituality (*Life* 11). Jesus might well have wanted some time alone with God, seeking his guidance through prayer and fasting. Only the Q tradition gives any indication of Jesus' temptations in the wilderness (Lk 4.1–13//Mt 4.1–11). While their heavy scrip-tural overtones make it unlikely that these passages go back to Jesus himself, their basic point – that Jesus spent his time work-ing out the implications of his new commission – is historically plausible.

## Jesus, John and execution

What was the relationship between Jesus and John after his bap-tism? Did Jesus' movement grow out of John's? Did the two min-istries overlap? And when, precisely, was the Baptist executed? Answering these questions with any degree of certainty is made problematic by the fact that the Markan and Johannine traditions assign different chronologies to the ministries of the Baptist and Jesus.

Mark (followed by Matthew and Luke) makes it clear that Jesus began his ministry only after the arrest of the Baptist (Mk 1.14); in fact, the two events are closely related, almost as if Jesus waited for John's removal before starting out on his own. John, however, has some overlap between the two men, during which time the Baptist is able to introduce Jesus to his disciples and the crowds (Jn 1.19, 26–7, 31, 36, 3.28–30, 10.41). Both accounts are theo-logically driven: for the Synoptics (as we have seen), the Baptist is Elijah who comes to prepare all things; it is only when his ministry is complete that Jesus' mission can begin. For John, however, the Baptist is not Elijah (Jn 1.21); his role is rather to act as a witness to Jesus' identity (Jn 1.15), a role he can best perform if there is some overlap between the ministries. Choosing between these two traditions is difficult, though I would tend to favour the Synoptic presentation over John's highly theological introduction scenes. (It has to be acknowledged that a number of scholars do trust John's report of an overlapping ministry here, such as Dunn, D. M. Smith, P. Fredriksen and Meier.) All we can say with any confidence is that Jesus began his ministry towards the end of John's career, and possibly after he had already been imprisoned.

But what led to John's imprisonment and execution? Once again, the accounts in the Synoptics are broadly corroborated by Josephus. Early on in his reign, Antipas entered into a politically expedient alliance with the daughter of Aretas IV of Nabataea, whom he later divorced in favour of Herodias, the wife of his half-brother Herod Philip (not the tetrarch, *Ant.* 18.110, 136). The marriage was unlawful because his half-brother was still alive (Lev 18.16, 20.21). According to Mark and Matthew, John the Baptist was arrested because he publicly criticized Antipas's actions (Mk 6.17, Mk 14.3). Later on, at Antipas's birthday party, Herodias persuaded her daughter (whom Josephus names as Salome, *Ant.* 18.136) to dance for the tetrarch. He was so entranced that he offered her anything she wanted, even half of his kingdom. After consulting with her mother, the girl asked for the head of John the Baptist; bitterly disappointed, Antipas had to comply. The story has a legendary air, and the details are reminiscent of both the biblical tale of Esther and Jezebel's hatred of Elijah in 1Kings 18-22, but the central claim that John criticized Antipas's marriage may well be historical. Quite apart from the illegality of the union, the divorce of Aretas's daughter was politically dangerous and Antipas would not have wanted a popular holy man continually drawing attention to it.

Josephus' account of John's death is much briefer. He does not mention John's criticism of the marriage (or Herodias's schemes), though he does note Antipas's domestic arrangements in a passage just prior to this one, perhaps indicating that he too saw a connection (*Ant.* 18.109–115). For Josephus, Antipas was worried that John's large following might lead to insurrection, so he had him imprisoned in the fortress of Machaerus and executed (*Ant.* 18.116–19). The account is perfectly compatible with that of Mark's: even if John was not inciting rebellion, his eschatological language and promise of imminent redemption and judgement had a clear political dimension (all the more if John was criticizing Antipas himself and holding him up as an example of an immoral ruler). Not surprisingly, the tetrarch decided to take action quickly, to nip the movement in the bud before trouble could break out.

Assigning precise dates to these events is difficult. Luke suggests that John's movement started in the 'fifteenth year of Tiberius Caesar' (Lk 3.1), or roughly 29 CE. It is less clear, though, when he died. Josephus's account of his death is reported as a 'flashback' while narrating Aretas's successful campaign against Antipas in 36 in retaliation for the tetrarch's treatment of his daughter (Josephus seems to have shared the popular view that Antipas' resounding defeat was retribution for his execution of John, as *Ant.* 18.119 shows). The Baptist's death clearly occurred some time before 36, but it is impossible to date it precisely. (We shall return to chronology in Chapter 11.)

Some time around John's arrest, aged about 30 years old (Lk 3.23), Jesus embarked on his own, independent ministry. It is clear that he continued to hold the Baptist in high esteem (Lk 7.24–28a// Mt 11.7–11a), that he retained much of his predecessor's outlook and perhaps conducted a baptizing ministry himself early on (if baptism had not been a feature of Jesus' ministry it is difficult to see why it was taken up by the early church.[7]) In several important ways, though, Jesus' activities differed from those of John's, and it is to his distinctive ministry that we now turn.

# CHAPTER SEVEN

# Jesus' message

Jesus' public ministry had two interrelated aspects: what he said and what he did. Although the two are closely intertwined, we shall look at his distinctive message in this chapter, and consider his activities as a healer and exorcist in the next.

## The reign of God

Scholars are generally agreed that Jesus' central message revolved around the 'Kingdom of God.'[1] The phrase is hardly used by John (who generally prefers the more inclusive language of abiding friends to hierarchical kingdoms) and Matthew prefers 'Kingdom of Heaven' (a Jewish way of avoiding referring to God). Yet 'Kingdom of God' language is common to both Mark and Q (and at least once in the Greek fragments of *Gos.Th.*) and clearly goes back to Jesus himself.

But what did Jesus mean by the phrase? Although 'Kingdom of God' is not used in the Hebrew Scriptures, most people would have had little difficulty in understanding it. Many biblical passages speak of the kingship of God, who chose Israel to be his people, who reigns over them in a special sense and who would one day be acknowledged even by non-Jews.[2] The prophets were often critical of the reigning monarch and longed for a future age when God himself would rule his people (Is 33.22, 52.7–11), and by the first century this had turned in some circles into a hope for God's eschatological reign (this is clear in *Ps.Sol.* 17.3, *Test. Moses* 10.1, 3., 9 and *1Enoch* 63.1–4). The Greek word translated 'kingdom' (*basileia*) refers not so much to a *place*, a geographical region or realm, as to *God's active reign* over the human world. The Kingdom of God, then, is a shorthand way to describe what the world would be like if God were in control, and to symbolize his reign of justice, mercy and peace.

Nearly all of Jesus' sayings can be subsumed under this overarching theme: descriptions of the kingdom, its arrival, the need for followers to prepare themselves, and the total commitment demanded by those who would be part of it. But when and how would this kingdom come about? Was it something entirely in the future, or already present within Jesus' movement? And would it be inaugurated by God in a great cataclysmic event, or by human beings?

One of the most divisive issues in historical Jesus scholarship revolves around what is usually referred to as Jesus' 'apocalyptic outlook' (see Chapter 1). The word 'apocalyptic' takes its name from a genre of literature, the apocalypse. These texts take a number of different forms, but they generally involve a visionary who reveals heavenly truths, calls for a radical change in behaviour, and foresees God's final victory over the forces of evil, ensuing judgement and cosmic renewal. The debate centres on whether Jesus held an 'apocalyptic eschatology': did he expect the Kingdom to be inaugurated by the imminent arrival of God, cosmic judgement and world transformation? Or did he imagine that the Kingdom was already present within the community of believers, and that society would be gradually transformed through Jesus' radically new ethical behaviour? We shall look at both sides of the argument.

## An apocalyptic Jesus?

The view that Jesus was an apocalyptic prophet has a long pedigree. It established itself as the majority view following the work of Weiss and Schweitzer in the early twentieth century and is particularly championed today by Sanders and Allison (see Chapter 1).[3] There are several strong points in its favour:

1  First is what is sometimes referred to as the 'apocalyptic continuum'. As we saw in the previous chapter, John the Baptist was an apocalyptic preacher, Jesus came to him for baptism and continued to hold him in high esteem. Paul and early Christianity also expected Jesus' imminent return and the establishment of the kingdom in apocalyptic terms (see 1

Thess, in particular). It would seem only logical to suppose that Jesus, too, held such a view.

2   Apocalyptic literature clearly enjoyed some popularity within the Palestinian Judaism of Jesus' day. An apocalyptic eschatology can be found in a variety of roughly contemporary documents: the *Psalms of Solomon*, the *Ethiopic Book of Enoch*, *4 Ezra*, the *Testaments of Abraham* and *Moses*, and several of the documents from Qumran. These texts variously envisage a period of judgement and earthly tribulation, followed by the establishment of God's reign and an earthly paradise.[4] While some have linked apocalypses to disenfranchised and alienated groups at times of persecution, this cannot be established with any degree of reliability (we actually have very little idea as to the identity of most of the authors of these works). Nothing, then, rules out the idea that Galilean peasants under Antipas might have embraced a future hope for God's kingdom in apocalyptic terms.

3   Mark 13 and parallels is saturated with apocalyptic imagery, and several of Jesus' sayings explicitly announce the imminent arrival of God's eschatological reign: Mk 9.1, 10.23, 13.30. We might add to this a number of parables which encourage people to watch for the coming of the Lord; sayings concerning the future vindication of the Son of man; and pronouncements of eschatological woes on contemporaries.[5] Even if the authenticity of some of these passages might be challenged, the number of them within the tradition strongly suggest that Jesus was remembered as someone who spoke in apocalyptic terms.

4   Jesus' sexual ethics presuppose that his was the last generation. Jesus says nothing about the necessity of marriage and having children. Instead, the stress is on the celibate lifestyle in preparation for the beginning of a new age. Jesus expected a final tribulation, a general resurrection into a new age when people would be like angels, and marriage and childbirth were no longer needed (Mk 12.25, Mt 22.30, Lk 20.35–6).

5   The early church interpreted Jesus' death and Resurrection in an apocalyptic manner, an interpretation which makes most sense if Jesus held an apocalyptic eschatology. His death was

accompanied by apocalyptic events: darkness on the earth, an earthquake and resurrection of the dead (Mt 27.51–3). Paul saw Jesus' Resurrection as the 'first fruits of those who have fallen asleep' (1Cor 15.23), that is, the beginning of the eschatological harvest. And even the Fourth Gospel, which has minimized much of the apocalyptic outlook characteristic of the Synoptics, sees Jesus' death as 'the judgement of the world', bringing down the reign of Satan (12.31, 16.11). Once again, whatever the historicity of various points of this tradition, its widespread nature across so many sources suggests that Jesus' message was seen in apocalyptic terms from an early date.

There are strong reasons, then, for concluding that Jesus held an apocalyptic view in which God would intervene in human affairs and establish his kingdom on earth. But what arguments are there against this?

## A non-apocalyptic Jesus

One of the earliest challengers to the apocalyptic Jesus was the British scholar C. H. Dodd, who in the 1930s stressed the 'here and now' element to much of Jesus' teaching (often referred to as 'realized eschatology'). Jesus often speaks in ways that suggest that the kingdom is already here – for those with eyes to see. Since the 1980s, this position has been championed by Marcus Borg and the Jesus Seminar (for whom apocalyptic denial is an article of belief).[6] The principal arguments are as follows:

1  The 'apocalyptic continuum' may not be as self-evident as it appears. Jesus clearly broke with John the Baptist on a number of issues (most notably rejecting John's ascetic lifestyle), so there is no need to assume that he maintained the Baptist's apocalyptic outlook. Furthermore, the intense apocalyptic eschatology of the early church may have *originated* with the resurrection. If so, it might have been read back into Jesus' earlier message, which was then overlaid with an apocalyptic colouring.

**2**   Dodd argued from the 'parables of crisis' that Jesus' own ministry had created the supreme crisis in history, to which hearers must respond in the present.[7] The focus was, thus, on the contemporary world, not a future age.

**3**   Proponents of the non-apocalyptic Jesus often appeal to specific sources. We saw earlier that some argue for different layers within the hypothetical Q document, with wisdom sayings belonging to an earlier layer than apocalyptic material. The *Gospel of Thomas*, too, is largely wisdom literature, with little in the way of apocalyptic material. Those who think that *Gos.Th.* preserves early material, or who see the earliest literary strata of Q as closer to the words of Jesus, conclude that Jesus was a wisdom preacher with little interest in future eschatology. (See fuller discussion in Chapter 2.)

**4**   The Son of man passages have come under particular scrutiny. This unusual term was clearly one of Jesus' favourite ways to speak of himself (see below), and sayings incorporating the term are often broken down into three types: those in which Jesus refers to his humility or authority (Mk 2.10, 28, Lk 9.58); those which speak of the passion and Resurrection of the Son of man (e.g. Mk 8.31 pars); and those which speak in apocalyptic terms of the final vindication of the Son of man (Mk 13.26, 14.62, Lk 12.40). The last category clearly echoes the apocalyptic vision of Dan 7.13 (which speaks of 'one like a Son of man') and, in the view of proponents of the non-apocalyptic Jesus, are best ascribed to post-Easter Christian reflection rather than the historical Jesus himself.

**5**   A number of Jesus' sayings suggest that the kingdom is already present within his movement (see in particular, Mt 12.28// Lk 11.20, Lk 17.20–21), or that God's promises are being fulfilled here and now through Jesus' words and actions (Mt 13.16–17//Lk 10.23–4). A number of parables, too, suggest that the kingdom is here already, unnoticed and growing slowly (Mk 4.30–2 par.). Even if these are not all authentic, their presence within the tradition must be explained.

It is probably fair to say that few scholars have been completely swayed by these considerations, and the dominant position is still to acknowledge a strongly future apocalyptic dimension to Jesus' teaching. It is, however, undeniable that there is an element of the 'here and now' in his preaching. The presence of these sayings in as early a source as Q suggests that it was a component of Jesus' message from the first, though this aspect would clearly have been stressed and perhaps enlarged upon by the early church as the first expectations of an imminent return of Jesus faded.

## Jesus the prophet

Discussions over the extent of Jesus' apocalypticism can mask the fact that the closest analogies to him are Israel's prophets and their announcement of the coming Day of the Lord.[8] This was to be a day of turmoil and judgement, a 'cruel day of wrath and fierce anger', when the wicked would be destroyed. And although the timeframe is not specified, it is clearly 'near and hastening fast' (Zeph 1.14).

Where Jesus went beyond some of the prophets (including John the Baptist), however, was his ability to see more clearly what lay over the horizon. The Day of the Lord was not so much an end in itself as the establishment of the Kingdom, the renewal of the world and human beings within it. Like Isaiah, Jesus could see in his imagination what the Kingdom might look like. Indeed Isaiah 35 might have provided a blueprint: the blind will see, the deaf will hear, the lame shall leap, the dumb will sing, and all creation will become fertile (Mt 11.2-6//Lk 7.18-23). There is a greater optimism about the future in Jesus than in some of his rather pessimistic prophetic counterparts. So strong was his focus on the final goal that there is a sense that the Kingdom is already establishing itself through his announcements and miracles. Once more there are echoes of Isaiah where one of the great passages of the book finishes with the joyful sense that God has already fulfilled his promises (Is 48.20–1).

For both Jesus and the prophets, the announcement of the end is fundamentally an ethical call. Joel puts its clearly:

'Yet even now,' says the Lord,
'Return to me with all your heart,

With fasting, with weeping and with mourning;
And rend your hearts and not your garments.'
Return to the Lord, your God,
For he is gracious and merciful,
Slow to anger, and abounding in steadfast love,
And repents of evil'. (2.12–13)

Like John the Baptist, Jesus knew that what God wanted was not the annihilation of the wicked, but repentance. This is the heart of Mark's summary of Jesus' message: 'The time is fulfilled, and the kingdom of God is at hand; repent, and believe in the gospel' (Mk 1.15). Repentance, as the quotation from Joel shows, is not simply about asking forgiveness for misdeeds, but radically re-orientating one's life back towards God. And much of Jesus' teaching concerns ethical instruction (a good deal of it from Q and found particularly in Matthew's great Sermon on the Mount). Some of Jesus' most quoted and loved sayings belong to this material: the command to love one's enemies and pray for persecutors (Mt 5.44//Lk 6.28, 35); to give alms and fast in secret (Mt 6.4, 17-18); not to serve God and Mammon (Mt 6.24//Lk 16.13); and not to judge others (Mt 7.1-2// Lk 6.37-38). We might call this an *interim ethic*, showing people how to prepare themselves and to live in readiness for the final consummation of all things.

In many respects, the Lord's Prayer perfectly encapsulates Jesus' message. It contains both a future hope that God will come soon to establish his kingdom on earth, but also an acknowledgement of the ethical expectations imposed on followers as they wait:

Father, hallowed by thy name.
Thy Kingdom come.
Give us each day our daily bread;
and forgive us our sins,
for we ourselves forgive everyone who is indebted to us;
and lead us not into temptation.
(Lk 11.2-4; with some differences, Mt 6.9-13)

Whether Jesus actually taught his disciples to pray in this way (as most scholars assume), or whether the prayer is best seen as a summary of themes and emphases within Jesus' preaching (so Crossan), it neatly sums up Jesus' central concerns.

# The restoration of Israel

Although couched in religious language, Jesus' message had clear *political* implications. As we saw with John the Baptist, any talk of judgement and a new age inevitably involved political upheaval, even if those who heard the message had no interest in taking up arms themselves. Talk of a kingdom, even *God*'s Kingdom, had a clear nationalistic dimension. Many of the texts speaking of God's future reign envisaged the ingathering of the scattered people of Israel and the reconstitution of the twelve tribes. Israel's enemies would be judged, foreign overlords cast out and God alone would be king (Deut 30.1–10, Ezek 37.15–28).

That Jesus also thought in this way is indicated by his appoint-ment of twelve disciples. Although their historicity is sometimes challenged, two factors suggest that they were a feature of Jesus' ministry. First, they are mentioned in all our early sources, includ-ing Paul (1Cor 15.5). Second, they quickly lose any relevance in the early church, and within two or three decades most have disappeared from the scene. It is difficult to see why they would have been created by the first Christians, only to be abandoned so quickly. That Jesus appointed twelve men for a particular task, then, is virtually certain. An intriguing feature, however, is that while the lists in the Gospels agree on the more prominent mem-bers, there is some uncertainty regarding the names of the lesser known ones (compare Mk 3.17–19 and pars.). This strongly sug-gests that the *symbolic value* of the disciples as 'the twelve' was more significant that the precise identity of every member. But what did they symbolize? In a Palestinian context, this could only be the *twelve tribes of Israel* (as Mt 19.28//Lk 22.30 makes clear). The ten northern tribes had been swept away in the Assyrian con-quest of the eighth century, and by Jesus' day only the two south-ern tribes remained. The restoration of the original twelve tribes continued to be a deeply held hope which would be manifested in the final golden age (Zech 8.7–8, *Bar* 5.5, *Pss. Sol.* 11.1–9). The presence of the twelve, therefore, symbolized the restoration of Israel, the re-establishment of Israel as it had once been in the days of David and Solomon. (Once the Gospel spread to a Gentile context, this particular element lost its relevance and was down-played.) Jesus' message was clear: through his movement Israel would be reconstituted as in the days of old, and this time God would be king.

The proclamation of the Kingdom of God, then, was not simply a harmless idea in the mind of a pious holy man, but a deliberate and provocative challenge to would-be followers to forsake all other forms of power and control and to re-orient themselves to God. But what language did Jesus use to express his ideas? His manner of communication seems to have been quite distinctive and it is worth pausing to consider some of his common modes of speech.

## Aphorisms

Jesus' most characteristic way of speaking in the synoptic Gospels is by means of pithy sayings (more technically known as aphorisms). These are snappy, witty pronouncements, often resembling proverbs. They are commonly found in wisdom literature, and Jewish collections of such sayings include the books of Proverbs, Ecclesiastes and Ben Sira. Many aphorisms are vivid, often shocking, and frequently force people to think about the world or their values in a new way. They might abruptly demand the reversal of social norms, cleverly turn questions on their heads or offer wise advice. Examples include Jesus' direction to pay to Caesar what belongs to Caesar and to God what belongs to God (Mk 12.17); his prediction that to those who have, more will be given (Mk 4.25); his comment that no one can enter a strong man's house without first binding him (Mk 3.27); and his direction to leave the dead to bury their own dead (Mt 8.22). More than 100 aphorisms are linked to Jesus, many of which are in Q. Some may simply be proverbs which have been ascribed to him later on, but even so, a great many must be authentic and it is reasonable to conclude that Jesus was genuinely remembered for his clever sayings.

## Parables

If the aphorisms are most numerous in the sayings tradition, Jesus' parables are the most strikingly original. The Synoptics contain around 40 parables from a variety of sources (Mk, Q, special Lukan and Matthean material), many of which undoubtedly go back to Jesus. Although John contains no parables, there are parabolic elements in 10.6, 16.25 and 29, and the 'I am' sayings characteristic of this Gospel may well be a development and reflection on earlier parables (so that, for example, 'I am the good shepherd' is a reflection on the parable of the shepherd and his sheep). The word 'parable' comes from the Hebrew *mašal*, meaning riddle, proverb, metaphor and can refer to a broad spectrum of sayings, from the three words said to be a parable in Luke 4.23 ('physician heal yourself') to the much longer and complex narratives of the Lost Son (Lk 15.11-24) or the Wedding Feast (Mt 22.1-14//Lk 14.16-24). Some are more accurately described as similies ('the Kingdom of God is like . . .'), others have allegorical overtones (such as the parable of the wicked tenants, Mk 12.1-9), but nearly all have an element of surprise, a dramatic twist at the end.[9]

Parables were not commonly used by religious preachers. A few can be found in the Hebrew prophets, most notably Nathan's parable to David in 2Sam 12.1–10, and a few more are scattered about rabbinic writings, where their purpose is more commonly to explain the Scriptures. The closest analogies in the Graeco–Roman world are Aesop's fables, though they lack any religious dimension. Jesus used parables first and foremost to describe some aspect of the Kingdom of God, comparing it to settings and actions familiar to his audience. Examples might be the famous parable of the sower (Mk 4.2–9 and pars.) or the Good Samaritan (Lk 10.30–37). Several parables express the quiet growth of the Kingdom (the seeds in Mk 4.3–8 and pars; the mustard plant in Mk 4.30–32 and pars.; the leaven raising the dough in Mt 13.33//Lk 13.20-1). Others say something about God's love, mercy and concern for every individual (for example, the three parables in Luke 15). Jesus draws on contemporary rural Galilean life and the experiences of his audience: farmers, fishermen, women breaking bread, a woman searching for a lost coin, day labourers, absentee landlords and their tenants. He invites his hearers into the familiar surroundings, only to have their comfortable expectations challenged at the end. The stories draw on well-known Jewish themes: God's providential love, his justice tempered with mercy, and his concern for the poor and oppressed. While the proclamation of the Kingdom was new and challenging, the portrait of God was thoroughly familiar.

Mark 4.10–12 ascribes a very odd saying to Jesus. Alone with his disciples, and prior to providing them with a highly allegorical explanation of the parable of the sower (which most scholars assign to the early church), Jesus says:

> To you has been given the secret of the kingdom of God, but for those outside everything is in parables; so that they may indeed see but not perceive, and may indeed hear but not understand; lest they should turn again, and be forgiven.

The implication of these verses seems to be that Jesus' parables are designed to be opaque, that they deliberately obscure the Gospel, and prevent people from understanding. This seems to be completely opposed to the more natural reading of his use of parables outlined above. While Jesus probably realized that not everyone would understand or accept his parables, it is inconceivable that they were *intended to prevent* people turning to God. The key to understanding this passage lies with the recognition that the quotation is taken from Isaiah 6.9–10, commonly seen as the prophet's reflection on what he saw as the failure of his ministry. What we seem to have here is a later reflection *by the early church* on why so many people failed to respond to the message. Israel's rejection of Jesus and his teaching could only be explained as part of God's mysterious purpose. If so, the passage tells us more about the frustrations of the earliest Christians than it does about the purpose of Jesus' parables.[10]

## Sounds like Jesus

Besides his distinctive message, Jesus seems also to have used three distinctive expressions. The first is the solemn use of *Amen* to lend his words authority (see, for example, Mt 5.18, Jn 1.51, etc). The word was used in both Hebrew and Aramaic to endorse the words of others (Num 5.22, Deut 27.15–26) or in liturgical contexts (as it is found commonly in the psalms). Jesus' endorsement of his *own* words would presumably have been unusual and was remembered as a characteristic manner of his speech, perhaps to add emphasis or authority to his pronouncements.

Second, Jesus' address to God as *abba* (father) in prayer also seems to have been distinctive (Mk 14.36). While there is some evidence that contemporary Jews might address God in this way, it was not common. The fact that Paul preserved the Aramaic word in Greek letters sent to predominantly Gentile Christian audiences (Gal 4.6, Rom 8.15), suggests that *abba* had a special place in the tradition. Writing much later, the evangelists have simply translated the term into the Greek word for 'father', *patēr* (for example in the opening of the Lord's prayer). Contrary to popular opinion, *abba* was not a childish form of address (rather like 'daddy'), though it did clearly encompass ideas of intimacy, sonship and filial love. All this suggests that Jesus had a particularly strong, personal sense of the fatherhood of God, which was distinctive enough for his followers to have remembered it.

The third and final expression linked to Jesus is the more complex 'Son of man'. Although the term, in both the singular and plural form, is found in Greek texts of Jewish provenance (the Septuagint, for example, or Philo of Alexandria), it is not a natural expression in Greek and clearly goes back to an Aramaic original. Furthermore, the expression as it consistently occurs in the New Testament with the definite article (*the* Son of man) is unparalleled in any ancient literature, rendering Jesus' use of the term highly unusual. In the Gospels, the expression is Jesus' typical self-designation (even John preserves it, though to a lesser extent than do the Synoptics); it never causes any confusion amongst onlookers, and sometimes parallel texts substitute the term simply with 'I' (compare, for example, Mt 16.13 with Mk 8.27 and Luke 9.8). We saw above that some of the sayings have close links with Daniel 7.13, and that the historicity of these has been disputed. But assuming that the majority of sayings are genuine, what did Jesus mean by this strange term?

An earlier generation of scholars assumed that the Son of man was a *title* in first century Palestine, denoting an apocalyptic figure. And while Schweitzer famously suggested that Jesus predicted the arrival of a heavenly Son of man who would inaugurate the eschatological age (as we saw in chapter 1), most took it that Jesus claimed to be none other than the Son of man himself. There is, however, little evidence that Son of man was ever a title at the time of Jesus. The term is used rather vaguely in *1Enoch* 46.1–4 and *4Ezra* 13.1–4 to refer to the heavenly Son of man in Daniel, but both of these texts may well be later than the time of Jesus. A more recent approach, therefore, has been to argue that the phrase was

a circumlocution for 'I' (so Geza Vermes) or simply means humans
in general (so Maurice Casey), though once again the evidence for
such usages at the time is scarce.[11]

Perhaps all we can say is that the term reflects Jesus' own, distinctive way of referring to himself. It stresses his shared humanity,
but also his particularity (*the* Son of man), perhaps underlining his
sense of having been chosen for a special purpose by God. While it
is quite likely that the early church embellished some of the sayings
with ever-clearer echoes of Daniel 7 (eg Mk 14.62//Mt 27.64), it is
by no means impossible that Jesus began to make some kind of a
connection with the Danielic Son of man himself, particularly as
he reflected both on his role as the one announcing God's eschatological age, and, as his death became increasingly likely, as he
hoped for some kind of future vindication.

The use of Amen, *abba* and Son of man, then, all seem to reflect
Jesus' distinctive manner of speech, expressions which struck his
hearers as both unusual and memorable, and for that reason were
preserved by the tradition. His talk of God's Kingdom spoke to the
imagination of his first-century hearers. It dared them to believe in
God's reign as an imminent possibility, to hope for the reconstitution of Israel as in the days of old and to dream that the hopes of
the Jewish prophets were about to be fulfilled. In the next chapter,
we shall look at the other side of Jesus' ministry: his miraculous
works as both a healer and exorcist.

# CHAPTER EIGHT

# Healer and exorcist

That Jesus healed the sick and exorcized demons in a way that struck onlookers as miraculous is virtually certain. While the First Quest attempted to explain away these great deeds and the Second quietly ignored them, more recent studies have restored Jesus' miraculous healings to a central place, seeing them as an integral aspect of his teaching on the Kingdom of God.[1] This chapter will analyse Jesus' healings and exorcisms in their historical context, before exploring their connection with his message (the so-called 'nature miracles' will be left until the next chapter). Finally, in the light of Jesus' words and deeds, we will ask who Jesus thought he was.

## The evidence

How can we be so sure that Jesus was a miraculous healer? First, Jesus is presented as a healer in all major strands of the tradition (Mark, Q, special Matthean and Lukan material, and John), and as a powerful exorcist in all but John (who presumably fails to record any exorcisms because he sees the Cross as the final, decisive defeat of Satan). Second, as we saw in Chapter 2, Josephus describes Jesus as 'one who wrought surprising feats' (*Ant.* 18.63). Although the authenticity of certain elements within this paragraph has been questioned, most modern scholars accept this relatively modest phrase as genuinely Josephan. Third, opponents of Jesus do not doubt his miraculous acts; their response is rather to deny that Jesus was acting with the power of God and to ascribe his works to a demonic force. The scribes in Mark 3.22, for example, accuse him of being possessed by Beelzebul, the prince of demons. Similarly, later rabbinic tradition responded to Christian preaching by describing Jesus as a magician or a sorcerer, terms intended to discredit and delegitimize his activities rather than to deny them altogether (*b.Sanh* 43a, 107b). The evidence suggests, then, that Jesus was remembered as a miraculous healer from very early on.

This portrait of Jesus is, of course, very difficult to accept for people in the twenty-first-century Western world. Most of us hold to a strictly rationalistic outlook in which there is little room for supernatural manifestations, demon possession, or any kind of healing beyond the bounds of what is medically likely. When analysing Jesus' healings and exorcisms, however, it is important to maintain a critical distance between the texts and our historical reconstruction. We need to steer a path between a naïve credulity which assumes everything happened just as the Gospels describe, and an overly sceptical approach which reduces the accounts to mere superstition on the part of the onlookers. Perhaps more so than any other strand of the Jesus tradition, the accounts of his healings and exorcisms have almost certainly been exaggerated and embroidered, twisted and shaped as they responded and adapted to new settings and cultural contexts. Stories of the miraculous, by their very nature, are likely to be magnified, and while this process began as soon as the stories started to spread around Galilee, it would have intensified significantly after Easter, in response to increasing claims about the identity of Jesus. Some stories, particularly the so-called nature miracles, may even have been created with the specific aim of expressing theological convictions about Jesus (as we shall see in the next chapter). All this means that it would be fruitless to attempt to remove later layers of tradition from the miracles and uncover a historical core. The most we can do in the discussion below is to look at the broad contours of the tradition and ask how we can best make sense of the miracles, and how Jesus' extraordinary abilities contributed to his message.

# Healings

The synoptic Gospels suggest that healings were a central part of Jesus' ministry and that it was his reputation as a healer that drew the crowds (John characteristically offers his own distinctive and much more theological picture in which seven carefully selected miracles, or 'signs', reveal something of Jesus' glory). In many respects, the excitement caused by Jesus is hardly surprising. Although the Essenes were renowned for their herbal remedies and some women might have achieved a certain degree of success in potions and midwifery, medical knowledge was in its infancy at the time and few people in rural communities could ever have hoped to gain access to any kind of skilled practitioner. Many conditions easily treatable today would have had debilitating effects in the ancient world. Deformity and disease, not to mention death itself, would have been far more prevalent than in our own sanitized society. The impact made by a holy man with a gift for healing can hardly be underestimated.

In addition to a number of summary passages, the Gospels record 17 healings performed by Jesus. We hear of him healing lepers, restoring sight to the blind, hearing to the deaf, stopping a woman's flow of blood, repairing withered arms, enabling a paralytic to walk and three revivications (Jairus's daughter in Mark, the widow of Nain's son in Luke, and Lazarus in John). While other healers commonly used spells or incantations (features which could easily lead to the charge of being a magician and sorcerer), Jesus seems to have avoided these methods. We occasionally hear of him using spittle (Mk 7.31–37, 8.22–26, Jn 9.6–7), but more commonly he heals simply by touching or declaring the person cured. It is, of course, possible that the Gospels have toned down any magical elements in Jesus' healings; interestingly, Matthew avoids Mark's suggestion that the woman with a haemorrhage was healed by touching Jesus' garment (which might imply that the garment had magical powers), and makes it clear that it was Jesus' words which were efficacious (compare Mt 9.20–26 with Mk 5.24–34). But the almost complete absence of these elements in the tradition suggests that Jesus' method of healing was simply by the authority of his words.

It is important to note that Jesus was not the only figure in the ancient world associated with miraculous powers. Jewish contemporaries could boast Honi the Circle Drawer who, during a drought in the first century BCE, drew a circle around himself and refused to leave until God sent just the right kind of rain for the crops. A century later, the Galilean Hanina ben Dosa left a more extensive record. He was believed to have been able to heal the sick through prayer, to have asked God to stop the rain, to be able to withstand the bite of a lizard which had killed several people in a town, and to have miraculously lengthened a number of beams so that a house could be built (a similar story is recorded of the infant Jesus in the *Infancy Gospel of Thomas* 13). Like Jesus, both these rather forceful personalities were known as teachers and scholars as well as miracle workers, and both had a close, familiar relationship with God, to the extent that outsiders often thought their attitude disrespectful.[2]

In pagan circles, the god Asclepeius was credited with bringing sight to the blind, voices to the mute and the ability to restore paralysed limbs, and many flocked to his temple at Epidauros. Apollonius of Tyana, too, was a noted first-century healer, and is said to have raised an aristocratic young lady from her funeral procession in one instance. Even the Emperor Vespasian was credited by no less an authority than Tacitus (*Histories* 4.81) with restoring sight to a blind man and the use of a paralysed hand to another. While we might want to retain a certain level of scepticism in all these cases, and stories have doubtless grown in the telling, it seems reasonable to suppose that there is a degree of historicity to at least some of them.

Parallels between Jesus and Jewish and pagan contemporaries, however, should not mask important differences between them. No one else is credited with as many healings and exorcisms as Jesus, nor is any other healer said to act with the same power and intensity. There is no evidence for a 'type' of healer to which Jesus conforms (contra Vermes). In fact, as Eric Eve has pointed out, miraculous activities were relatively uncommon in Jewish tradition, being associated above all with the prophets (particularly Moses, Joshua, Elijah and Elisha) and the great saving events of the Exodus–conquest. While Jesus' great deeds would have certainly contributed to his growing fame and renown, on a more significant level they would have marked him out in the eyes of his contemporaries as a true spokesman of God and authenticated his prophetic commission (a theme we shall return to in the next chapter).

## Exorcisms

The belief in demons was real and widespread in the first-century world, and was accepted in Jewish contexts just as much as pagan. The question in an ancient mind was not *what* caused a particular medical condition, but *who* caused it? And how might a hostile demon be appeased?

Jesus' contemporaries had a number of ways to protect themselves against demons – special amulets to ward off evil spirits, magical papyri containing incantations and, when all else failed, exorcists to drive them out. In the Scriptures, David exorcized King Saul's evil spirit through his music, a story which was developed and expanded by first-century writers.[3] Another famous Jewish exorcism was that of Asmodeus, a demon who had killed a woman's six husbands on their wedding nights. The book of Tobit describes how the seventh husband smoked the heart and liver of a fish in his bridal chamber and frightened the demon away (Tob 3.7–16; 6). Josephus, too, tells of how a fellow Jew named Eleazar exorcized some men in the presence of Vespasian. The exorcist put a ring to a man's nose with a special root under its seal and, when the demon came out, he recited an incantation and ordered the evil spirit to jump into a bowl of water (*Ant.* 8.46–8). Belief in demons is also attested at Qumran: one text credits Abraham with exorcizing an evil spirit from Pharaoh, and another is a collection of incantations against demon possession.[4] Sometimes the evil spirit was believed to have been sent by God as a punishment, sometimes the possessed person was simply unlucky.

Along with various summary statements, the synoptic Gospels describe six accounts of exorcisms performed by Jesus: the man in the Capernaum synagogue, the Gerasene demoniac, the Gentile woman's daughter, a possessed boy, a man who was unable to speak and Mary Magdalene's seven demons.[5] The cause of the problem is known by a variety of terms: demons, evil spirits, or unclean spirits. Although some accounts are more complex than others, they broadly follow a similar pattern to those associated with other Jewish exorcists: Jesus invokes the evil spirit and orders it to leave, it does so violently and the account concludes with a demonstration of the efficacy of the exorcism. Where Jesus departs from other exorcists, though, is the lack of incantations, amulets or other symbolic objects. As with the healings, his authoritative command is enough for even the strongest demon to obey.

## Making sense of the miracles

Jesus' cures have often been seen as psychosomatic, effective not so much because of any great powers inherent in Jesus but because of the faith of sufferers in his ability to cure them. More scientifically, some have tried to explain the miracles by appealing to sociological distinctions between *illness* and *disease*. The former describes the impact of the condition on the sufferer in terms of his or her alienation from society, while the latter describes the medical condition itself. So, for example, Crossan argues that although Jesus was unable to cure people's diseases (the leprosy or the flow of blood still remained), he was able to heal their illnesses, in that he was able symbolically to restore them to their place in society. As a gifted folk healer, he understood people's cares and concerns, their sense of alienation, and all that stood in the way of a true and fulfilled existence.[6]

This theory does have a certain attractiveness. A number of sociological studies have suggested that 'demon possession', in particular, is often a response to domestic, social and political stress, and is especially prevalent in occupied territories as a response to imperialism and colonialism.[7] The 'demon' allows people to give vent to ideas and assertions which might otherwise be socially unacceptable and politically dangerous. It is possible that the rise of Roman power in the East led to widespread feelings of disenfranchisement and despair which manifested themselves in demonic possession. The encounter with Jesus, his authoritative voice and conviction that God was about to act decisively in history might then have been enough to 'cure' such people. The persuasiveness of this thesis depends to a large extent on one's picture of first-century Galilee – the more oppressed and disenfranchised the peasants, the more likely such a proposal appears. If, however, Galilean life, despite its occasional outbursts and underlying tensions was reasonably stable under Antipas, the explanatory power of the theory is weakened.

Similarly, the sociological explanation of the miracles appears at first sight to draw a certain degree of support from the fact that much in the tradition involves the healing and restoration of social relations. Healing a leper was a clear way of allowing a previously excluded person back into society, and the same could be said for the epileptic boy, the widow of Nain's son, and the daughters of the Syro-Phoenician woman and Jairus, all of whom were restored to their parents. The Gerasene demoniac was clearly rescued from a liminal existence and returned to his townspeople, while Peter's mother-in-law was released from her sickbed and able to perform her domestic chores. Yet the stories themselves give no hint that Jesus got to know the people he healed, or that he made any attempt to understand their emotional, psychological or social problems. Instead, as we have seen, he healed instantaneously, often with nothing but a word, and those who saw his actions interpreted them as miraculous (it is difficult to see how a leper could have returned to society unless his disease had actually left him). Social sciences, then, may help to make sense of Jesus' healing activity to some extent, but overall they do not help us to understand the conviction of Jesus' earliest followers that what they were witnessing was God's power breaking into their lives in spectacular acts. In the end, how much of the miracle tradition we are willing to accept as historical is probably determined by our own worldview and where we draw the line on the spectrum of plausibility. Assuming, however, that something is behind the Gospel reports, we need to look now at the link between Jesus' miracles and his preaching.

## The significance of the miracles

At a general level, Jesus' healings and exorcisms demonstrated his extraordinary abilities; they enhanced his prophetic authority and established him as someone through whom God was active. More specifically, though, the Hebrew Scriptures often associated miraculous healings with the coming age. The prophet Isaiah announced a time when the deaf would hear and the blind would see, the lame would leap, and the dumb would speak[8] – the very passage quoted by Jesus in response to John the Baptist's question from prison (Lk 7.18–23//Mt 11.2–6). Jesus spoke of the imminent reign of God and the restoration of Israel, and those witnessing the miracles in this context would understand that through his great deeds the Kingdom of God was in the process of being realized. The miracles were examples of the Kingdom breaking into people's lives, concrete expressions of what it would be like to live under God's reign. This is particularly clear in a passage from Q:

> . . . if it is by the finger of God that I drive out the demons, then be sure the kingdom of God has already come upon you. (Lk 11.20//Mt 12.28)

The full manifestation of the Kingdom was in the future, but the miracles gave a dramatic foretaste of what the Kingdom would be like and assured listeners of the truth of Jesus' words.

The miracles also seem to have been intended to evoke repentance. This is illustrated by another Q passage:

> Alas for you, Chorazin! Alas for you, Bethsaida! If the miracles performed in you had taken place in Tyre and Sidon, they would have repented long ago, sitting in sackcloth and ashes. (Lk 10.13//Mt 11.21).

The point is not so much that those who are healed or exorcized have themselves repented (often there is little indication of this), but rather that the miracles, as witnessed by others, are manifestations of God's power acting through Jesus. They both confirm the truth of Jesus' message and give it a concrete reality. Jesus' words and deeds, then, were inextricably interwoven; his words proclaimed the imminence of the Kingdom while his actions gave a foretaste of what that Kingdom would be like. Both together demanded immediate repentance.

Although Jesus preached his message primarily to poor rural peasants, those to whom Isaiah had promised good things, the miracles symbolically express the inclusivity of the Kingdom. Jesus shows a complete disregard for the age, gender and social status of those he heals (even perhaps healing the occasional Gentile, see Mark 5.1–20 and 7.24–30). All could potentially enter the Kingdom, and the requirements were the same for everyone: they needed to repent, believe in God's saving work and follow him. So urgent was Jesus' call that on one occasion he is said to have commended a would-be disciple to 'Leave the dead to bury their own dead' (Mt 8.18–22//Lk 9.57–62). The only explanation for this deeply offensive statement, which flagrantly ignored a fundamental religious duty, is Jesus' utter conviction that the Kingdom was about to dawn and the demand for a present response.

## Who did Jesus think he was?

All of this leads to one crucial question: how did Jesus see his own role in the Kingdom of God? This, though, is one of the most difficult areas in historical Jesus studies. We have no access to Jesus' motivations and can only attempt to imagine how he saw his role in relation to his wider ministry. Furthermore, although the Gospels are full of what initially appear to be helpful titles for Jesus – Messiah, Son of God, Son of David (even Word of God and Saviour of the World in John!) – these are the product of many decades of Christian speculation on Jesus, fine-tuned through fierce controversies with Jewish opponents and reflecting an influx of new ideas from the Gentile world. As we shall see in the next chapter, it is quite likely that some of Jesus' followers began to see him as Messiah during his lifetime, but is it a role he himself would have welcomed, or even accepted?

On a very basic level, it is difficult not to imagine that Jesus had a strong sense of vocation; that since his baptism by John he felt himself chosen for a special purpose. Aspects of his ministry link him with a range of Scriptural figures. We have already seen that his announcement of God's imminent arrival and the call for repentance put him firmly within the prophetic tradition; his miracles link him to Moses, Joshua, Elijah and Elisha; his social critique to Amos and Hosea; his vision of the future to Isaiah; and his prediction of the fall of the Temple (which we shall look at in Chapter 11) to Jeremiah. How many of these associations derive from early Christian speculation and how much to Jesus himself is impossible to determine, though it is likely that Jesus saw himself as God's spokesman in the scriptural tradition. Given the apocalyptic dimension to his preaching, it is likely too that he saw himself as God's last envoy, the one who would announce the close of his own age and the inauguration of the next.

Does this mean that he saw himself as the Messiah? Certainly it is not a title that Jesus seems to have welcomed. He never refers to himself in this way and appears to distance himself from the term, particularly when its royal, victorious connotations were to the fore (see Mk 8.27–30 and pars.). It is true that Jesus chose twelve men to represent the twelve tribes *in addition to himself*, suggesting that he, too, would have some role in the future Kingdom. Yet he seems to have been remarkably cagey about assigning roles in the new age, either to himself or to others (see the question of James and John in Mk 10.35–44). Jesus' preaching concerned *God* and *God's kingly reign* rather than himself; it was only later, in the post-Resurrection church that Jesus became the centre of his own preaching. He may have had a general sense of being anointed, of being chosen and appointed for a particular task, but whenever he spoke about his own role he preferred to do so in terms of the Son of man. While this may show a link in Jesus' mind between his own actions and the Danielic Son of man ushering in God's golden age, it simultaneously served to emphasize his ordinariness and humanity.

Bruce Malina has reminded us that personality in the ancient Mediterranean world was composed not simply of a person's own view of him or herself, but was inextricably bound up with the views of the larger community.[9] What others thought about Jesus, then, is just as important in working out Jesus' role as his own self-perception. In the next two chapters we shall turn our attention to this topic – first to his family and supporters, and then to his opponents.

# CHAPTER NINE

# Family and supporters

We shall begin our investigation into Jesus' supporters with his family and see that there is evidence that during the ministry itself these relations were strained. This seems to have led Jesus to move his centre of operations to Capernaum, and to redefine his 'family' as those who accepted his message – his closest disciples, both men and women, and the crowds more generally. We shall look at each of these groups in turn and end with a consideration of who Jesus' followers supposed him to be.

## Jesus' family

The Synoptics record a story in which Jesus' mother and siblings hear that he is 'beside himself' and come to take him home, only to be rebuffed by Jesus (Mk 3.21, 31–4 and pars.). Later on, Jesus' preaching in the synagogue at Nazareth strikes his hearers as arrogant and presumptuous, prompting him to remark that 'a prophet never lacks honour except in his home town, among his own relations and his own family' (Mk 6.1–6 and Mt 13.53–58; in Luke's dramatic scene the townspeople even try to kill him, Lk 4.16–30). John, too, notes that Jesus' brothers had no faith in him and urged him to take his ministry to Judaea (Jn 7.1–5). The family tension which stands behind all of these scenes is doubtless authentic.

Reasons for these strained relations are not difficult to imagine. Like many people at the time, Jesus belonged to a large family, with four brothers and a number of sisters (Mk 6.3, Mt 13.55). Perhaps the family initially felt obliged to offer hospitality to Jesus and his companions, hospitality which would quickly have drained their resources. And if Joseph was now dead (as the reference to his mother alone in Mk 6.3 suggests), Mary may well have expected Jesus (as the eldest son?) to take charge of the family, to arrange his sisters' marriages, and to provide for them financially. Perhaps his brothers saw Jesus' lifestyle as an abdication of his responsibilities, a desertion which increased the pressure on themselves and their own families. There is evidence of a reconciliation later on – two evangelists put Mary in Jerusalem at the end of Jesus' ministry and his brother James emerged as leader of the Jerusalem church following a vision of the resurrected Jesus.[1] At the earliest stages, though, the family seem to have been unsupportive, leading Jesus both to redefine his 'true family' as those who accepted his message (Mk 3.31–4 and pars.; Lk 11.27–8), and to make his centre of operations elsewhere.

## Capernaum

Quite apart from providing relief from strained family relations, Capernaum offered a number of advantages over Nazareth. Situated on the northwest shore of the Sea of Galilee close to the border with Philip's territory, it was one of the larger villages in the area, with a population of roughly 600–1,500.[2] The thriving fishing community was a centre of regional trade, and could boast easy access to other settlements around the lake. Mark suggests that it was the home of Jesus' most prominent disciples, Peter, Andrew, James and John.[3] If so, personal links and the expectation of ready sources of hospitality might have been another reason for the choice of this particular town. Jesus became so closely linked with Capernaum that Matthew could simply refer to it as 'his own town' (Mt 9.1).

Tradition associates Jesus with a number of activities in Capernaum: the call of a tax collector variously known as Levi or Matthew; an exorcism in the synagogue; his instruction to Peter to catch a fish with a coin in its mouth to pay the Temple tax; and several healings – an army officer's servant, a paralysed man and Peter's mother-in-law.[4] Whatever we make of individual stories in this list, Jesus was clearly remembered as having preached and healed in the town. Large crowds are also said to have gathered (Mk 1.32–3, 2.2 and pars.), some perhaps anxious to be healed, others attracted by the novelty and wit of the new holy man.

There is also evidence, however, that Jesus was not entirely happy with his reception in Capernaum. The town is condemned in a Q passage, along with Bethsaida and Chorazin, for a lack of repentance when confronted by Jesus' mighty works (Mt 11.23// Lk 10.15). Perhaps the townsfolk were happy enough to have a successful healer in their midst but refused to repent and prepare themselves for the Kingdom. It may well have been a sense of frustration with his experience in Capernaum that convinced Jesus to embark on an itinerant mission. Rather than stay in one place and waste time in discussions with those who refused to believe, he would take the message to others in the surrounding fishing villages and rural settlements. And rather than wait for people to come to him, he would seek out new people and confront them with his urgent message of the approaching Kingdom.

As he made his way around lower Galilee, Jesus was accompanied by various groups of disciples, both male and female, and large crowds. We shall now look at each of these in turn.

## Disciples: the twelve

We have already seen that Jesus was accompanied by twelve male disciples, a group whose importance lay primarily in their symbolic value as representatives of the twelve tribes of Israel soon to be restored in the Kingdom of God. We have also seen that the names of these men were not entirely fixed in the tradition, perhaps indicating that the constitution of the twelve varied from time to time. Most important were an inner group of disciples, consisting of Peter, James and John. These men were with Jesus at some of the most crucial stages of his mission – the raising of Jairus's daughter and the garden of Gethsemane – and were largely responsible for the continuation of the movement after his death.

We know very little about the disciples themselves. The fact that Zebedee, the father of James and John, owned a boat and was able to hire labour (Mk 1.20) suggests that some at least had a certain amount of economic security before their call. It is also reasonable to infer that they had been open to new ideas and were looking for God's saving acts in their lives. We have seen that the Fourth Gospel's suggestion that some of these men were introduced to Jesus by John the Baptist seems to be theologically driven, but it is by no means impossible that some of the twelve had previously been attracted to the Baptist's movement. Although Jesus' message had different emphases to that of the Baptist, its broad parameters had much in common with that of his predecessor.

The Synoptics suggest that the disciples made a complete break with their families after their call (Mk 1.16–20 and pars.). Other clues, however, suggest that while Jesus was active in Galilee, the disciples maintained some connections. In Mark 1.29–31, for example, the whole group enjoyed hospitality at Peter's house, and in Mark 2.15–17 it was the turn of Levi. While Jesus was in Capernaum, some of the group may have simply gone home, to reduce the pressures of catering for a large body of men. Other members of the twelve might well have had families and friends in nearby Bethsaida, Chorazin or Gennesaret, on whose generosity Jesus and his disciples might have depended when in those towns. Once the company embarked on their journey to Jerusalem, though, the disciples must have made a much cleaner break with their families. Jesus' promise that eternal life would be granted to those who had 'given up home, brothers or sister, mother, father or children, or land' for his sake doubtless reflects something of the complete commitment expected by the movement (Mk 10.28–30, Lk 18.28–30). Luke's Jesus even demands that followers *hate* their families (Lk 14.26) and allows would-be followers neither to bid their relatives farewell nor to bury a dead father (Lk 9.59–62). The Gospels, of course, were written to encourage discipleship, often at times of difficulty and even persecution; their depiction of the unquestioning faith of the first disciples was clearly intended to inspire and strengthen subsequent disciples. There is no reason, though, to suppose that Jesus did not demand total allegiance from followers, particularly once he turned his face towards Jerusalem and the eschatological nature of his message became increasingly urgent.

As Jesus and his company made their way to the southern region of Judaea, they would often have had to depend on the generosity and hospitality of people they met on the way. Sometimes they may even have had to sleep in the open (Mt 8.20). Throughout all of this, the small band were accompanied by a group of women – and it is to these that we now turn.

# Disciples: women

Since the 1980s it has been common to emphasize the presence of women in Jesus' movement. It is often claimed that Jesus was particularly open to women, welcoming them into his inner group and proclaiming an egalitarian Kingdom. Frequently, Jesus' attitude towards women is contrasted with what is seen as a restrictive and oppressive attitude towards women in contemporary Jewish society, thus setting a liberating Jesus against a thoroughly patriarchal Judaism. The anti-Jewish tone of this argument is all too clear, as Jewish feminists have been quick to point out. Historically, too, it has little to recommend it: there is no evidence that Jewish women in Palestine led particularly restricted lives (in fact, women throughout the Empire were enjoying greater freedom than ever before in this period). Women certainly flocked to hear Jesus, and his parables and sayings reflect women's lives and experience, but there is nothing in these images which challenges conventional feminine roles. And though Jesus (like the prophets before him) had a great deal to say about poverty and riches, and what we might call economic equality in the coming Kingdom, he says nothing about gender equality. This should not particularly surprise us: all ancient societies were patriarchal, and there are no examples of egalitarianism as we would understand it in any contemporary context, whether Jewish or Graeco–Roman. Tempting as it might be to see Jesus as a 'feminist', the evidence cannot support such a claim. Women play a role in his movement not primarily because of Jesus' radical social views but rather because Jewish society of the time allowed them to act in these ways.[5]

Mark mentions a large group of women at Jesus' cross, including three named individuals: Mary Magdalene; Mary, the mother of James the Younger and of Joses; and Salome (Mk 15.40–41). These women, he says, had been with Jesus in Galilee where they followed and 'ministered' to him. The likeliest interpretation of this is that the women were responsible for domestic arrangements, cooking and serving at table, as the little group made its way around Galilee. Luke puts his reference to the women who accompanied Jesus much earlier, naming only Mary Magdalene, Joanna, the wife of Chuza, Antipas's steward, and Susanna (Lk 8.1–3). These women have all been healed from various ailments, thus owing Jesus a debt of gratitude, and the manner in which they are presented casts them in the rather more respectable role of patronesses, providing financial support for the travellers. Although wealthier women like Joanna may well have been part of Jesus' group, Mark's picture of ordinary women (perhaps some of them wives or friends of the disciples?) engaged largely in domestic service is more likely to be historically accurate. There would have been nothing particularly strange or scandalous about men and women travelling as a group, particularly if the latter were seen to oversee domestic arrangements – men and women regularly travelled together to Jerusalem for the Passover and other feasts.

Considerable attention has been focussed in recent years on the figure of Mary Magdalene. Although she has a certain prominence in all four Gospels, it is striking how little we actually know about her. In addition to the passages cited above, she is said to have been the first to witness the risen Jesus in John 20.11–18. Through a convoluted process of linking the story of the sinful woman from the city who anoints Jesus in Luke 7.36–50 with the story of Mary (of Bethany) anointing Jesus in John 12.1–8, and the similarity of names, church tradition saw her as a repentant prostitute. Yet there is nothing in the biblical text itself to support such a reconstruction. Later Gnostic texts also accorded her a prominent place (which probably explains the desire of the church fathers to denigrate her). She was clearly a prominent female follower of Jesus, but there is no reason to assume that she had a particular relationship to him (in fact, modern studies which aim to 'enhance' her role by casting her as Jesus' wife only continue the attempts of the church fathers to demean her).[6]

Clearly, then, Jesus both preached to women about the coming Kingdom of God and welcomed them into it as it was being symbolically constituted on earth through his movement. As we saw in the last chapter, women as often as men were the recipients of Jesus' miraculous healings or exorcisms, and Jesus occasionally used examples from women's experiences in his preaching (such as the parables in Lk 15.8–10 and 18.1–8). But why were women attracted to Jesus and his movement? It is often claimed that the eschatological orientation of the group, as with other millenarian groups, led to a certain egalitarianism which women, in particular, found attractive. It is certainly possible that women were attracted by less rigid gender divisions within the movement and the fact that usual household concerns were now taking second place to an exciting and adventurous participation in Jesus' vision. Some women may also have been intrigued by Jesus' reputation as a healer and hoped to learn from him; it was often women in the ancient world who were most closely linked with the use of herbs, ointments and the healing arts. But even if (as I have argued) women's roles were largely domestic and Jesus did little to challenge this, there is nothing to suggest that these women were not as engaged and inspired by Jesus' message as were their male contemporaries. They had left behind their homes and families for the sake of the gospel just as the men had done. Like them they were swept away by Jesus' announcement of an imminent Kingdom of God and responded with repentance and belief in God's saving acts.

## Crowds

Throughout his ministry, Jesus continued to attract large crowds. Sometimes these appear to have been so large that they constrained his movements, forcing him to withdraw secretly, or to take to a boat on the lake to preach to them. A wide range of people seem to have sought Jesus out: people of high status (such as the rich young ruler), synagogue officials, tax collectors and, of course, the people with whom Jesus was particularly concerned, the poor and outcast. Almost all, however, appear to have been *Jewish*, and Jesus seems to have directed his mission predominantly, if not exclusively, to Jews.

Untangling this aspect of Jesus' ministry is complicated by the fact that the Gospels were written at a time when Gentiles were an integral part of the church, and the evangelists show a natural desire to locate the origins of Gentile inclusion firmly within the life and ministry of Jesus. So Mark includes a 'Gentile cycle', a series of stories in which Jesus heals and feeds Gentiles (Mk 7.24–8.21; see also Mt 15.21–39). Luke, however, has Jesus preaching only to Jews and leaves all contact with Gentiles to the book of Acts. This embodies Luke's theological scheme whereby the message was taken first to Jews and only to Gentiles when it was rejected, but it may have some basis in history. John, too, though he makes occasional allusions to a future Gentile mission (10.16, 11.55, 12.20–21), locates Jesus' ministry exclusively towards Jews and Samaritans. The Gospels occasionally show Jesus travelling beyond the boundaries of Galilee and Judaea, into Tyre, Sidon, the Decapolis and Caesarea-Philippi, but these were all part of Israel as it was in the glory days under David and Solomon. And while Jesus might occasionally have come into contact with or healed a Gentile, his message seems to have been directed first and foremost to Israel. A mission only to fellow Jews fits with the election of the twelve and the motif of the restoration of Israel. Presumably, like the prophets, Jesus envisaged a time when Gentiles, too, would be gathered to God's holy mountain (Is 2.1–4, Mic 4.1–4). Indeed, if there was nothing in Jesus' message which allowed for the inclusion of Gentiles it is difficult to see why the early church began to offer the message to them as early as it did (Acts 11.20–21). During the lifetime of Jesus, though, the message was taken only to the 'house of Israel' (Mt 10.6, 15.24).

## Who do people say that I am?

The large crowds associated with Jesus are reminiscent of those who flocked to John the Baptist at the River Jordan and anticipate those who flocked to the sign prophets two or three decades later. But who did the people think that Jesus was? How did they fit him into their view of the world? Jesus is said to have asked this very question, to which the disciples replied: 'John the Baptist; and others say, Elijah; and others one of the prophets' (Mk 8.27–30 and pars.; also Mk 6.15 and pars.). While the ensuing dialogue between Peter and Jesus arguably reflects the later beliefs of the post-Easter church, the response of the disciples here is illuminating and shows that popular perceptions of Jesus understood his activity firmly within the prophetic tradition. As we saw in the last chapter, miracles tended to be associated in Jewish tradition with Israel's prophets and the exodus-conquest story. Jesus' miraculous healings, then, placed him firmly in the context of Israel's mythic past, and established him not only as the prophetic spokesman for God but also as one announcing future national deliverance.

In particular, Jesus' audience might have associated him with Moses who had been responsible for a spectacular series of miracles in the Scriptures (Ex 13–17); indeed a 'prophet like Moses' was popularly associated with the End Times (Deut 18.15–22). Or they might have associated Jesus with his namesake, Joshua, who led the Israelites into the Promised Land (Josh 1–4). Perhaps, as Galileans, they favoured Elijah and Elisha, northern prophets associated with a series of miraculous deeds (1Kgs 17–2Kgs 13). If John the Baptist had foretold the imminent arrival of Elijah, some may well have made this connection with Jesus, and seen his presence as an indication of the imminent arrival of the eschaton. The fact that the sign prophets, later in the century, could invoke these great figures from the past suggests that they retained a current potency, and that people were only too eager to see spectacular events of the past re-enacted in their own times.

Some of Jesus' followers presumably understood his message better than others. John 6.15 records an attempt by some to make him king. Whatever we make of this verse, it is likely that some did misunderstand Jesus and took his talk of a kingdom to imply that he harboured political pretensions. If so, they must soon have been disappointed. It could not have taken long for people to realize that the Kingdom preached by Jesus was not going to be established by humans through a violent call to arms, but by God.

But did some see Jesus as a non-violent eschatological king, along the lines of the Davidic messiah outlined in *Pss.Sol.* 17 – an ideal judge, king and shepherd, who in the coming era would reign under the ultimate authority of God? Might they, in other words, have seen him as some kind of messiah, perhaps with a future kingly role in the kingdom he proclaimed? Certainly the Synoptics suggest that Jesus' disciples had begun to see him in messianic terms (Mk 8.29 and pars.). Peter's confident proclamation here clearly owes a great deal to the post-Easter church and its convictions both that Jesus was 'the Messiah' and that the Hebrew Scriptures (when read properly) provided a blueprint for his role. On a broader, more general level, though, Jesus' talk of God's approaching Kingdom, coupled with his mighty works and clear prophetic activity, might well have led them to wonder if Jesus might well be some kind of anointed End Time prophet. If the disciples were capable of seeing Jesus in this way, then others who gathered to hear his message might well have also shared the same hopes. In fact, Pilate's decision to execute Jesus as 'King of the Jews' (which we shall consider in Chapter 12) makes little sense unless Jesus was seen by at least some as a kingly messiah.

The crowds, then, most likely saw Jesus as a charismatic leader who derived his authority not from the traditional power structures of the day (Temple, priesthood and Torah), but from his own authoritative personality and his prophetic ability to speak for God. His words and actions were deeply entwined with both Israel's past and the nation's hopes and aspirations for the future. Jesus may not have fitted into any one pre-existing script, but his activities were recognizable to his audience and tapped into some of their deepest longings for deliverance. Quite how they made sense of his role would have varied, but some presumably already began to see him as God's long-prophesied anointed one even during his lifetime.

## Stories about Jesus

The Gospels make it clear that Jesus' reputation spread quickly and widely. We do not need to wait until the late first century for tall stories and exaggerated claims to be made about him. Quite probably, the Galilean villages were buzzing with incredible tales of Jesus' actions almost as soon as he made his first appearance.

It is probably in this context that we need to understand the origins of the so-called 'nature miracles'. This group includes two miraculous feedings (the 5,000 and the 4,000), accounts of Jesus walking on water, stilling the storm, cursing a fig tree and the Transfiguration. It is often noted that while Jesus' healings and exorcisms demonstrate his *authority*, the nature miracles are all concerned with his *identity*. As told in the Gospels, these stories do not advance the plot, they are witnessed only by the disciples and they are heavily overladen with scriptural allusions.[7] In fact, it is possible sometimes to detect subsequent layers of scriptural additions. The feeding of the 5,000, for example, despite its Eucharistic overtones and links with the story of the manna in the wilderness (Ex 16), seems at its heart to be a retelling of Elisha's feeding of the 100 men in 2 Kings 4.42–4. And the stilling of the storm, which in its present form has echoes of the crossing of the Red Sea (Ex 14), has much in common with the story of the Galilean prophet Jonah (1.1–16). Once Jesus became linked in popular imagination with prophetic figures such as Elisha and Jonah, it is easy to see how stories associated with the great men of old were retold in connection with him. The saying, reported in Q, that 'something greater than Jonah is here', may well have encouraged such imaginative reapplication of stories (Mt 12.41//Lk 11.32). As tales were passed around the post-Easter church, they acquired new overtones and allusions. In the accounts of walking on the water and stilling the storm, Jesus' words echo the voice of God in Is 43.1–2, and the stories as a whole were gradually seen as examples of God's triumph over the waters of chaos and rescue of his people.[8] By this stage, the stories were not so much accounts of Jesus' activities as post-Easter illustrations of his divinity. The Transfiguration, too, illustrates Jesus' divine sonship, and the Christian belief that he had fulfilled both the Law and the prophets (Mk 9.2–8 and pars.).

It is possible that some kind of historical event lies at the heart of these stories, but equally likely that their origin and development derives exclusively from connections made by followers, first to the prophets and then later to the increasingly high Christology of the early church. It was not unknown for great men to be linked with extraordinary abilities in the contemporary world: Philo, for example, presents Augustus as the 'averter of evil' who calmed the terrestrial storms and healed pestilences (*Legatio* 144–5) and Nero, too, had a storm-stilling to his credit (Calpurnius Siculus, *Eclogue* iv.97–100).[9] As time passed, Jesus, just as much as Augustus or Nero, might be associated with extraordinary powers which surpassed anything he was ever able to do on earth.

Most of these developments, however, come from a time well beyond that of Jesus. We need to return to Jesus' ministry now and look at those who chose not to follow him. Clearly, the Galilean prophet was a controversial figure whose message had a polarizing effect: large crowds flocked to him to see his miracles and to hear his preaching of the Kingdom, while others were suspicious of the source of his power and mistrustful of his intentions. The most serious objections to Jesus would come from the priestly leaders in Jerusalem (as we shall see in Chapter 12); in the next chapter, however, we shall confine ourselves to early opponents, those who rejected Jesus' message in Galilee and one ruler who might well have been more than a little interested in Jesus' activities.

# CHAPTER TEN

# Opposition in Galilee?

Although Jesus attracted large crowds throughout Galilee, it is clear that not everyone was swept away by his ministry. As we would expect from any popular figure, he attracted a range of opponents and detractors. Some wished to debate theology with him, others may have been more fearful of any political repercussions, yet others presumably regarded him with deep distrust. We shall look at opposition to Jesus in this chapter under two headings: the Pharisees and Herod Antipas.

## Jesus and the Pharisees

We saw in Chapter 1 that older studies of the historical Jesus tended to assign a central place to his debates with the Pharisees. It was here that Jesus' completely new conception of God's love, mercy and forgiveness could be contrasted with the sterile, legalistic 'Jewish' view of God, represented above all by the Pharisees. Modern research on the Pharisees has come a long way in recent years (as we shall see below), and these caricatures of both the Pharisees and contemporary Judaism are no longer sustainable. Furthermore, it is now clear that the Pharisees of the Gospels reflect the often turbulent 'partings of the ways' between the emerging Christian movement and its Jewish parent in the late first century. Stories of conflict over Sabbath observance, food laws and purity were preserved in the tradition (and probably intensified), because they proved useful as the early Christian congregations attempted to define themselves against their synagogue neighbours. Some of the intense hostility shown by Jesus towards Pharisees (such as the series of woes in Matthew 23), even if it has a historical kernel, doubtless reflects the sense of hurt and outrage experienced by the evangelists' communities at the hands of contemporary Pharisaic synagogue leaders. And the suggestion that Jesus was seen as a blasphemer by the Pharisees in Mark 2.7 and pars. is probably also a retrojection of later, post-Easter disputes. To appreciate the historical Jesus' relationship with the Pharisees, we need a clearer picture of what they were really like at the time.

The Pharisees were a lay movement, probably originating around the time of the Maccabean revolt in the second century BCE. Josephus (who claims to have been a Pharisee himself, *Life* 12) suggests that there were around 6,000 of them in the early first century.[1] Although it is likely that some were based in Galilee (as Mk 2.18–19, 24 suggests), the majority were around Jerusalem in the south. Central to Pharisaism was the meticulous interpretation of the Law, both the written Torah and their own oral traditions.[2] Pharisaic discussions from this period (as preserved in the earliest rabbinic texts) reveal lively and strident debates on matters such as table-fellowship, ritual purity, food production and preparation, and tithing. All of this shows a concern with purity and distinctiveness. They seem to have striven to keep the laws of Levitical purity in their own homes, just as the priests did in the Temple. In other words, they aimed to maintain a state of permanent 'Temple holiness' in their day-to-day activities. This would have necessitated keeping themselves apart from ordinary people to some extent and probably explains the origins of their name (Pharisee means 'separated ones').

There is some debate as to how influential the Pharisees were in the first century. E. Rivkin argued that the group maintained an active political involvement from their origins in Hasmonaean times, though the difficult reign of Herod, and continued on under direct Roman rule. On the basis of certain passages from Josephus,[3] he claimed that they were a powerful and authoritative scholarly group with particular influence over judicial and educational matters. J. Neusner, however, concluded that by the time of Jesus, the Pharisees had lost their political influence and had withdrawn into an inward-looking movement centred in the home. The reality was probably somewhere between these two extremes. Under Roman rule, the Pharisees had no formal religious or political position in Judaean society; the day-to-day running of the nation was left to the aristocratic priesthood in Jerusalem (as we shall see in the next chapter); it was the high priest and his advisers who made laws and judged legal matters. Similarly, as S. Mason has shown, although Pharisees were active in synagogue life, there is no evidence that they controlled the synagogues prior to the war with Rome (again, the priests seem to have been in charge). Yet their previous political power and the high esteem in which they were held by ordinary people probably means that they retained a level of social influence far beyond their actual authority.[4] What the Pharisees thought clearly mattered to many ordinary people and several of their broader religious ideas were adopted by the masses, particularly their beliefs in angels, resurrection and fate.

Jesus criticized the Pharisees' love of money, presumably indicating that some at least were affluent (Mt 6.24//Lk 16.13–15); he himself advocated a far more radical renunciation of worldly wealth (Mk 10.21 and pars.). In general, however, he clearly approved of the Pharisees' pursuit of righteousness, though he criticized their preoccupation with parading it before other people.[5] He told his followers that their righteousness needed to exceed that of the Pharisees and scribes (Mt 5.20), and that they should aim at perfection (Mt 5.45//Lk 6.36). In ideas which the Pharisees would no doubt have endorsed, Jesus made it clear that true righteousness flowed from the right attitude of the heart, true repentance and humility before God.

The Pharisees, for their part, would certainly have been interested in Jesus. As a holy man and preacher they would have wanted to know his views and how he justified them from Scripture. The issues about which they debate are what we might expect: in Mark it is Sabbath observance (2.24, 3.2), purity (7.1–8) and divorce (10.2–9). The latter was clearly a matter of current debate at the time and the Pharisees were themselves split in their interpretation of the ruling of Deuteronomy 24.1, which allowed a man to divorce his wife if he found 'some indecency in her'. The stricter house of Shammai allowed divorce only for unchastity, while the more lenient house of Hillel allowed a man to divorce his wife for a range of misdemeanours. Jesus' response in Mark (though ameliorated to some extent by Mt 19.9) went beyond even the strictest Pharisaic views and allied him with the more uncompromising Essenes, who did not countenance divorce in any situation. Matthew charac-teriztically escalates Pharisaic hostility or adds them where Mark mentions only the more general 'scribes' (local officials and legal experts); a feature which probably tells us more about the strained synagogue-church relations in Matthew's environment than about the historical Jesus.[6]

It is important to recognize that there is never any question in these disputes of Jesus *breaking* the Law. There are only two places where this possibility is even raised. First, Jesus' *disciples* are chal-lenged in Mark 2.23–8 with breaking the Sabbath by plucking ears of corn. Although he justifies their actions, Jesus is not himself shown as taking part in this (nor do we know for sure precisely what was permitted in Galilee at the time). Second, Mark 7.19 interprets certain words of Jesus to be annulling the food laws ('Thus he declared all foods clean'). By almost universal agree-ment, however, this was not Jesus' intention and the explanation was added by Mark for his largely Gentile (non-Law-observant) audience.[7] If Jesus had been as explicit as this regarding dietary laws, the endless controversies of the early church on the topic are inexplicable (see Acts 10.11–17). In Matthew, Jesus came not to abolish the Law but to fulfil it (5.17–19), and the series of antitheses which follow suggest that he went beyond the requirements of the Law, demanding a higher righteousness of his followers (5.21–48). The issue, then, was not so much whether Jesus kept the Law as his *interpretation* of various points.

More controversial is the question of purity regulations (laid out especially in Lev 11–15).[8] Ritual purity was an important aspect to the Jewish faith in Jesus' day and a wide range of things could make a person ritually unclean (either temporarily or for a longer period of time). Many of them were simply normal bodily func-tions – menstruation, ejaculation, childbirth, or contact with a corpse, unclean animal or person – and so most people would have been unclean quite frequently. The usual way to deal with this was to wait for a prescribed length of time and to immerse oneself in a ritual bath (known as a *miqveh*; on the presence of these in Galilee, see Chap. 5). Uncleanness was not the same as sin, and only really became an issue when someone wanted to go into the Jerusalem Temple (where high levels of purity were demanded). There is no evidence that synagogues excluded those who were ritually impure, nor that impure people were routinely shunned (though it is easy to see why those with leprosy or certain types of demon possession might have been avoided for other reasons). Even the Pharisees, who maintained a high level of personal purity, did not impose their standards on others.

What, then, was Jesus' attitude to ritual purity? There is a certain amount of disagreement on this issue among Jesus scholars, with writers as diverse as Dunn and Crossan arguing that Jesus paid little attention to purity, and Sanders, Flusser and Vermes maintaining that it was important to him. Living at a considerable distance from the Temple, it is possible that Galileans tended to be rather more lax (or perhaps simply different) in their interpretations of the purity laws.[9] It is clear, too, that Jesus was quickly believed to have been able to touch impure people without himself contracting impurity (see, for example Mk 1.40–45, 5.25–34), a feature which may well have led to a relativizing of purity matters within the Christian movement. Yet there is nothing in the tradition to suggest that Jesus preached a general disregard for purity regulations. We have seen that he submitted himself to John's baptism, with its strong connection to ritual purity; it is also clear that Jesus' apostles continued to attend the Temple after his death, which would have required them to maintain a certain level of ritual cleanliness. Purity was important to many religious groups at the time, not just Jews, and was a necessary element of holiness and preparation for contact with the divine. The issue, once again, as far as the Pharisees were concerned, was Jesus' *interpretation* of purity requirements – how purity was to be achieved and maintained within his following and to what extent it was expected in everyday life.[10] (Once Christianity began to spread into the Gentile world, purity requirements were abandoned along with the rest of the Law.)

There was much in Jesus' teaching with which contemporary religious thinkers might have agreed: his insistence on the centrality of love and concern for one's neighbour are found in a variety of Jewish sources, and his saying about the Sabbath being for man and not man for the Sabbath is echoed in 2Macc 5.19 and b.*Yoma* 85b. Few would have disputed that it is what comes out of a person that makes him or her pure or impure (Mk 7.15), and no one would have objected to his healing on the Sabbath by an authoritative command. Where the Pharisees particularly parted company with Jesus, however, seems to have been on the matter of table-fellowship.

## Table fellowship

Bound up with Jesus' proclamation of the Kingdom were his shared meals with followers. Luke particularly likes to show Jesus as a guest, visiting his hosts and sharing his teaching with them.[11] Who a person ate with in the ancient world – just as today – had extremely important social and cultural implications, and Jesus' extension of table-fellowship to a wide range of people from a diversity of backgrounds had a very clear message. The meals were symbolic enactments of the messianic banquet of the End Times (Is 25.6, 2Bar 29.5–8, Mt 8.11, Lk 14.15), and a sign that these hopes were about to be realized in the coming Kingdom.

It is clear, though, that not everyone regarded these shared meals positively. In a Q passage, Jesus' opponents characterize him as 'a glutton and a drunkard, a friend of tax collectors and sinners' (Mt 11.19//Lk 7.34). The 'scribes of the Pharisees' take offense at his eating with 'tax collectors and sinners' in Mark 2.15–17 and pars.; and in Luke 19.7 a wider group of observers are taken aback by Jesus' decision to eat at the home of Zacchaeus, the chief tax collector. On a purely social level, eating with a mixed group of people would have been unusual and questionable behaviour, especially in a religious teacher and healer whose successful ministry would make his association with undesirables rather suspect. Clearly Jesus' eating habits were deeply objectionable to some and highly questionable to others.

But who were these table companions? And what precisely was the cause of Jesus' offence? It is often pointed out that tax collectors were generally despised in both Graeco–Roman and Jewish literature. Whether they operated in a supervisory capacity like Zacchaeus, or at a more minor level collecting transport tolls or fishing rights, their livelihood allowed them a great deal of scope for personal gain. They also, almost by definition, were required to work closely with the ruling powers – whether Herodian or Roman – and would have been regarded as collaborators and quislings. The term 'sinners' covered a much broader group of people. Clearly it included those who lived their lives outside the Law, presumably with little, if any, interest in following its precepts. But it probably also encompassed a grey area, where it might be a matter of debate as to whether a person was a 'sinner' or not. Women were particularly vulnerable here. Poor women often had little power over their own lives and might easily fall into prostitution; others might have found themselves in situations judged immoral by the more pious but without any personal ability to change their circumstances. The label 'sinners' was, thus, to a large extent an assessment by outsiders, whose judgements would have been coloured by their own assumptions and prejudices.

Which understanding of 'sinners' best fits Jesus' associates? E. P. Sanders famously suggested that Jesus ate with people who were outside the Law and that he made no demand on them first to repent. This would certainly explain the hostility of the Pharisees, who would have been appalled at Jesus' choice of companions.[12] Yet this is perhaps the aspect of Sanders's work which has been most criticized by other scholars. It is true that calls for repentance are not as prevalent in the tradition as we might expect, but Mark makes it central in his summary of Jesus' Gospel (Mk 1.15) and it is difficult to see why Jesus would have abandoned the Baptist's demand on this issue. In all likelihood, then, Jesus' table companions had responded to his message by repenting of their past lives. Yet even if this was the case, and their inclusion in Jesus' group signalled their commitment to his moral vision in the future, Jesus' easy acceptance of them may well have been troublesome to outsiders. How could they be sure that their repentance was genuine, particularly since there was no sign that they had followed the obligations laid on them by the Law? (We are not told that Jesus, any more than John, asked people to demonstrate their repentance through sacrifice in the Temple.) There might well have been the suspicion that Jesus had abandoned any kind of purity in his fraternizing with these people. And on a more theological level, Jesus' table companions raised profoundly difficult questions: if tax collectors and sinners were really to be the first into the Kingdom, with little more than a cursory nod in the direction of repentance, what was the point of living a righteous life? From a religious teacher, even one who unquestionably kept the Law himself, this was deeply perturbing.

Read in this way, 'tax collectors and sinners' is a shorthand label for undesirables, coined by Pharisees and perhaps other pious ones who refused to believe that some people could ever change their ways. Had they genuinely believed that these 'sinners' had turned to God, they would doubtless have been only too pleased. As it was, a certain cynicism (which in some cases may well have been warranted) meant that they saw in Jesus' shared meals not symbols of the messianic banquet, but a blatant disregard for true repentance and adherence to the Law. Jesus' behaviour would have been deeply unsettling to his Pharisaic contemporaries, and would have raised serious questions regarding his message and his claim to speak for God.

In all this we need to remember that the Pharisees engaged in *dialogue and debate* with Jesus, often it was heated, and sometimes both sides would have left the argument frustrated and annoyed. But there were never any attempts by the Pharisees to *kill* Jesus. The note that they plotted his death (Mk 3.6 and pars.) is undoubtedly a later attempt to increase Pharisaic hostility towards Jesus. The Pharisees were not in a position to kill anyone, they had no reason to wish to do away with Jesus, and when he was eventually executed the people who handed him over to Rome were not the Pharisees but the chief priestly rulers. In Galilee, though, there *was* a potentially deadly threat to Jesus, and that came from the Jewish tetrarch, Herod Antipas.

## Antipas

One rather curious aspect of the Jesus tradition is that he is never said to have preached in the Galilean cities. We hear of his ministry in Nazareth, Capernaum, Bethsaida and a host of small villages and remote locations, but no story is located in Sepphoris or Tiberias. This is all the more surprising, given the fact that Sepphoris was only an hour's walk from Nazareth (Jesus might well have known people there), and Tiberias's shoreside location made it easily reachable from other settlements regularly found on Jesus' itinerary. As we saw in Chapter 5, Sepphoris, and later Tiberias, were Antipas's administrative centres, hubs of bureaucracy and local government, the very core of the tetrarch's power in the region. The cities were the natural homes of the Herodians (Mk 3.6, 12.13–17//Mt 22.15–22), Antipas' officials, political supporters and retainers. Although Jewish, many of the inhabitants were wealthier and perhaps more cosmopolitan and Hellenized than people in the surrounding areas.

It is, of course, possible that stories recording Jesus' preaching in these cities have simply not been preserved. Alternatively, Jesus may have preferred preaching to rural folk who might have better understood his pastoral images and metaphors. But a further option, which merits serious consideration, is that Jesus deliberately avoided the cities. Perhaps the fate of John the Baptist was still very much in his mind, leading him to take steps to avoid a confrontation with the tetrarch. Luke suggests that at least two of Antipas's courtiers were attracted to the new movement (Lk 8.2–3, Acts 13.1); if so, he could hardly have been unaware of Jesus and his activities. The Synoptics maintain that he kept an eye on Jesus and saw him as a second Baptist (Mk 6.14–16 and par.). The passage as it now stands forms an introduction to the account of the Baptist's beheading, but is may well go back to a genuine historical tradition that Antipas began to be concerned about Jesus, or at least that Jesus and his closest followers feared that he might.

Luke's gospel has a number of other traditions involving Antipas. In 9.7–8, he expresses a desire to see Jesus, and in 13.31 a group of Pharisees (here presented in an uncommonly positive light) warns Jesus that the tetrarch wants to kill him. In reply, Jesus refers to Antipas as 'that fox' (a reference to his cunning cleverness? or his inferiority as a ruler?) and acknowledges that he must leave Galilee 'because it is unthinkable for a prophet to be killed outside Jerusalem' (13.32–3). Whatever the historicity of the exchange, Jesus doubtless was only too aware of the risks he ran in Galilee. Once he had made up his mind to take his message to Jerusalem, it would have been important to avoid open confrontation with Antipas and no doubt prudent to avoid the cities altogether. If there is any historical core to the 'feeding of the five thousand,' it may also be significant that Luke locates this large gathering near Bethsaida, that is, territory ruled by Philip rather than Antipas.[13]

As far as the tetrarch was concerned, Jesus was clearly not a conventional military threat – his followers were not armed and there seems to have been no serious hint of insurrection. Jesus' words explicitly urged non-violence and non-retaliation, even in the face of injustice (for example Mt 5.11–12, Mt 5.38–48//Lk 6.27–36). Nor is there any indication that Jesus ever openly attacked Antipas or his government (though his strict upholding of marriage could have harboured an implicit critique of the tetrarch's private life). But talk of a kingdom could be dangerous, and dreaming of and proclaiming a Kingdom of God implied at the very least that the kingdoms of Antipas and his Roman patrons were sadly deficient. Most importantly, though, the presence of large crowds would have been cause for concern, just as they had been before in the case of the Baptist. It is unlikely that Jesus could have continued his ministry for long in Antipas's territory.

In the end, though, it was not Antipas who executed Jesus in Galilee, but Pilate in Jerusalem. And what led to his death was not feasting with undersirables, or even attracting large crowds, but his actions in Jerusalem shortly before Passover. Before moving on to Jesus' last days in Jerusalem, however, we need to consider one more chronological matter – exactly how long did Jesus' ministry last?

## The length of Jesus' ministry

The precise length of Jesus' ministry is debated, as, too, are the number of visits that he made to Jerusalem. Mark's gospel (followed by Matthew and Luke) suggests that Jesus was active for about a year with one fateful visit to Jerusalem at the end. John's gospel, though, suggests a longer ministry. He mentions the Passover three times (Jn 2.13, 6.4, 11.55), implying a period of over two years (and longer still if the unnamed feast in 5.1 is also the Passover). Throughout this lengthy ministry, Jesus goes to the capital city at least four times for a variety of feasts (Jn 2.13, 5.1, 7.2, 10.22). Both traditions, however, have literary and theological colouring.

John is anxious throughout his Gospel to show Jesus as the fulfilment of Jewish feasts and institutions. He is the new wine replacing the water of Jewish purification, the new manna in the wilderness, the new paschal lamb and so on. The evangelist makes his points by constantly bringing Jesus to Jerusalem where he can be seen to supersede a variety of 'feasts of the Jews'. Clearly, this deeply theological interpretation could only have been penned once Christians began to see themselves as something distinct from (and in their view, superior to) their Jewish neighbours, but John's overtly theological use of material does not necessarily mean that a longer ministry is itself unhistorical. The theological

gloss may well have been inspired by a straight-forward recollection that Jesus' ministry lasted two to three years. A longer
period would allow time for development within Jesus' outlook,
and is advocated by a number of scholars (for example, Meier,
Fredriksen and D. M. Smith).

Mark presents a geographical scheme in which all the Galilean
material is found in the first section of the Gospel (Mk 1.14–9.28),
Jesus and his followers journey to the capital in a central section (9.29–10), and the Jerusalem material is confined to the end
(chs 11–16), thus creating the impression that the ministry lasted
only one year. This, too, has an air of artificiality, with the heavy
brooding pointers to Jerusalem underscoring the importance of the
Passion narrative, the climax to Mark's gospel. Again, a theological interpretation does not necessarily rule out a broadly historical
portrayal. A shorter ministry would bring Jesus into line with the
sign prophets who appeared in the wilderness only two decades
later and would explain how he managed to avoid Antipas.

A variety of other alternatives are also possible. Jesus' ministry
might have lasted one year, but he may have visited Jerusalem more
than once (the suggestion that the branches at the 'triumphal entry'
belong to the festival of Tabernacles, when people carried braches
of greenery, is intriguing[14]). Or perhaps the ministry lasted several years, but Jesus only visited the holy city once. It is impossible
now to know. However, the shorter ministry as it is presented in
Mark is probably still the dominant scholarly position today (advocated, among others, by Sanders, Crossan and Dunn), and will be
assumed in the following chapter.

# CHAPTER ELEVEN

# Jerusalem

Some time in the early 30s CE, Jesus and his disciples joined the throng of pilgrims making their way to Jerusalem. Galilee was about 100 miles to the north of the holy city, slightly more if pilgrims followed the traditional route and bypassed Samaritan territory by crossing to the east of the Jordan, and the journey would have taken around a week. It is hardly surprising that the Synoptics make this long trek central to their recollections of Jesus, filling it with his teaching on the meaning of discipleship, the disciples' misunderstandings of the Kingdom, and a general sense of anticipation and expectation.

Most pilgrims went up to Jerusalem at least a week before the start of the festival to purify themselves, to spend time in the holy city and to prepare themselves spiritually. Jesus and his companions also seem to have arrived early, on what is known by Christians as Palm Sunday. The city would have been quickly filling up with tens of thousands of pilgrims from all over the world. Many were from Palestine and its surrounding areas, but some were from the Jewish Diaspora, joined by an occasional intrepid traveller from Parthia, making a once in a lifetime trip to the feast.[1] The city would be full to bursting, and many would have been forced to stay in the surrounding towns and villages, or even outside in tents (a chilly option given Jerusalem's high altitude). Jesus and his disciples seem to have stayed two miles away in Bethany, perhaps with their friends Mary, Martha, and Lazarus (Jn 12.1, Mk 11.11-12//Mt 21.17).

## Jerusalem

By the first century, Jerusalem was at the height of its influence and prestige. Inspired by his patron Augustus, and drawing on a range of innovative Roman architectural developments, Herod had completely transformed the city into a fitting reflection of his own splendour and magnificence. It could boast grand Roman-style homes for the wealthy inhabitants of the Upper City, a lavish palace, a range of entertainments (including a theatre), and elaborate tombs and monuments beyond the city walls. Most dramatic of all, however, was the remodelling of the Temple Mount. In a great feat of engineering, Herod extended the sacred precinct so that it was one of the largest in the world, surrounded it with Roman-style colonnades and porticoes, and completely rebuilt the inner sanctuary in white limestone and gold, turning the huge complex into one of the great visitor attractions of the ancient world.

Jerusalem was both the most Jewish and the most Hellenistic city in Israel.[2] It had been strongly influenced by prevailing Hellenistic culture since Hasmonaean times, and Hellenistic influence showed no signs of abating in the first century. Pilgrims, traders and tourists flocked to Jerusalem from all over the Roman Empire, many Diaspora Jews moved back permanently (hence the synagogue(s) in Acts 6.9), and all brought their own cosmopolitan outlook with them. Visitors to the city would have heard both Aramaic and Greek in the city's narrow streets (and perhaps, on occasion, a little Latin). Although inhabitants generally welcomed Graeco–Roman culture, it was not simply a question of absorbing new ideas. Newer outlooks and perspectives were only assimilated through a complex process of alteration and adoption, rendering Greek ways compatible with basic Jewish beliefs. Those which proved ultimately incompatible with indigenous customs were simply jettisoned. Thus, while Jerusalem in many respects resembled cities throughout the Roman Empire, a visitor would have been struck by the complete lack of images and statues or any kind of figurative art. The large number of ritual baths in the city, along with a particularly high use of stone rather than pottery vessels (for purity reasons), would again signal that although a visitor might be in a Hellenistic city, its inhabitants were largely Jewish.

Why did Jesus go to Jerusalem? To some extent, of course, he went simply to observe the feast of Passover, as he had probably done many times before (on Galilean attendance at Passover, see Chapter 5). There would be crowds in the holy city, and his message would be guaranteed a ready audience. Yet this is only a small part of the explanation. As the capital of the great shepherd-king David, and the site of the Temple built by his son Solomon, Jerusalem was full of symbolic and religious associations. None were more aware of this than the prophets, who saw it as the holiest place on earth, God's dwelling place and the centre of the nations. One day, the scattered tribes of Israel would return to Jerusalem along with the Gentiles, and all would enjoy a blissful existence (see particularly Is 60–2, Ezek 40–8). By the time of Jesus, a 'Jerusalem theology' continued to be prominent in much contemporary literature and many eschatological visions of a glorious age centred on a restored or heavenly city.[3] Any Jewish preacher had to reckon with Jerusalem, particularly one who prophesied the restoration of Israel and looked for the establishment of God's kingdom on earth. Jesus' presence in the city, then, was both a prophetic announcement that the promises associated with Jerusalem were about to be realized and an apocalyptically charged declaration that God's arrival was imminent (see Luke 19.11).

Jesus not only preached in Jerusalem but also illustrated his message with a number of symbolic acts. Centuries before, the Jewish prophets had similarly used actions to intensify their words – we might think of the names of Hosea's children, or Jeremiah's smashed jar.[4] Already in Galilee, Jesus' choice of twelve disciples provided a vivid and dramatic demonstration of the imminent restoration of the tribes of Israel. Now, in Jerusalem, he performed three more symbolic acts: his entry into the city on a donkey, an incident in the Temple, and a last supper with his disciples. This chapter will look at each of these in turn, before turning to the plots of the chief priests, the date of Jesus' death and his betrayal.

## Entry into Jerusalem

Both the Markan and Johannine traditions agree that Jesus entered Jerusalem for the final time on the back of a donkey. His route from the north had taken him through Jericho and Bethany, from where he approached the city from the Mount of Olives on the east. He rode down from this wooded hill through the Kidron Valley and on into the town, as onlookers welcomed him and cried out in jubilation (Mk 11.7–10 and pars., Jn 12.12–15). The Gospels suggest that the sign was planned, that Jesus commanded two of his disciples to bring him an animal from a nearby village (Mk 11.1–6 and pars). If so, this would support reading it as an intentional prophetic act like those of the Hebrew prophets. But what did it signify?

For the evangelists, the scene emphasizes Jesus' *kingship*. Mark, for example, has him hailed as 'Son of David' directly before this episode (Mk 10.46–52); several features of the story are indicative of eastern royalty (such as carpeting the road, 2Kgs 9.13); and the cry of the crowd is replete with Davidic and messianic overtones. Luke makes Jesus' kingship explicit with the phrase 'Blessed is the King who comes in the name of the Lord' (19.38), while Matthew and John both quote a prophecy from Zechariah 9.9:

Rejoice greatly, O daughter of Zion!
Shout aloud, O daughter of Jerusalem!
Lo, your king comes to you;
Triumphant and victorious is he,
Humble and riding on an ass,
On a colt the foal of an ass.

The question, of course, is whether Jesus also saw his sign in this way. Was it a deliberate re-enactment of Zechariah 9.9? Or was the biblical passage added later, as the earliest Christians set about searching their Scriptures for messianic proof-texts?

Choosing between these alternatives is not easy. The wider context of Zechariah 9 concerns God's holy war and triumph over Israel's enemies; once the conflict is at an end, the Davidic king rides into Jerusalem to begin a peaceful rule over a restored land and people. The passage clearly looks forward to the revival of the Davidic dynasty, but the difficulty is that there is no evidence that anyone in the first century regarded Zechariah 9.9 in particular as a messianic prophecy. Neither the Dead Sea Scrolls nor any other literature from the period seem to have expected a royal figure to ride into Jerusalem on the back of a donkey.[5] If Jesus' symbolic act was inspired by Zechariah 9.9, then, it is by no means clear that his audience would have made the connection. It is perhaps more likely that links with the earlier prophet were made later, once Jesus' kingship had firmly established itself in the minds of the early Christians.

What, then, did the sign mean? Taking their cue from the passage in Zechariah, many people tend to stress the element of humility in this scene, regarding a donkey as a particularly lowly means of transport. The reference to humility, however, concerns the king's attitude towards God and has nothing to do with the donkey. The important point about the animal is that its rider comes in peace – one might want to ride into battle on a stallion, but donkeys' robust constitutions, dependability and natural caution made them ideal for all other journeys. In the Old Testament we hear of Abraham saddling his ass (Gen 22.3); the 30 sons of Jair touring the land on their donkeys (Jdg 10.3–4); and Solomon riding a mule to his succession (1Kgs 1.33, 38). The normal way for pilgrims to enter the city was on *foot*; the very wealthy and infirm might have ridden in, but this would have been the exception. Jesus' decision to ride into Jerusalem, then, set him apart from the crowd and must have appeared to be a claim to some kind of authority. Perhaps he intended it to emphasize his own status as God's anointed envoy; or perhaps he saw it as symbolic of God's imminent arrival in his holy city and the establishment of the Kingdom. At all events, the symbolic act drew attention to Jesus' entry to the city and his prophetic authority.

It is important to appreciate, however, that the event – particularly as it is described in Mark – does not seem to have been too large. In the press of the Passover crowds, it is likely that only Jesus' immediate disciples and those who had joined him on the journey knew what was going on. Even they may not have been entirely clear about what the sign meant. We are not told that Jesus offered any kind of an explanation to onlookers, and quite likely different people understood what they saw in differing ways. Some may well have taken it as an unspoken claim to kingship, in effect a declaration that Jesus was the Davidic messiah come to claim his royal city. If a growing number of onlookers had not begun to harbour such hopes, the role of this charge in Jesus' eventual crucifixion is difficult to explain. Thus, while Jesus himself may not have planned his action as a deliberate echo of Zechariah 9.9, there were doubtless some who increasingly saw him as the focus for their messianic hopes.

The small scale of the event explains why there seem to have been no immediate repercussions. Word may well have reached the Jerusalem leaders that the holy man from Nazareth had entered the city mounted, but the incident would have been over quickly and there was no reason for them to take action. In all probability, they decided to watch him and to monitor his movements in the crowded city. If so, they did not have long to wait. According to Mark, Jesus performed a second symbolic act the very next day.

# Incident in the temple

Mark's account of Jesus' demonstration in the Temple runs as follows: Jesus entered the Temple, drove out those who bought or sold there, overturned the tables of the money changers, upset the seats of the pigeon sellers and prevented anyone from carrying anything from one court to another. He accompanied his actions with words drawn from the prophets: Is it not written, 'My house shall be called a house of prayer for all the nations'? But you have made it a den of robbers.' When they heard what had happened, the chief priests and scribes sought to kill Jesus (Mk 11.15–18 and pars., Jn 2.13–7).

As with the entry into Jerusalem, it is important to appreciate the scale of this incident. Two features suggest that Jesus did not create a major disturbance. First, these events took place in the outermost court of the Temple, the Court of the Gentiles, a huge expanse the size of 12 football stadia. A demonstration by one man in such a place would only have been noticed by those immediately around him. Second, Jesus was not arrested by either the Levitical police on duty throughout the Temple or by the Roman soldiers posted above the Temple porticoes. Once again, this suggests a relatively small incident, one that was over almost as soon as it had begun. Jesus' action, then, was not an attempt to disrupt cultic activity, still less a political coup (there is no suggestion that his disciples did anything but watch). Instead, it was a symbolic act, like the triumphal entry before it.

What, then, did the act symbolize? In view of the centuries of Christian scholarship which have been devoted to this passage, it may be useful first to clear the ground by outlining what modern scholars do *not* think that Jesus opposed.

- There is no indication that Jesus was *opposed to sacrifice*. Cultic activity, with its ritual slaughter of countless animals by highly trained butcher-priests, may strike many Westerners as the very antithesis of true and heartfelt devotion. Blood sacrifice, however, was the normal expression of religious piety in every ancient culture. Sacrifice might be seen as a gift to the god (usually when the offering was completely consumed by the fire) or as a meal which ensured the divine presence within the community (usually when part of the offering was returned to the worshipper). The Hebrew Bible itself lays out strict guidelines for the yearly round of sacrificial offerings, from the daily sin offerings to the much more complicated offerings at festivals. The sacrifices were in direct continuity with the sacrifices offered by Noah after the flood, and symbolized God's covenant with Israel. They expressed people's thanks to God, obtained his mercy and forgiveness, and ensured the stability of the seasons, the fertility of the soil and the fruitfulness of the crops. Many believed that what went on in the Jerusalem Temple was an imitation of the angelic worship of God in heaven. It is inconceivable that any first-century Jew could have been 'against sacrifice', and if Jesus really held such a view, it is incredible that such an attitude has not shown up elsewhere in his teachings.[6]

● A second, related point is that Jesus was not against the *Temple itself*. Both Christians and Jews have learnt to manage without a Temple ever since Titus burnt the Jerusalem sanctuary to the ground in 70 CE. In the time of Jesus, though, the Temple was the very heart of the Jewish faith. It was the centre of holiness, the place where God's presence was strongest, and the cosmic link between heaven and earth. What went on in the Temple had significance not only for Israel but for the whole world. There is no contrast between prayer and cultic activity in Jesus' words in Mark 11.17: the Temple *was* a house of prayer (see Acts 3.1). Jews might bring their sacrifices, but more often those resident in Jerusalem would simply gather in the sanctuary to pray and to reflect on God's graciousness. If Jesus had been against the Temple *per se*, it is very strange that his followers continued to gather there according to the early chapters of Acts. Matthew's readers clearly worshipped at the Temple while it still stood (Mt 5.23–24), and Paul uses Temple imagery in a constructive and positive way.[7] Later on, Christians needed to define themselves apart from the Temple, and it is probably to this period that supersessionist passages such as Stephen's speech in Acts 7.48–50 or John 2.19–22 belong.

- Jesus was not against the Temple's *exclusivity*, or Jewish exclusivity more generally. The note that the Temple should be a house of prayer 'for all the nations' (Mk 11.17, derived from Is 56.7) makes little sense in its setting: Jesus was standing in the Court of the Gentiles, and there was nothing to stop non-Jews entering this outermost precinct. In all probability, Mark's phrase is designed to appeal to his largely non-Jewish audience. We have already seen that Jesus' mission was very much directed towards Israel, with the promise of national renewal and restoration under God's rule at its heart. It is hardly likely, then, that he would have objected to the Temple's exclusivity.

- It is also doubtful that Jesus was against the *commercialism* of the Temple (though this is still maintained in a nuanced form by some).[8] There was nothing improper going on in the outer court of the Temple. The money changers were collecting the half-shekel Temple tax, payable by all adult male Jews. The tax had to be paid in Tyrian shekels, owing to their high silver content, and many people chose to pay when they arrived at the Temple for Passover. The pigeon-traders, too, were selling sacrificial birds whose ritual purity could be guaranteed. People were not compelled to buy their animals in the Temple, but it would clearly be convenient for many to do so. There is no indication that anyone was doing anything improper here. It is, of course, possible that some money changers might have weighted their scales, that pigeons were sold at exorbitant prices, or that the high priests exercised some kind of monopoly on the traders, but there is no evidence for such abuses, or for this being at the heart of Jesus' critique. The reference to the Temple as a 'den of robbers' (Mk 11.17) may sound like a reference to unjust commercial activity, but it is important to remember that even if these were the actual words of Jesus, robbers do not usually practice their skills in their own 'den'! Whatever abuses may have occurred seem to be *outside* the Temple, not within its walls.

If Jesus was not fundamentally against sacrifice, the Temple, Jewish exclusivity or the presence of traders, what then was the meaning of his demonstration? Following the work of E. P. Sanders, most scholars nowadays understand his actions as symbolizing the Temple's *destruction*. Jesus' actions encompassed a wide range of Temple activities – without the pigeon traders there could be no individual offerings, without the Temple tax there could be no communal offerings, and without the priests and Levites moving from one court to another, cultic activity in the vast Temple complex would grind to a halt. His activities symbolically stopped the Temple's functioning – if only for a moment – and powerfully symbolized its end. In line with his apocalyptically charged message, then, Jesus saw that God was even now preparing to destroy the Temple and to establish his Kingdom on earth (see also Mk 13.2). Whether he imagined, in line with other apocalyptic thinkers, that God would establish a new, heavenly Temple is unclear. Perhaps he saw himself as God's agent, not only announcing the end of the Temple, but in some ways bringing it about. This, too, is ambiguous, though the recurrent charge, albeit by unsafe witnesses, that Jesus would himself destroy the Temple (Mk 14.58, Jn 2.19–20), suggests that his precise role was open to question.

The image which Jesus' actions would most have evoked in his contemporaries, however, was that of the prophets of old – Amos, Micah, Isaiah, Hosea and Jeremiah. Each of these spoke out against the Temple; it was not that they were against sacrifice or festivals, but they clearly saw that these were not the most important things. What God really wanted was obedience, kindness, morality and justice.[9] Jeremiah was particularly close to Jesus: twice he prophesied the destruction of the Temple (chapters 7 and 26) and wore a yoke about his neck to symbolize the impending Babylonian victory (Jer 27.2, 17, 29.10–11). The presence of an ethical dimension in Jesus' outburst is quite probable. We have already seen that his vision of the Kingdom of God in Galilee was one in which economic divisions of rich and poor were dissolved, where widows and orphans could live in security, and where oppression and exploitation would have no place. In Jerusalem, Jesus must have been forcibly struck by the vast inequalities between the excessively wealthy and the destitute, between those who lived in luxury and the needy and distressed. It was perhaps no worse than any other city of its day, but the extremes of social injustice were too apparent to ignore. Besides, Jerusalem's special place as God's city placed additional ethical demands on its population. Like the prophets before him, Jesus countered the people's complacency with his announcement of God's imminent arrival and the destruction of the Temple.

## The chief priests and the plot to kill Jesus

Speaking against the Temple could get a person into serious trouble. Jeremiah was threatened with death for prophesying its destruction, and his words provoked a furious reaction among the people (Jer 26.1–15, 38.1–5). Closer to the time of Jesus, a Jewish peasant named Jesus ben Ananias who was in Jerusalem for the autumn festival of Tabernacles in 62 CE echoed the words of Jeremiah in the following lament:

A voice from the east,
A voice from the west,
A voice from the four winds;
A voice against the sanctuary,
A voice against the bridegroom and the bride,
A voice against all the people.

Finding it impossible to silence the man, the leading Jews handed him over to the Roman governor, Albinus, who declared him to be a madman before having him scourged and released. Ben Ananias continued his mournful dirge until he was killed by a Roman missile in 70 CE, only a few months before his prophecy was fulfilled (*War* 6.300–9).[10]

Jesus of Nazareth was more of a danger than either Jeremiah or Ben Ananias. First, he had a band of followers who had come down with him from Galilee. Even if Jesus himself was no threat, there was no knowing what his disciples might do. And second, Jesus not only spoke against the Temple but also performed a symbolic act in the holy place itself. Once words translated themselves into actions, the priestly leaders were bound to take note.

Mark is quite clear that those who plotted Jesus' death were the chief priests and scribes (Mk 11.18, 14.1–2). The chief priests were a group of aristocratic priests from whose ranks the High priest was chosen. Originally, the high priesthood had been hereditary and for life, but Herod the Great had taken it upon himself to appoint and depose incumbents at will, a practice followed by Rome. This led to a number of competing high-priestly families in Jerusalem, and the unprecedented phenomenon of the presence of ex-High priests (such as Annas in Jn 18.19, 22, Lk 3.2 and Acts 4.6). Until the reign of Agrippa I in 41 CE, the high priesthood was dominated by the family of Annas (or Ananus, as Josephus calls him): the old man himself had served as the first appointee of Rome from 6 to 15 CE, and three of his sons along with his son-in-law Caiaphas also held the office in this period. Religiously, the High priest acted as a figurehead of Jews everywhere; he held overall responsibility for the smooth running of the Temple and was the one who stood before God to atone for the nation's sins on the Day of Atonement. Politically, he was expected to oversee the day-to-day running of Jerusalem; to mediate between the Roman prefect and the people; and to maintain law and order. Caiaphas, the High priest at the time of Jesus, held office from 18–37 CE (losing his post only a few months after Pilate was also deposed). His long incumbency must have brought a much-needed stability to the role. It also suggests that he and Pilate worked well together, and that Rome could trust him to deal with any political disturbances.[11]

There is no reason to assign particularly cynical motives to Caiaphas and his chief priestly advisers. The maintenance of law and order, while good for Rome, was also good for the Jewish people. Realistically, the pursuance of a generally acquiescent policy towards Rome was the only way to survive – both for the priests and the people. Of supreme importance to the chief priests was the preservation of the Temple. The revolts after the death of Herod had spread right into its outer courts, some porticoes had even been burned in the conflict; that time, the Temple had escaped without defilement, but the threat that an uprising might escalate and bring down the wrath of Rome was always a real one. It is with some degree of historical plausibility that the chief priests in John's gospel worry that if Jesus is allowed to continue, the Romans will come and destroy both the Temple and the nation (Jn 11.48). At the feast of Passover, with its clear political overtones and large crowds, the threat of insurrection was all the greater. Most importantly, the Temple had to be safeguarded and the sacred ritual performed in the appropriate manner. Any disruption might halt the sacrificial rites and bring down God's wrath, not only on the priests but also on the nation as a whole. With his message of God's imminent

Kingdom, and his habit of drawing attention to himself, Jesus was too much of a loose cannon to be allowed to continue. What was the life of a deluded peasant, they might have reasoned to themselves, when the house of God was at stake?

Did Jesus foresee his impending death? The Synoptics include three passion predictions in which he sees the events of his passion and Resurrection with increasing precision (Mk 8.31, 9.31, 10.33–34 and pars.). Quite probably, the present form of these sayings goes back to the early church, which was anxious to stress Jesus' foreknowledge and acceptance of his divinely willed death. While details may have been increased with hindsight, however, the broad substance of this material may well go back to a historical memory that Jesus *did* see death as a possible outcome. The lot of a prophet was customarily associated with rejection and death,[12] and after John the Baptist was executed it would have been strange if Jesus had not speculated on his own possible fate. (Indeed, we have already seen that the Lukan Jesus already anticipated his death in Jerusalem while still in Galilee, Luke 13.31–35.) After his authoritative entry into the city and his demonstration in the Temple, it must have been clear both to Jesus and his followers that the situation was becoming particularly tense. And once his death became possible, perhaps even likely, it is not implausible that Jesus began to reflect on what his impending death might mean for the coming Kingdom.

The demise of a prophet did not necessarily invalidate his message. Jesus might have imagined that his death would inaugurate the Kingdom, or that it would provide the catalyst for God's arrival and deliverance of his people. While his followers would later interpret Jesus' execution in the light of a range of scriptural ideas (the Psalms of the suffering righteous,[13] the suffering servant of Is 52–3, the Danielic Son of man in Daniel 7 and Isaac in Gen 22), it is quite possible that a *broad* application of some of these texts may have originated with Jesus himself as he considered his fate. Before his death took place, however, Jesus had time for one last symbolic action, a final meal with his friends.

## Last supper

The historical events associated with Jesus' last meal with his disciples and the institution of the Eucharist are particularly difficult to unpick. It is almost certain that the versions that we now have reflect post-Easter speculation on the meaning of Jesus' death, particularly its sacrificial and covenantal nature. We possess five different versions of Jesus' words at this gathering: Paul's account in 1Cor 11.23–26; Mk 14.22-5 followed by Mt 26.26–9; Lk 22.15–20 which has similarities to both Paul and Mark; and *Didache* 9–10, a second-century Christian manual. Although there are similarities between them, none are identical, and each probably reflects Eucharistic language current in its author's own particular gatherings.

The earliest of these versions is Paul's in his first letter to the Corinthians. The letter is usually dated to around 53–5 CE, and since Paul is quite clear that this is traditional material (1Cor 11.23), it is likely to have been a version current in at least some churches within a decade or so of Jesus' death. He writes:

> The Lord Jesus on the night when he was betrayed took bread, and when he had given thanks, he broke it, and said, 'This is my body which is for you. Do this in remembrance of me.' In the same way also the cup, after supper, saying, 'This cup is the new covenant in my blood. Do this, as often as you drink it, in remembrance of me.' For as often as you eat this bread and drink the cup, you proclaim the Lord's death until he comes. (1Cor 11.23–26)

Even very early material, however, may well have undergone quite considerable transformation. Whether the element of memorial (do this in remembrance of me) makes sense *before* Jesus' death is open to debate. So, too, is the clear hope of Jesus' imminent return – Jesus preached the coming of God, rather than his own return. But the basic contention of all these traditions, that Jesus, sensing the end was near, gathered with his disciples for one more meal as he had done many times before in Galilee, is highly plausible. They assembled in a borrowed 'upper room', for one more evening of fellowship and friendship, fearful of what the next few days would bring. There might well have been feelings of anxiety, foreboding, perhaps even excitement in the room, and overarching everything was the powerful Passover story of God's past redemption of his people, and the hope that he was about to do so again.

Two snippets from the tradition may allow us even more insight into this last gathering.

● Mark ends his account with Jesus' affirmation that 'I shall not drink again of the fruit of the vine until that day when I drink it new in the kingdom of God' (Mk 14.25 and pars.). Of all the elements here, this saying has the ring of authenticity. Sharing a meal with his friends, and aware that his days were numbered, Jesus might well have spoken of the imminence of the Kingdom, particularly if he thought that his death might in some way help to bring it about. Mark is quite clear that Jesus shared this meal only with 'the twelve' (Mk 14.17// Mt 26.20), even though it is clear that Jesus had many other supporters in Jerusalem, some of whom had followed him from Galilee (Mk 15.41). The reference both to the Kingdom and to the twelve suggests that ideas of the restoration of Israel and the inauguration of the Kingdom were not far from anyone's minds.

● Luke adds the following words at this point:

> You are those who have continued with me in my trials; and I assign to you, as my Father assigned to me, a kingdom, that you may eat and drink at my table in my kingdom, and sit on thrones judging the twelve tribes of Israel (Lk 22.28-9; see also Mt 19.28).

Whether or not these precise words belong in this context, their sentiment may again go back to the last evening. They have a sense of handing over the reigns, much as Elijah threw his cloak over Elisha, nominating him as successor (1Kgs 19.19). Aware of the coming threat, Jesus gathered with his disciples and spoke to them one more time of the kingdom and of the need for them to continue his work. Perhaps he shared the bread and the wine as a symbol of their participation in the work of announcing the Kingdom. Later, as the disciples reflected on this last evening, the very elements of the meal began to take on symbolic resonance, as his broken body on the cross and his spilled blood of the new covenant.

## The date

When did this last meal take place? The question has particular relevance not only for the meal itself but also more specifically for the date of Jesus' death. By our modern reckoning, the meal took place on Thursday night and Jesus died on the Friday. Jewish days, however, began at sundown, or approximately 6 pm; both the last meal and the crucifixion, therefore, took place on the same day. But what was the date? The Gospels offer conflicting reports here. The Markan tradition (followed by Matthew and Luke) is quite clear that Jesus' last meal was a Passover celebration, the *seder* meal (Mk 14.12-16) and that Jesus died on the day of Passover, or the 15th day of the Jewish month of Nisan. John, however, is equally clear that Jesus died the day *before* the Passover, on the Day of Preparation, the day that the lambs were sacrificed in the Temple (Jn 13.1, 18.28, 19.14), or Nisan 14. Both agree that Jesus died the day before the Sabbath (a Friday); the question revolves around whether that day was the Passover itself, or the prior Day of Preparation.

Some have tried to harmonize the two accounts by suggesting that more than one calendar was used in Jerusalem at the time. These attempts, however, have not won wide scholarly support, and most argue that we simply have to choose between the two dates. Matters are complicated further by the highly theological nature of both traditions. For the Synoptics, the Eucharist is the new Passover meal. Recalling the events of Jesus' death in the context of the Passover story highlights God's new act of deliverance and his new covenant with his people. For John, however, Jesus dies as the Passover lamb, the sacrificial offering for the sins of the world. His death fits with John's interest in seeing Jesus as the fulfilment and replacement of a series of Jewish symbols and institutions, from the Temple and various feasts, to the manna in the wilderness and Jewish purification rites.

Although the Markan chronology has had its proponents (most notably J. Jeremias), this is one of the rare cases when the majority of scholars favour John's date over Mark's (so Brown, Crossan, Dunn and Meier) – and for good reasons. Mark is full of inconsistencies:

- In 14.2, the chief priests decide to have Jesus killed before the feast 'lest there be a tumult amongst the people', but in the subsequent story, Jesus is arrested on the very night of the Passover. It is difficult to imagine that the high priest and his advisers gathered to try Jesus on one of the holiest nights of the year.

- Within the meal itself, although some of the elements we might expect of a Passover meal are present (the wine, the reclining disciples, the singing of hymns at the end), other important aspects are not mentioned (the Passover lamb, the bitter herbs, any re-enactment of the exodus story).

- In Mark 15.42–6, we are told that the body needs to be buried quickly because of the imminent arrival of the Sabbath. The author seems to have forgotten, however, that in his presentation Jesus dies on the even more sacred day of Passover, a day on which it would have been difficult for Joseph of Arimathaea to buy a linen shroud (15.46).

John's account is not entirely without problems – we still need to believe that the High priest and his entourage were able to meet with Pilate on the afternoon of the Day of Preparation when their presence was needed in the Temple – but his account is at least internally consistent. Furthermore, Paul gives no indication that he sees the last meal as a Passover meal, and his interpretation of Jesus as a paschal lamb may offer some support for the Johannine dating (1Cor 5.7). If we are forced to chose between these two traditions, that of John seems to be the most likely, suggesting that Jesus died on the Day of Preparation, or Nisan 14.

A third possibility is that neither date is precise. In the ancient world, just like today, deaths (and also births) at certain times could take on special meaning. We often talk about someone dying 'at Christmas' without necessarily meaning that the person died on 25 December; the point is simply that the person's death occurred around about then, a time when, traditionally, families should be celebrating together. The connection with the feast makes the loss all the more poignant. Theological conflations of time are common in the ancient world. Some early church fathers regarded the destruction of the Temple as God's punishment on Jews for the death of Jesus, even though the two events were separated by 40 years. And mediaeval Jews had no difficulties in dating the end of Jewish kingship to the fall of the Temple, even though the last king (Agrippa II) died a generation later.[14] Religious memory has always operated with a certain latitude towards historical fact, particularly in the pursuit of deeper theological truths. If Jesus' death occurred at Passover (in the sense of being *around about*

Passover), it is easy to see how two different traditions might have developed in the course of time. One linked his death with that of the *paschal lamb* on the day of Preparation (and which now forms the basis for John's Passion narrative) and another focussed more on the *last supper*, fixing the inauguration of the Eucharist at the same time that Jews were celebrating the Passover (giving the dating familiar to us from Mark).

Historically, it is likely that Jesus was executed some days before the feast; this would explain Mark 14.2, which gives the impression of an older tradition into which elements more closely connecting Jesus' death to the Passover festival have been grafted. It may still have been on a Friday, the day before the Sabbath (a dating on which all the Gospels agree); the point is that the Passover celebrations themselves may well have been the following week. If this was the case, then the precise *year* of Jesus' death is no longer recoverable. The commonly held assumption that Jesus died in either April 30 or 33 is based on astronomical calculations relating to years in which Nisan 14 fell on a Friday.[15] If, in fact, neither tradition is historical, then such calculations are no longer relevant. All we can say with any confidence is that Jesus died some time between around 29 and 33 CE (any later and Pauline chronology becomes problematic).

# Betrayal?

All four Gospels suggest that Jesus was betrayed by one of his closest friends, Judas Iscariot, one of the twelve. Although the early Christians might have found some scriptural echo of this in David's betrayal by a close associate (2 Sam 15.31), this detail is almost certainly historical. The presence of a traitor within Jesus' inner group was too embarrassing to have been invented. Instead, it is clear that early Christian efforts were directed towards showing that Jesus knew that he was about to be betrayed and incorporating this betrayal into the divine plan (Mk 14.21 and pars.).[16] John even has Jesus sending Judas on his way (Jn 13.27). Precisely *why* Judas betrayed Jesus is difficult to determine. Mark gives no reasons, Matthew assumes that he did it for money (Mt 26.15), and Luke and John can only imagine that he was possessed by Satan (Lk 22.3, Jn 13.2, 27). Modern scholars have offered a range of speculations. Perhaps he was a disillusioned nationalist, no longer inspired by Jesus' talk of a kingdom. Perhaps he was impatient and hoped that by forcing a confrontation between Jesus and the Jewish authorities, he would bring matters to a head. Perhaps he had doubts, perhaps he lost his nerve, or perhaps the Temple officials got to him or his family in some way.[17] But none of these suggestions can be proved, and we have to admit that Judas' precise motives are now lost.

What Judas seems to have betrayed to the authorities was Jesus' location that particular night. Consequently, when Jesus and his disciples left their upper room and crossed the Kidron Valley into the Garden of Olives, Judas slipped away to inform the Temple police. With the arrival of the arresting party, the disciples fled, leaving Jesus to be taken to the high priest's palace alone.

# CHAPTER TWELVE

# Trial and execution

The one thing that we know for sure about the historical Jesus is that he died, and that he died in the most gruesome, cruel and shameful of ways – on a Roman cross. What is less clear, though, is the reason for his execution. We saw in the last chapter that certain activities connected to his last week would have worried the chief priestly leadership, specifically his demonstration in the Temple. But how did the Roman governor Pontius Pilate become involved? What were the charges against Jesus? And is there any way to see past the contradictory Gospel trial narratives to what actually happened in the course of Jesus' final few hours? We will begin with a consideration of the Gospel accounts themselves.

## The Gospel Passion narratives

In Chapter 2, we noted the difficulty of using the Gospels as historical sources. When it comes to the passion narratives, however, the difficulties become all the more intense. The Cross was a huge embarrassment to the early church; Jesus' followers quickly began both to reflect deeply on what had happened and to sift through their Hebrew Scriptures in an attempt to find explanations. Thus, the Gospels are saturated with Old Testament quotations and allusions, particularly to the suffering servant of Isaiah 52–3 and the Psalms, showing that the traumatic events were all part of God's plan. While most scholars recognize a degree of embellishment here, disagreements revolve around the *extent* to which the Scriptures have inspired the Passion narratives. Crossan, for example, argues that there is very little solid historical recollection here; for him, the texts are 'prophecy historicized', stories inspired by and created from scriptural texts (see Chapter 2). R. E. Brown, however, represents a more moderate majority who assume that scriptural echoes have overlaid a basic story and may even be responsible for some of the details (the darkness over the land? the dividing of Jesus' clothes? his last words?), but that the *general framework* is probably fairly reliable.[1]

In all probability, the earliest Christians had a reasonably good idea of the sequence of events after Jesus' arrest, despite the confusion and anxiety of the night. Even if his closest followers kept a low profile, Jesus still had plenty of sympathizers in Jerusalem, people who could have watched his movements and kept the disciples informed. Everyone would have been anxious for news, and, doubtless, the city's crowded rooms were buzzing with rumour and speculation. Furthermore, once Jesus was safely in Roman custody, the Jewish authorities would have wanted it to be known that that they did not support his movement and that they had handed him over for sentencing. There was no need for secrecy or evasion; the judgement of the chief priests carried its own weight and authority.

But what about the details of Jesus' last few hours, specifically the courtroom scenes and the exchanges between Jesus, the Jewish leaders and Pilate? The Gospels vary enormously at this point, offering a variety of reconstructions. Most people, relying on countless Christian dramas, films and musicals, have a harmonized picture of events in which aspects of each of the Gospels are slotted into a reasonably coherent sequence which goes something like this: Jesus is arrested, tried briefly by the High priest, then in more detail by the entire Jewish council, charged with blasphemy and sent to Pilate. The Roman governor reopens the case, unsuccessfully attempts to pass Jesus over to Herod Antipas, declares Jesus innocent and washes his hands of the matter, but is finally forced to send Jesus to the cross at the insistence of the chief priests and the people. There are two difficulties with this reconstruction: first, it is not found in *any* of the Gospels; second, many of these events are recorded in only *one* Gospel.

It can come as a surprise, for example, to discover that a formal nighttime Jewish trial scene is *only* found in Mark 14 and its Matthean parallel; Luke knew this account but chose to replace it with a much briefer morning interrogation (Lk 22.66–71). Pilate's dramatic washing of his hands and the cry of 'all the people' – 'his blood be on us and on our children' – is found only in Matthew

27.24–25. The trial in front of Herod Antipas is narrated only by
Luke 23.6–12, and John alone includes a quiet hearing in front
of the High priest (18.19–24), together with a long and complex
trial before Pilate, in which the governor famously asks 'What is
truth?' (18.38). It is clear that in the trial narratives, perhaps more
so than any other part of Jesus' ministry, theological, apologetic
and contemporary concerns have played a large part in the way the
accounts are constructed:

- *Mark* wrote for people, who were themselves called upon to
  stand before synagogue councils and governors (Mk 13.9). His
  interweaving of Peter's denials with Jesus' confident assertion
  of his identity before the High priest shows his audience how
  they themselves were expected to behave in a formal trial.[2]

- Writing in a context of church–synagogue hostility, *Matthew*
  used the trial scenes to increase Jewish responsibility for
  Jesus' execution. His Pilate uses a Jewish ritual from Deut
  21.1–9 to declare himself innocent of Jesus' death, while his
  Jewish crowd accepts responsibility with its infamous cry,
  'his blood be on us and on our children'.

- Directing his work towards non-Jews, *Luke* portrayed Jesus
  as a guiltless prophet and martyr, unjustly sent to his death.
  His Pilate three times declares Jesus innocent and the scene
  with Herod shows that two high-status men clearly saw no
  harm in him (see Deut 19.15).

- By common consent, the whole of the first half of *John*'s gospel has been a lengthy and public 'trial' of Jesus before his
  Jewish opponents, who tried to arrest him as early as chapter
  7 and finally condemned him in his absence in chapter 11.[3]
  There is little need in this Gospel for a further Jewish trial
  after Jesus' arrest, and the evangelist is free to turn his attention to a complex Roman trial, which will expose the short-
  comings of all earthly rulers, both Jewish and Roman.

The safest conclusion to draw from all of this is that while the
broad outline of events may be assumed to be historical, the
details of the various interrogations owe much to the theological
outlooks of the evangelists. Once again, this should not surprise
us. Jesus' followers probably had little access to what was going

on behind closed doors, and even if they did, by the time the Gospels were written, the trial narratives were powerful vehicles for theology and rhetoric rather than the kind of 'accurate historical reporting' that we prize so much today. An earlier generation of scholars expended much effort into trying to reconstruct a pre-Markan passion narrative, and on the vexed question of whether Luke's many alterations reflect his use of an alternative source (the latter, in my view, is unlikely). While these studies are useful, all they really tell us is that the Passion narratives have a long history of adaptation and embellishment. The extensive alterations made by Matthew and Luke to their Markan source are clearly evident, and it is only reasonable to suppose that Mark and his predecessors made equally free use of their own traditions.

In the following discussion, I shall assume that Jesus was arrested, tried briefly by both the Jewish and Roman authorities, and sent to the cross. Crossan would object that a provincial like Jesus would not have merited any kind of a trial, and that the Roman authorities would have agreed before the feast that troublemakers were to be dealt with severely. In his view, Jesus was simply rounded up after the disturbance in the Temple, led out of the city and executed; there was no Jewish 'trial' of any kind, and no Roman of particularly high rank need have been involved. He is undoubtedly right to stress the brutality of the Roman regime, and the appallingly low value set on human life, particularly that of a person of no social status. Yet the story of Jesus ben Ananias (whom we met in the last chapter) clearly illustrates that high-level involvement (both Jewish and Roman) in an unusual case was quite possible. John the Baptist, too, was dealt with by the tetrarch himself, according to both the Synoptics and Josephus. Furthermore, Josephus's account of Jesus asserts that he was handed over by 'our leading men', in a phrase which by common consent has not been altered too substantially by later Christian editors. Although much in the Gospel narratives goes back to the theological and pastoral art of the evangelists, then, the basic building blocks seem reasonably reliable.

## The arrest and Jewish hearing

We saw in the last chapter that Jesus was probably arrested some time before the feast and was taken first to the High priest's palace. Although the precise location of this building is no longer known (there are several competing sites),[4] it was probably one of the lavish mansions in the wealthy Upper City.

What happened next is difficult to determine. With its rowdy false-witnesses, accusations and formal verdict, Mark's trial scene resembles a kangaroo court; the judges have assembled with the intention of convicting Jesus and the whole affair is presented by the evangelist as a travesty of justice (Mk 14.55). John's gospel, in contrast, presents a quiet, dignified hearing before the High priest and one or two attendants (Jn 18.19–24). Most scholars at this point tend to follow John.[5] While we cannot be sure that he had a better source than Mark, his presentation does seem to exhibit a greater air of verisimilitude than anything found in the Synoptics. John, at least, seems to have known how cases *might* have operated in first-century Judaea. Most importantly, perhaps, the very existence of a formal, fixed Jewish council known as *the* Sanhedrin has been repeatedly called into question in recent years. Commentaries often refer to tractate *Sanhedrin* of the Mishna, written about 200 CE, which refers to a council of 72 members, both Pharisees and Sadducees, which met to debate legal and religious matters. There is, however, no evidence for such a council in the first century and most scholars see this as nothing more than a product of rabbinic wishful thinking – how the rabbis would structure their government if they and not Rome were in charge. The most up-to-date research suggests that the High priest alone made all the decisions, and while he often summoned a group of aristocratic, priestly advisers, it was an *ad hoc* group which would have changed depending on the matter at hand.[6] Jesus, then, was probably heard by Caiaphas and perhaps his father-in-law, Annas, as John suggests. As the head of a priestly dynasty, Annas would have been a highly respected and influential man whose opinion would have held some weight. Other advisers might have been summoned, but the hearing was probably brief and discreet. It is quite likely that Caiaphas had already made the decision to hand Jesus over to Rome before the arrest. As far as he was concerned, Jesus was a threat to the smooth operation of the Temple at Passover; the excitement generated by his message could easily lead to trouble, a riot perhaps, and disastrous Roman intervention.

What was the specific Jewish charge against Jesus? In many respects, the Jewish authorities did not need a formal charge and might well have confronted Pilate with a range of concerns: that

Jesus claimed to speak with God's authority; that he had already
caused trouble in the Temple; that he had a following; that he was
a skilled healer and exorcist; and that many were already seeing
him as a messianic liberator, perhaps even hailing him as king. A
Roman governor could not have ignored the appearance of such a
figure at the tense Passover festival.

It is perhaps more likely, though, that the chief priests did select
a specific charge. They would have wished to justify their actions,
both to themselves and to the crowds gathered for the feast, and a
definite charge would have carried more weight. Our sources offer
a range of alternatives. Mark 14.64 (followed by Matthew) suggests that the accusation was *blasphemy*, which in the first century
included not only speaking against the Jewish God or institutions,
but also appropriating God-like abilities to oneself. Luke sees the
basic charge as 'perverting the nation' (Lk 23.2, 5, 14), while in
John Jesus is arraigned as an 'evildoer' (Jn 18.30), someone who
has made himself both the son of God and king (Jn 19.7, 12).
In Matthew, the Jewish leaders refer to Jesus as an imposter, or
one leading others astray (Mt 27.63), a charge repeated in *b.Sanh*
43a. Some of these charges show clear theological development:
Mark's blasphemy makes better sense as a reflection of Jewish
allegations against Christians in the late first century rather than
something from the lifetime of Jesus, and John's accusations reflect
the author's high Christology.[7] There is enough evidence, however, to suggest that the basic charge went back to two passages
in Deuteronomy: that Jesus led Israel astray and that he acted as a
false prophet (Deut 13, 18.21–2). The penalty for both was death.
By letting it be known that Jesus was a deceiver of the people, the
priestly leaders doubtless hoped to drain him of his legitimacy.
He might look and behave like a prophet, but they denied that he
truly spoke for God.

But why did Caiaphas need to pass Jesus to Rome? Could a
Jewish charge not be dealt with by a Jewish death penalty, such as
stoning? Whether Jewish courts had the power of capital punishment under Roman rule is a highly contested issue. While John
18.31 seems to rule out the possibility, a number of isolated cases
in the first century suggest that, in some instances, it may have
been possible, particularly regarding infringements of the Jewish
Law.[8] Irrespective of the legalities, however, it might have seemed
advisable to Caiaphas and his colleagues to pass this particular

prisoner over to Pilate. As a potential 'King of the Jews', Jesus easily came within Rome's jurisdiction, and the chief priests needed to attend to the festival preparations and their own purity. Besides, handing over a prisoner would store up good relations with the governor and might prove useful as a negotiating tool at a later date. Thus, the transfer was not an attempt to escape complicity in the execution, but a matter of expediency. Pilate and Caiaphas could work together on this particular case.

## Pontius Pilate

Pilate was usually based in the coastal city of Caesarea Maritima (Casearea on Sea), which had been built by Herod I in the manner of a thoroughly Graeco–Roman city with a magnificent harbour, civic amenities and pagan temples. All the Roman prefects had made their headquarters there, effectively transforming the largely Gentile city into a new administrative provincial capital. At festivals, though, Pilate came to Jerusalem with a detachment of auxiliary troops, in case of riots or disturbances. Passover was always a particular problem: the festival celebrated the exodus from Egypt, national liberation from bondage, and was a time when political hopes and messianic dreams might be expected to be at their height. Josephus notes wryly that most insurrections took place at Passover (*War* 1.88). Ironically, however, Pilate's presence may have exacerbated discontent: the sight of pagan troops riding into Jerusalem and standing guard along the Temple porticoes could have only contributed to hostility and resentment. The governor installed himself in the Roman headquarters, or *praetorium*, which was almost certainly the magnificent palace built by Herod the Great in the western part of the city (not the Antonia Fortress as traditionally assumed). Visiting Herodian rulers – Antipas and his brother Philip, for example – would have had to make do with the older and less imposing Hasmonaean palace. (See Figure 12.1 for the map of Jerusalem at the time of Jesus)

Pilate was a Roman knight, belonging to the equestrian order, or the lowest rung of the Italian nobility. Quite probably, he had served in the Roman army, coming to the Emperor Tiberius's attention perhaps for gallantry or tactical abilities on the battlefield. His title prefect (*praefectus*) was a military title. The small yet turbulent region of Judaea had only been a Roman province for 20 years, and Pilate's job was clearly to keep order and to use his auxiliary troops to bring the people into line. It may not have been the best appointment in the Roman world, but it was a provincial governorship, nonetheless, calling for both military skill and diplomacy and might have led to more prestigious posts later on.

Pilate is one of the few characters in the Gospel tradition to have left an impact in the wider historical record. We are fortunate enough to have accounts of his governorship from two first-century Jewish authors, Philo of Alexandria and Josephus. Both, however, are hostile towards him. Philo, in particular, talks of Pilate's 'venality, his violence, his thefts, his assaults, his abusive behaviour, his frequent executions of untried prisoners, and his endless savage ferocity' (*Embassy to Gaius* 302). As with the Gospels, we need to be cautious in our use of these two aristocratic authors: neither Josephus nor Philo had any time for a low-ranking Roman governor like Pilate and were quick to accuse him of insensitivity and misrule.

The accounts, however, do allow us to build up a partial picture of Pilate's term of office. Soon after his arrival in the province in 26 CE, the prefect brought into Jerusalem troops displaying images of the emperor on their standards. Regarding this as a flagrant breech of the second commandment, many Jews protested at the provincial headquarters in Caesarea. After almost a week, Pilate relented and withdrew the regiment.[9] It had probably seemed absurd to Pilate that Jewish sensitivities could govern which troops he, as Roman prefect, could deploy in Jerusalem. He might have begun his governorship with a break with previous conventions, but he was at least reasonable enough to see that his heavy-handed actions had been a mistake, and was willing to compromise in the interests of peace. We hear of two later incidents involving Pilate: unrest at his use of golden shields inscribed with the name of the emperor in his Jerusalem headquarters and a riot which was put down with some violence following a protest concerning a new aqueduct.[10] Pilate finally lost his post after dealing too brutally with an armed messianic uprising among the Samaritans in 36 CE (see Chapter 3). What comes over most clearly from these stories is both Pilate's expectation that he should be boss in his own province and his determination to keep the peace, whatever the cost. The fact that he lasted a decade in a province that clearly did not welcome Rome and all it stood for is a testament to his efficiency.[11]

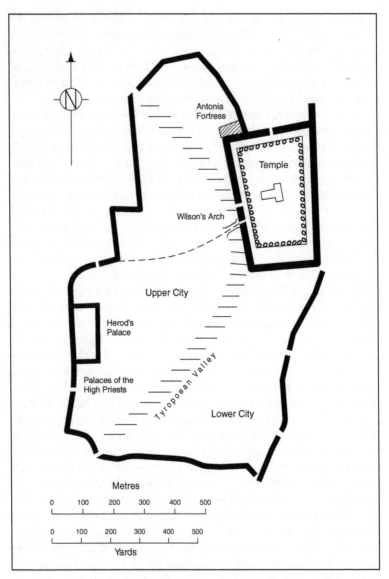

Figure 12.1 Map of Jerusalem at the Time of Jesus.

Pilate and the Jewish authorities must have had a reasonably good working relationship. It was not an equal one by any
means – the Roman governor was responsible for appointing the
High priest – but Pilate found Caiaphas already in office when he
arrived in the province and seems to have had no reason to depose
him, suggesting that the two men worked well together. What was
good for Rome in terms of the maintenance of law and order was
also good for Jews. If Pilate had received a deputation from the
chief priests asking that Jesus be eliminated as a false prophet
or a troublemaker, it is unlikely that he would have deliberated
long. Roman justice would not have been particularly concerned
with the life of a provincial, especially one with a following in a
crowded city at a festival celebrating national liberation. But it
is doubtful in any case that the high priestly deputation was the
first time that Pilate had heard about Jesus. Even if the ministry
had lasted only a year, the governor's spies and informers would
have kept him abreast of the situation. If the chief priests had not
handed Jesus over, Pilate might well have acted himself. Jesus'
proclamation of the Kingdom of God had clear political implications, and whatever Jesus' own view of Roman rule, his message
could serve as a rallying cry for those of a more nationalistic per-
suasion. Pilate would have remembered John the Baptist; perhaps
Antipas had told him that the movement seemed to centre around
one man, that he had hoped to nip things in the bud and that
by executing the leader things seemed to have subsided. Seen in
this context, Pilate's decision both to act, and to act against Jesus
alone, makes good historical sense.

The complex Roman legal system was applicable only to citi-
zens. Provincials, or non-citizens, were tried according to *cognitio
extra ordinem*, which meant that the governor had sole discretion
in how to hear a case, what witnesses to call (if any), and what
sentence to impose. Jesus, of course, fell into this category, and
though there might have been commonly held principles, there
would have been no fixed rules for the way in which Pilate held
his interrogation. It is unlikely, in any case, that the interview
lasted long: all Pilate needed to do was to establish that Jesus
was the ringleader and that without him the movement would
dissipate. The presence of a paschal amnesty and a jeering crowd
are difficult to substantiate historically. There is no evidence for
an amnesty in any contemporary literature and it is difficult to

imagine a Roman governor offering a volatile Passover gathering a choice between prisoners, especially if one were a popular insurrectionary. There may be some historical basis to the Barabbas story – perhaps he benefitted from a single act of clemency sometime during that fateful Passover, and Christians later contemplated the injustice of his release and Jesus' execution. The Gospels as they now stand, however, are more interested in emphasizing the Jewish people's choice of a revolutionary leader and their rejection of the Messiah than furnishing us with accurate accounts of Jesus' trial.

Some clues to the direction of the proceedings against Jesus can be gleaned from the *titulus*, the statement of the crime which hung above the cross. Both the Markan and Johannine traditions agree that it read 'King of the Jews' (Mk 15.26 and pars., Jn 19.19). Clearly Pilate regarded Jesus as a political agitator with some kind of messianic pretensions, or at least someone who might inspire those hopes in others. Popular perceptions of Jesus, along with his triumphal entry into Jerusalem and talk of a kingdom would all have contributed to the charge. Once Pilate was sure that Jesus was a troublemaker, he would have sent him to the cross, a penalty reserved for slaves, robbers and political agitators.

## Death and burial

Crucifixion was one of the most horrific forms of ancient torture. It was excruciatingly painful, deeply humiliating (victims were naked), and people could often take several days to die of shock, exhaustion and, finally, suffocation. Victims were usually scourged first (see Mk 15.16–20 and pars.), and would walk to the place of execution carrying their own crossbeam (Mark suggests that Jesus was so weakened that he was helped by Simon of Cyrene, 15.21 and pars.). At the appropriate place, the victim's arms were attached to the crossbeam by means of nails, or occasionally ropes; the beam was then hoisted onto the upright and finally the *titulus* was attached. In Jesus' case, as we have already seen, it read 'King of the Jews'. Pilate may well have regarded Jesus as a kingly aspirant, yet it is difficult not to detect a note of irony and scorn in the title. A scourged and dying man was hardly the kind of king first-century Jews dreamed of, and the title served as a grim reminder that a similar penalty would meet anyone else who dared to challenge the kingship of Rome.

If the Gospels are accurate, Jesus' death seems to have been mercifully swift, taking only six hours in Mark (from 9 am to 3 pm; Mk 15.25, 33) and even less time in John, where Jesus is only crucified after midday but is still dead before sunset (Jn 19.14, 31). According to Mark 15.34, he died with words from Ps 22 on his lips: My God, my God, why have you forsaken me? (Mark gives these words in Aramaic: *Eloi, Eloi, lema sabachthani*).[12] The psalms of lament, to which this psalm belongs, were often used in the early church to understand Jesus in the role of the righteous sufferer. It is possible, though, that Jesus began this process himself. Did he die quoting the psalm? And did he intend to call to mind only the first verse, as a cry of dereliction? Or, more probably, did he remember the whole psalm in which the righteous sufferer is finally vindicated? Did he still hope, even on the cross, that God would intervene and establish his Kingdom? And did those followers who dared to watch, if only from a distance, see his crucifixion as the beginning of the End Times? Is this why recollections of his death are coloured with eschatological imagery – the darkening of the sky (Mk 15.33 and pars.), the tearing of the Temple veil (Mk 15.38 and pars.), and even an earthquake and the emptying of tombs (Mt 27.51b–53)?

Part of the horror and shame of crucifixion was that most victims were deprived of burial, particularly when their crime was linked to treason.[13] The last thing Rome wanted was for a rabble-rouser to be seen as a martyr, and bodies were often left on the cross as carrion until nothing more remained, a gruesome reminder of the fate of those who opposed imperial rule. We saw in Chapter 1 that Crossan argued that this was Jesus' fate. The apostle Paul and the Gospels, however, all agree that he was buried and a number of texts do suggest that burial was not unknown after crucifixion (Cicero, *Verr.* 2.5.45; Philo, *In Flaccum* 10.83–4). In 1968, the bones of a young man named Yehohanan found in Jerusalem with a four-and-a-half inch nail through his ankle added concrete proof that some were buried after execution. (In the case of Yehohanan, his family were obviously unable to remove the nail, which had lodged itself in his bone.)[14] Although crucified as a rebel, Jesus had not led an armed revolt and the Roman governor might well have been content to allow his burial. The fact that it was a feast, too, may have persuaded Pilate to grant certain concessions in the interests of preserving the peace.

Jews tended to bury their dead quickly, generally on the same day on which they died. The need for a swift burial (before sundown) would have been all the more intense if the following day was a Sabbath (Mk 15.42). A text from Deuteronomy relates directly to executed criminals:

> When someone is convicted of a capital offence and is put to death, and you hang him on a gibbet, his body must not remain there overnight; it must be buried on the same day. Anyone hanged is accursed in the sight of God, and the land which the Lord your God is giving you as your holding must not be polluted. (Deut 21.22–3)

Both Philo (*Flaccum* 83–5) and Josephus (*War* 4.317) suggest that this practice was followed in Jewish circles at the time, particularly at festivals. The Jewish leaders, along with other pious Jews, would have thought it fitting and appropriate to bury Jesus as soon as possible. There is nothing inherently implausible, then, in the Gospel claim that a Jewish leader by the name of Joseph of Arimathaea had Jesus buried that same day.

But who exactly was Joseph? In Mark, he is a respected member of the council who was 'looking for the kingdom of God' (15.43). He acted bravely in asking for the body of Jesus (15.43), but there is no indication that he was particularly favourably disposed towards Jesus. Later Gospels struggled with Joseph's role: Luke makes him a 'good and upright man' who had dissented from the council's purpose and action (23.50–51), while Matthew makes him a wealthy disciple (27.57) and John casts him as a secret disciple who, with Nicodemus, gave Jesus a regal burial (19.38–42). The implication in Mark, however, is that Joseph is a pious Jew who, in accordance with the command of Deut 21.22, oversaw Jesus' interment. Quite probably, he had been specially appointed by the Jerusalem leadership to dispose of the bodies of executed criminals. The Synoptics's interest, unsurprisingly, lies only with Jesus, but John notes the request for *all the bodies*, including the two robbers crucified along with Jesus (19.31).

The clear implication of all of this is that Jesus was buried in shame. As one condemned by a Jewish court, he could expect nothing better.[15] Joseph's intervention clearly shows that he expected no deputation from either Jesus' family or his disciples. Nor is there any hint of cooperation between Joseph and Jesus' followers in the actual burial itself.[16] Jesus had none of the trappings of a normal Jewish burial: no washing and anointing, no funeral procession, no 'gathering to the fathers' in a family grave, no eulogies and no period of formal mourning. From start to finish, the burial was ignominious and dishonourable.

Although the shame of Jesus' burial is still clearly visible within the canonical Gospels, the evangelists show an understandable desire to dignify his final resting place. In Mark, he is laid in a rock-hewn tomb (Mk 15.46), in Luke and John he is placed in a *new* rock-hewn tomb (Lk 23.53, Jn 19.41), and in Matthew he is put to rest in *Joseph's own unused* tomb (Mt 27.60). Rock-hewn tombs, however, could only be afforded by the wealthiest members of Jerusalem society; it is hardly likely that a crucified criminal would have ended up in such a place. The stress on the *newness* of the tomb is doubtless to prepare for the accounts of the empty tomb; if Jesus' was the only corpse present, there could clearly be no problems over identification. It is almost impossible that the tomb belonged to Joseph himself; travel any distance with a corpse would have been difficult, owing to the approaching Sabbath, and a Jewish aristocrat would hardly have had a rock-hewn tomb close to a place of execution.

A later rabbinic text refers to the maintenance of burial places for those killed by capital punishment (*m.Sanh* 6.5; see also the reference to a burial site for foreigners in Mt 27.7–8). R. E. Brown suggests that what is envisaged here is not a mass grave but the type of individual trench grave associated with the burial of the poor. It might have been five or six feet long and a couple of feet deep.[17] Although Christian tradition clearly found the idea offensive, it is highly likely that Jesus' body ended up in a poor man's grave reserved for criminals.

As far as the Jewish leaders were concerned, Jesus' ignominious demise was proof (if any were needed) that he could not have been God's spokesman. Many ordinary Jews, too, saw their hopes dashed (Lk 24.19–21a). No text in the Hebrew Scriptures expected a Messiah who would die, especially in such discreditable circumstances. The disciples, too, presumably had little idea of how events would unfold in only three days time.

# CHAPTER THIRTEEN

# Resurrection

It might be argued that Jesus' burial marks the end of what we can say about the historical man with any degree of plausibility. Christian claims regarding his Resurrection, however, have been so crucial in terms of determining the future of his movement that a book on the historical Jesus which did not examine the Resurrection would be lacking an important element. Although the event itself is not open to historical investigation, we can at least examine the *effects* of the Resurrection on Jesus' earliest followers.

The claim that Jesus rose from the dead is undoubtedly very early. Paul, in the 50s, could already speak of it as part of the tradition he inherited:

> I delivered to you as of first importance what I also received, that Christ died for our sins in accordance with the Scriptures, that he was buried, that he was raised on the third day in accordance with the Scriptures. (1Cor 15.3–4)

Belief in the Resurrection was clearly central to Paul and is referred to many times in his letters.[1] So powerful was the idea that it even began to redefine God, who could now be referred to as 'the one who raised Jesus' (Rom 4.24, Gal 1.1). The fundamental claim was not that Jesus had been glorified, or exalted, or even vindicated (though all of these were assumed), but quite specifically that *God had raised him from the dead*. In order to understand this remarkable assertion, we need to look first at Jewish concepts of resurrection in the time of Jesus before turning our attention to the Christian texts themselves.

# Jewish views on resurrection

Given the variety of Jewish beliefs in the first century, it should come as no surprise to learn that speculations regarding resurrection and afterlife were far from uniform or consistent.[2] In the earliest parts of the Hebrew Scriptures there is no concept of any kind of life after death; the dead simply go to Sheol, a dark place devoid of God's presence (rather like the Greek Hades). There is no sense of resurrection, whether corporate or individual, and no associated suggestion of rewards and punishments. The psalmist puts it clearly:

> This is the fate of those who have foolish confidence,
> The end of those who are pleased with their portion.
> Like sheep they are appointed for Sheol;
> Death shall be their shepherd;
> Straight to the grave they descend,
> And their form shall waste away;
> Sheol shall be their home. (Ps 49.13-14)

The emphasis in ancient Israel was on the present mortal life; blessings and retribution would befall a person only in his or her appointed time on earth.

Things began to change in the exilic period, where ideas of a national corporate resurrection start to emerge. This is clearly the assumption behind Ezekiel's vision of the dry bones (Ezek 37.1–14) and Isaiah's song of Israel's deliverance (Is 26.19). But the most important developments were to occur in the last two centuries BCE, as Jews were increasingly influenced by Hellenistic culture and ideas of *individual* resurrection start to appear. The Maccabean revolt, in particular, raised difficult questions about those who had remained loyal to God and suffered martyrdom. Surely, some Jews reasoned, these people would receive a posthumous reward? And what of those who had denied their ancestral traditions – were they to suffer no retribution? One of the earliest texts to speak clearly of individual resurrection is Dan 12.2–3, written about 167–4 BCE:

> And many of those who sleep in the dust of the earth shall awake, some to everlasting life, and some to shame and everlasting contempt. And those who are wise shall shine like the brightness of the firmament; and those who turn many to righteousness, like the stars for ever and ever.

The 'dust of the earth' here is probably a reference to Sheol. At some appointed time in the future, all will be raised and judged according to the way they conducted their earthly life. The 'wise' do not seem to be rewarded with physical bodies but seem rather to be like stars, taking their place in an angelic assembly.

Another roughly contemporaneous group of texts have been gathered together in the work known as *1Enoch*. Together, they exhibit a variety of perspectives on resurrection. The oldest section, the *Book of Watchers*, differentiates between the fate of the righteous and sinners. The latter remain in Sheol while the 'spirits of the souls' of the former are raised to a new life in a second Eden close to the Jerusalem Temple (see *1Enoch* 22.5–13, 25.5–6). The *Animal Apocalypse* is quite clear that the bodies of the righteous will be transformed into white beasts in the new Jerusalem (*1Enoch* 90.34–8), while both the *Epistle* and the *Similitudes (or Parables) of Enoch* – like Daniel – see the righteous shining like angels or stars in heaven (*1Enoch* 104.2–6, 71.16–17).

One text which clearly expects some kind of a physical resurrection is 2 Maccabees 7 (written around 100–63 BCE). The text tells of the martyrdom of a pious Jew named Eleazar, along with his seven sons and their mother. The second son died expressing the hope that 'the King of the Universe will raise us up to an everlasting renewal of life, because we have died for his Laws' (2Macc 7.9). After suffering mutilation, the third announced his certainty that he would receive his limbs back in a heavenly existence, and their mother encouraged them throughout their ordeal with the conviction that the Creator of the world would restore life and breath to them once more (2Macc 7.10–11, 23). Clearly, while there is to be no resurrection of any kind for their persecutors (2Macc 7.13-14), this text assumes that the martyrs will have their earthly bodies restored in preparation for a heavenly existence.

The Pharisees believed in an afterlife, and by the time of Jesus, a general expectation of some kind of final resurrection seems to have been widespread.[3] What all the above texts have in common is an assumption that the resurrection will take place *on the last day*. Even works which envisage some kind of postmortem sifting see this as a precursor to a final judgement and resurrection. Thus, discussions of the afterlife tend to be very much tied up with eschatological ideas. If people are to be judged, it is clear that this is in the context of a general judgement associated with God's saving power and the final defeat of sin, evil and death. And though individuals will be judged according to their own righteousness, this is always seen in the context of a *general resurrection* of all the faithful. Beyond this, however, there was little agreement on what the body would be like (a shining star, or still recognizably human?), where it would be (in heaven, or on a transformed earth?), and even who precisely would be raised (everyone, or just the righteous?). And while Jewish speculation does not make the common Graeco–Roman distinction between a body and a soul, it is clear that even those texts which speak of resurrection in the most physical ways still envisage a body which has been transformed in some manner, rather than a crude resuscitation. Quite obviously, first-century Jews (rather like their modern counterparts!) were in a realm where all talk of resurrection, by its very nature, had to be symbolic and metaphorical.

That Jesus also shared this widespread belief in resurrection is shown in his debate with a group of Sadducees. In contrast to his opponents, who denied any kind of afterlife, Jesus explained that when people rise from the dead they are 'like angels in heaven' (Mk 12.25 and pars.). Aside from this, however, Jesus appears to have had little to say on the subject of resurrection. The Synoptics claim that he predicted his own Resurrection (Mk 8.31, 9.31, 10.33–4 and pars.), but these passages have so clearly been worked over after the event that they are of dubious use historically. He makes several references to 'Gehenna', the fiery place where the wicked are punished after death, but without explaining precisely what he imagined it to be like.[4] Quite probably, Jesus expected to be raised on the last day, along with his fellow Jews. If he believed that God's intervention in history would be very soon (as I have argued in Chapter 7), then he may well have imagined an imminent judgement and resurrection. There is no indication, however, that he expected his own, individual Resurrection to take place soon after his death. Such a view would have been extremely odd in an ancient Jewish context.

Why, then, did Jesus' followers believe so intensely – and with such certainty – that he had been *raised from the dead*? None of the canonical Gospels describe the Resurrection itself (a gap filled by the fanciful *Gos.Pet.* 34–42), but they do outline two of its effects: the empty tomb and reports of appearances to a number of Jesus' followers.[5] We need to look at each of these in turn.

# The empty tomb

The story of a small group of women discovering Jesus' empty grave early on a Sunday morning is well known and, with a number of variations, is told in all the Gospels (Mk 16.1–8 and pars., Jn 20.1). Not all scholars, however, are convinced of the historicity of this scene. It is often pointed out that Paul never mentions an empty tomb, even though he carefully notes Jesus' burial (1Cor 15.4). His clear separation of 'physical bodies' from 'raised spiritual bodies' in 1Corinthians 15.42–50 also seems to reduce the need for an empty grave. The earliest explicit mention of the tradition is found in the Gospel of Mark, written roughly 40 years after the events it describes. Strangely, this account ends with the women's silence regarding their experience (Mk 16.8). Bultmann saw this as Mark's way of indicating why it was that the story had not been told before, in effect an acknowledgement of the fact that it was actually a later legend. The tale, he argued, had been put together by Jewish Christians who believed that the Resurrection had to be physical, and that if the Resurrection was true (as they believed), then the tomb must have been empty.[6] Several modern scholars, such as G. Lüdemann, W. Marxsen and Crossan, similarly see the story of the empty tomb as a metaphor, as picture language expressing the early Christians' deep conviction that Jesus had been raised from the dead.[7] These scholars would place more historical trust in the *resurrection appearances* of Jesus, which are at least referred to by Paul, than in the account of the empty tomb.

Yet, the story of the empty grave has its defenders. One of the strongest arguments for its historicity is its strangeness. As Wright notes, the account is remarkably free from the Scriptural allusions that permeate so much of the Passion narratives. And as he, Dunn and others observe, it seems unlikely that a fabricated account would cast women as the central characters. Women's testimony was not so highly regarded as that of men, and in a matter of this magnitude it was essential that their claims could be trusted. In fact, the later Gospels show an apologetic interest in having male witnesses corroborate the women's testimony: John 20.2–10 includes a visit to the tomb by Peter and the Beloved Disciple, while Luke 24.12 (a later addition to the Gospel) similarly brings Peter to the scene. If the story of the empty tomb was a late tradition, male disciples would surely have played prominent roles from the first. Other considerations also speak in favour of the empty tomb. The accusation of the Jewish leaders, preserved only in Matthew, that Jesus' disciples had stolen the body, does seem to be a grudging acceptance on the part of the authorities that the corpse was nowhere to be found (Mt 27.62–65, 28.11–15). And the complete lack of any kind of grave veneration until the fourth century shows, at least, a remarkable level of disinterest in the mortal remains of Jesus.

In the last chapter, I argued that Jesus' burial was dishonourable and that he would not have had the dignified tomb of Christian tradition (epitomized for many Protestants in the iron-age Garden tomb outside the walls of Jerusalem). This does not mean, though, that there was no grave to visit. What was envisaged was not a mass burial place but a poor man's trench grave. By the time the Gospels were written, this simple plot had been transformed into the altogether more fitting tomb of a Jerusalem aristocrat. Several details associated with the scene in the Gospels are clearly designed to counter objections: the women could not have gone to the wrong tomb (they made a careful note of its location); the body could not have been stolen (the stone was much too large); and Jesus was clearly raised from the dead (the angel[s] said so). Beneath all the later apologetic, however, is a reasonably consistent story in which the women who went to visit the grave once the Sabbath had passed were unable to find his body.[8] The likeliest explanation, it seems to me, is that they found the grave disturbed and empty.

The absence of a body, though, would not naturally have suggested to onlookers that Jesus had been raised from the dead. Any amount of more prosaic explanations might be possible: perhaps Jesus had revived in the tomb (a suggestion popular with First Quest scholars); perhaps his body had been relocated (this is Mary's assumption in Jn 20.2); or perhaps the body had been stolen (this was famously argued by Reimarus, and finds some corroboration in the suspicions of Matthew's Jewish leaders). As we have seen, resurrection as a concept was very much linked to apocalyptic End Time ideas and would not have presented itself as an obvious explanation for a missing corpse. Even scholars who accept the empty tomb tradition as historical argue that it is only in conjunction with the reported visions of Jesus that we have anything like a necessary basis for Christian claims of *resurrection*.

# Resurrection appearances

That Jesus' followers believed that he appeared to them alive again shortly after his Resurrection is virtually beyond dispute. Both Paul and the Gospels list a number of reported sightings of Jesus, though they are all rather different:

- Paul gives the following list in 1Corinthians 15.5–8:

  '... he appeared to Cephas [Peter], then to the twelve. Then he appeared to more than five hundred brethren at one time, most of whom are still alive, though some have fallen asleep. Then he appeared to James, then to all the apostles. Last of all, as to one untimely born, he appeared also to me.'

- Mark records no actual appearances (Mk 16.9–20 is generally agreed to be a later addition), but he did end his Gospel with the promise that followers would *see* Jesus in Galilee (Mk 16.7).

- Matthew's gospel includes a brief Galilean appearance, probably to complete the account he inherited from Mark (Mt 28.16–20).

- Luke has an appearance to two disciples on the road to Emmaus; a report of a sighting by Peter (but without details); and a further one to the remaining eleven disciples in Jerusalem (Lk 24.13–53). In Acts, the risen Jesus continues to appear to the disciples for a further 40 days (Acts 1.3–11).

- John has an appearance to Mary Magdalene and two to the disciples in Jerusalem (in chapter 20) and a longer one in Galilee (chapter 21).

The fact that the lists are different, both in terms of geography and participants, is not particularly surprising. While Paul wrote only 20 years or so after events, more than half a century had transpired before the later canonical Gospels were written. The stories reflect the evangelists' own particular interests, stressing the commissioning of Jesus' followers and the beginnings of the new community. The texts are equally uncertain as to what Jesus' resurrected body looked like. Sometimes the risen Jesus can pass through locked doors (Jn 20.19, 26), sometimes he cannot be recognized (Lk 24.13–32), but at other times he can eat (Lk 24.41-3) or invite disciples to touch him (Jn 20.27). Paul seems to have assumed that people experienced visions of Jesus, rather like his own on the Damascus road (see Gal 1.15–16). Once again, there was probably no unanimity among the earliest Christians as to how to describe what they saw. As time wore on, there was perhaps a natural desire to underline the physicality of the experience and to stress that the risen Jesus was indeed the one who had been crucified. Tales would be expanded, embellished, perhaps even invented. But in the earliest days there were visions, appearances (sometimes to many people), and a powerful communal sense that their leader had defeated death and was once more alive with them.

Something happened to change frightened disciples, hiding for fear of the Jewish authorities, into bold missionaries. Their central claim, though, was not that something had happened to *them*, but that it had happened to *Jesus*. It was not a case of their own feeling of empowerment, or a vague sense that Jesus' spirit was still with them, but the remarkable claim that God had raised him from the dead – and that they would soon share his triumph. For this to make any sense at all, stories of an empty grave and Resurrection appearances had to have been made in a *highly charged apocalyptic context* where the end was imminent and God's power was at the point of breaking into the world.[9] Only in such an atmosphere would appearances and an empty tomb be interpreted in an unparalleled way as a *resurrection*.

That this was indeed the case is quite probable. Jesus' whole ministry, as we have seen, had an apocalyptic orientation. He may well have interpreted his arrival in Jerusalem as the culmination of his eschatological prophecies, as a sign that the End Times were drawing near. And many of his disciples might well have seen his death in apocalyptic terms, as an earthly event which would signal God's intervention, judgement and restoration. These hopes and expectations would hardly have abated over the course of 48 hours, and the remarkable claims of both the women and those who saw the risen Jesus presumably stoked the flames of an existing and evolving eschatological fervour. In this context, they interpreted stories of an empty grave and appearances as indications that God had raised Jesus from the dead, that he was the first of a general end-time resurrection, and that they were witnesses to the last days and the dawn of the Kingdom.

It was within this eschatological framework that Paul understood the Resurrection of Jesus, set out most fully in 1Corinthians 15. Christ, he says, is the 'first fruits' of this general resurrection; just as all those who came after Adam must die, now all those who follow Jesus 'shall be made alive' (1Cor 15.20–23). If God has raised Jesus, then the time of judgement must be imminent. Soon all those who have died will be raised to new and spiritual bodies bearing the likeness of Jesus himself (1Cor 15.42-50). Those still alive, too, will hear the last trumpet and exchange their mortal natures for immortal ones. So confident was Paul that all this would soon take place that he could already talk of Christ's victory over death and the imminent resurrection of believers.[10] Matthew, too, regarded Jesus' death as the beginning of the general resurrection of the last days, a belief he illustrated with the scene of revivified bodies appearing in Jerusalem some days later (Mt 27.52–3).

The Christian claim was indeed a bold one, but it would have taken something of enormous magnitude to explain the sudden and unprecedented outpouring of devotion to Jesus among early Christians very soon after his death.[11] It was the Resurrection that made Jesus different from any other first-century messianic leader and ensured that his movement continued, while those of others (including John the Baptist) did not. Christian preaching was now focussed not simply on the Kingdom of God but on Jesus himself: that God had raised him from the dead, that believers needed to make a personal commitment to him, and that he would come again in glory. The new eschatological context meant that the Scriptures were read in new ways and the process of seeing Jesus as the fulfilment of prophecies and long-held hopes increased substantially. By now the historical Jesus was on his way to becoming the Christ of faith, not just the faith of those earliest followers who trusted in his promise of a new Kingdom, but a powerful Easter faith which would one day see him as nothing less than the Incarnate God.

# NOTES

## Introduction

1 Nikos Kazantzakis, *The Last Temptation of Christ* (London: Simon and Schuster, 1960); M. Baigent, R. Leigh and H. Lincon, *The Holy Blood and the Holy Grail* (London: Jonathan Cape, 1982); D. Brown, *The Da Vinci Code* (New York: Doubleday, 2003).

## Chapter 1

1 Analyses of the various quests abound. In addition to the opening chapters of most historical Jesus books, I have found the following particularly helpful: W. R. Telford, 'Major Trends in Interpretive Issues in the Study of Jesus' in B. Chilton and C. A. Evans (eds), *Studying the Historical Jesus: Evaluations of the State of Current Research* (Leiden: Brill, 1994): 33–74; C. Marsh, 'Quests of the Historical Jesus in New Historicist Perspective', *Bib Int* 5 (1997): 403–37; J. Carleton Paget, 'Quests for the Historical Jesus' in M. Bockmuehl (ed.), *The Cambridge Companion to Jesus* (Cambridge: CUP, 2001): 138–55; and D. S. du Toit, 'Redefining Jesus: Current Trends in Jesus Research' in M. Labahn and A. Schmidt (eds), *Jesus, Mark and Q: The Teaching of Jesus and Its Earliest Records* (Sheffield: Sheffield Academic Press, 2001): 82–124.

2 For an accessible edition of Reimarus (with introduction), see C. H. Talbert, *Reimarus: Fragments* (London: SCM, 1971).

3 One of the most famous and sensational of the Lives was that of French Catholic Ernest Renan, *The Life of Jesus* (London: Trubner, 1864; French orig. 1863). One of the last was Adolf Harnack's hugely popular *What Is Christianity?* (London: Williams and Norgate, 1901; German orig. 1900).

4 A. Schweitzer, *The Quest of the Historical Jesus* (London: A & C Black, 1954; trans. from the 3rd German edition by W. Montgomery): 4.

5  W. Wrede, *Das Messiasgeheimnis in den Evangelien* (Göttingen: Vandenhoeck, 1901). English translation: *The Messianic Secret* (Cambridge: Clarke, 1971).

6  J. Weiss, *Predigt Jesu vom Reiche Gottes* (Göttingen: Vandenhoeck & Ruprecht, 1892). English translation: *Jesus' Proclamation of the Kingdom of God* (Philadelphia: Fortress, 1971). A. Schweitzer, *Von Reimarus zu Wrede: Eine Geschichte der Leben-Jesu-Forschung* (Tübingen: Mohr, 1906). For an English trans., see n. 4 above.

7  A. Schweitzer, *Quest*, 401. This paragraph remained unchanged throughout all editions of the book.

8  R. Bultmann, *Jesus and the Word* (London: Ivor Nicholson and Watson, 1935): 14.

9  E. F. Scott, 'Recent Lives of Jesus', *HTR* 27 (1934): 1–31 (the quotation is from p. 1).

10  C. H. Dodd, *Parables of the Kingdom* (London: Nisbet and Co, 1935); T. W. Manson, *The Teaching of Jesus* (2nd ed. Cambridge: CUP, 1935); J. Jeremias, *Parables of Jesus* (London: SCM, 1954; German orig. 1947); *The Eucharistic Words of Jesus* (Oxford: Blackwell, 1955; 2nd Ger. Ed. 1949); *Jerusalem in the Time of Jesus* (London: SCM, 1969; German orig. 1923–1924).

11  C. G. Montefiore, *Some Elements in the Religious Teaching of Jesus* (London: Macmillan, 1910); 'Rabbinic Literature and the Gospel Teachings, What a Jew Thinks about Jesus', *Hibbert Journal* 33 (1934–1935); J. Klausner, *Jesus of Nazareth: His Life, Times and Teaching* (New York: Macmillan, 1929; Hebrew orig. 1922); R. Eisler, *The Messiah Jesus and John the Baptist* (London: Methuen, 1931).

12  A. Drews, *The Christ Myth* (London: T. Fisher Unwin, 1910; German orig. 1909). For a discussion of those who denied Jesus' existence, see R. Van Voorst, *Jesus Outside the New Testament* (Grand Rapids: Eerdmans, 2000): 6–16.

13  H. S. Chamberlain, *Die Grundlagen des Nuenzehnten Jahrhunderts* (Munich: Bruckmann, 1899); W. Grundmann, *Jesus der Galiläer und das Judentum* (Leipzig: Wigand, 1940). See the studies by S. Heschel, *The Aryan Jesus: Christian Theologians and the Bible in Nazi Germany* (Princeton: Princeton University Press, 2008); P. M. Head, 'The Nazi Quest for an Aryan Jesus', *JSHJ* 2 (2004): 55–89; and M. Casey, 'Who's Afraid of Jesus Christ?' in J. Crossley and C. Karner (eds), *Writing History, Constructing Reality* (Aldershot: Ashgate, 2005): 129–46.

14  E. Käsemann, 'Das Problem des historischen Jesus', *ZTK* 51 (1954): 125–53. Published in English as E. Käsemann, 'The Problem of the

Historical Jesus' in *Essays on New Testament Themes* (London: SCM, 1964).

15 G. Bornkamm, *Jesus of Nazareth* (New York: Harper, 1960; German orig. 1956).

16 N. Perrin, *Rediscovering the Teaching of Jesus* (London: SCM, 1967): especially 38–47.

17 J. Jeremias, *New Testament Theology. The Proclamation of Jesus* (New York: Scribner's, 1971).

18 For discussion, see C. Tuckett, 'Sources and Methods' in M. Bockmuel (ed.), *The Cambridge Companion to Jesus* (Cambridge: CUP, 2001): 121–37, here 132–3.

19 L. T. Johnson, *The Real Jesus: The Misguided Quest for the Historical Jesus and the Truth of the Traditional Gospels* (New York: Harper Collins, 1996): 130.

20 E. P. Sanders, *Paul and Palestinian Judaism: A Comparison of Patterns of Religion* (London: SCM, 1977). Useful discussions of the Third Quest include: J. P. Meier, 'The Present State of the "Third Quest" for the Historical Jesus: Loss and Gain', *Biblica* 80 (1999): 459–87; T. Holmén, 'The Jewishness of Jesus in the Third Quest' in M. Labahn and A. Schmidt (eds) *Jesus, Mark and Q: The Teaching of Jesus and Its Earliest Records* (Sheffield: Sheffield Academic Press): 143–62; C. A. Evans, 'Assessing Progress in the Third Quest of the Historical Jesus', *JSNT* 4 (2004): 35–54; and H. K. Bond, 'The Quest for the Historical Jesus: An Appraisal' in D. Burkett (ed.), *The Blackwell Companion to Jesus* (Oxford: Wiley Blackwell, 2010): 337–54.

21 Detailed critiques in B. Witherington, *The Jesus Quest: The Third Search for the Jew of Nazareth* (Carlisle: Paternoster, 1995): 108–12; and M. A. Powell, *The Jesus Debate: Modern Historians Investigate the Life of Christ* (Oxford: Lion, 1998): 62–4.

22 Detailed critiques in B. Witherington, *Jesus Quest*, 116–32, and M. A. Powell, *Jesus Debate*, 123–40.

23 Detailed critiques in B. Witherington, *Jesus Quest*, 145–51, and M. A. Powell, *Jesus Debate*, 60–2.

24 Detailed critiques in B. Witherington, *Jesus Quest*, 42–57; M. A. Powell, *Jesus Debate*, 75–92; and L. T. Johnson, *The Real Jesus*, 1–27, in particular (though the whole book is largely a critique of the seminar).

25 Detailed critiques in B. Witherington, *Jesus Quest*, 58–92; and M. A. Powell, *Jesus Debate*, 93–110. Upholders of the Cynic Jesus include B. Mack, *A Myth of Innocence: Mark and Christian Origins*

(Philadelphia: Fortress, 1988); and F. G. Downing, *Cynics and Christian Origins* (T & T Clark, Edinburgh, 1992).

26  For a critique of Meier, see L. T. Johnson, *The Real Jesus*, 126–33; M. A. Powell, *Jesus Debate*, 141–57; and the reviews by C. Marsh in *JSNT* 26 (2004): 374–6, and J. S. Kloppenborg in *Bib.Int* 12 (2004): 211–15.

27  Detailed critiques in B. Witherington, *Jesus Quest*, 219–32, and M. A. Powell, *Jesus Debate*, 159–77. Also, C. C. Newman (ed.), *Jesus and the Restoration of Israel: A Critical Assessment of N. T. Wright's Jesus and the Victory of God* (Downers Grove: IVP, 1999).

28  For discussions of Dunn's work, see the reviews by S. Byrskog and B. Holmberg in *JSNT* 26 (2004): 459–87, with response by Dunn. Against Bailey's work see T. J. Weeden, 'Kenneth Bailey's Theory of Oral Tradition: A Theory Contested by Its Evidence', *JSHJ* 7 (2009): 3–43. Dunn's response can be found in 'Kenneth Bailey's Theory of Oral Tradition: Critiquing Theodore Weeden's Critique', *JSHJ* 7 (2009): 44–62.

29  See, for example, the review by S. J. Patterson (himself an advocate of a non-apocalyptic Jesus) in *JBL* (2000): 357–60. It is too early for reviews of Allison's latest book, but see M. A. Powell, *Christian Century*, 18 April 2011.

# Chapter 2

1  Translation from R. Van Voorst, *Jesus Outside the New Testament*, 30–1. Van Voorst's book provides useful discussions of many of the texts examined in this chapter. See also, J. H. Charlesworth, 'The Historical Jesus in Light of Writings Contemporaneous with Him', *ANRW* 2.25.1, (1982): 451–76.

2  See R. Van Voorst, *Jesus Outside the New Testament*, 70–2.

3  R. Van Voorst, *Jesus Outside the New Testament*, 119. See also R. E. Brown, 'The Babylonian Talmud on the Execution of Jesus', *NTS* 3 (1957): 158–9.

4  The translation is from L. H. Feldmann, *Josephus LCL* IX 49, 51. On this paragraph generally, see discussions in G. Vermes, 'The Jesus Notice of Josephus Re-Examined', *JJS* 38 (1987):1–10; J. P. Meier, 'Jesus in Josephus: A Modest Proposal', *CBQ* 52 (1990):76–103; J. Carleton Paget, 'Some Observations on Josephus and Christianity', *JTS* 52 (2001): 539–624; S. N. Mason, *Josephus and*

*the New Testament* (2nd edn., Peabody, Mass.: Hendrickson, 2003): 225–36; and R. E. van Voorst, *Jesus Outside the New Testament,* 81–104.

5   Origen, *Contra Celsum* 1.47; *Commentary on Matthew* 13.55; Eusebius, *Church History* 1.11.8. It was popular for a short time at the beginning of the twentieth century to argue that an Old Russian version of Josephus' other major work, the *Jewish War,* contained the original version of this paragraph. Known as 'Slavonic Josephus', it presents Jesus as a political activist; see R. Eisler, *Messiah Jesus and John the Baptist.*

6   See, for example, *1Clement* 13.1–2, 46.8.

7   An example might be the Western text of Lk 6.5 in which Jesus, seeing someone working on the Sabbath, says, 'Man, if you know what you are doing, you are blessed, but if you do not know you are cursed and a transgressor of the Law'; or the paragraph on the adulteress often found in brackets at Jn 7.53–8.11.

8   For English translations of these texts, with useful introductions, see J. K. Elliott, *Apocryphal New Testament* (Oxford: Clarendon Press, 1995).

9   For a full discussion, see P. Foster, *The Gospel of Peter: Introduction, Critical Edition and Commentary* (Leiden: E. J. Brill, 2010).

10   See J. D. Crossan, *The Cross That Spoke: The Origins of the Passion Narrative* (San Francisco: Harper and Row, 1988); also, H. Koester, *Ancient Christian Gospels: Their History and Development* (Philadelphia: Trinity Press International, 1991): 216–30.

11   H. Koester, *Ancient Christian Gospels,* 75–128, and S. J. Patterson in J. S. Kloppenborg et al., *Q-Thomas Reader* (Sonoma: Polebridge Press, 1990): 77–123. See more generally, S. J. Patterson, *The Gospel of Thomas and Jesus* (Sonoma: Polebridge Press, 1993).

12   Sayings often argued to be authentic include *Gos.Th.* 39, 47, 51, 52, 58, 81, 82, 98 and 102.

13   C. Tuckett, 'Sources and Methods'; C. A. Evans, 'Gospels, Extra-New Testament' in C. A. Evans (ed.), *Encyclopedia of the Historical Jesus* (New York: Routledge, 2008): 261–5; J. D. G. Dunn, *Jesus Remembered. Christianity in the Making* vol I. (Grand Rapids: Eerdmans, 2003): 164–5; and A. D. DeConick, who suggests a rolling corpus of material, *Recovering the Original Gospel of Thomas: A History of the Gospel and Its Growth* (London: T & T Clark, 2005): esp. 113–55.

14   James M. Robinson, John S. Kloppenborg and Paul Hoffman, *The Critical Edition of Q: Synopsis Including the Gospels of Matthew and*

*Luke, Mark and Thomas with English, German and French Translations of Q and Thomas* (Minneapolis: Augsburg Fortress, 2000).

15  See in particular, John Kloppenborg's *The Formation of Q: Trajectories in Ancient Wisdom Collections* (Philadelphia: Fortress Press, 1987); 'The Sayings Gospel Q and the Quest of the Historical Jesus', *HTR* 89 (1996): 307–44; and *Excavating Q: The History and Setting of the Sayings Gospel* (Edinburgh: T & T Clark, 2000).

16  See the works by Crossan in the Bibliography; also B. Mack, *The Lost Gospel: The Book of Q and Christian Origins* (Shaftesbury: Element, 1993).

17  J. S. Kloppenborg, 'The Sayings Gospel Q', esp. 322–3, n. 70 and 331.

18  For the former position, see J. D. G. Dunn, *Jesus Remembered*, 147–60; and C. Tuckett, 'Sources and Methods'; for the latter, M. Goodacre, *The Case Against Q: Studies in Markan Priority and the Synoptic Problem* (Harrisburg: Trinity Press, 2002); and F. Watson, 'Q as Hypothesis: A Study in Methodology,' *NTS* 55 (2009): 397–415.

19  C. H. Dodd, *Historical Tradition in the Fourth Gospel* (Cambridge: CUP, 1963); D. M. Smith, 'Historical Issues and the Problem of John and the Synoptics' in M. de Boer (ed.), *From Jesus to John* (Sheffield: Sheffield Academic Press, 1991), esp. 255–6. See also, J. Ashton, *Understanding the Fourth Gospel* (Oxford: Clarendon Press, 1991): 36–8.

20  P. N. Anderson, F. Just and T. Thatcher (eds), *John, Jesus and History* (Atlanta: SBL, 2007). Works by Meier and Fredriksen can be found in the Bibliography.

21  For the view that the Gospels do, in fact, record eyewitness testimony, see R. Baukham, *Jesus and the Eyewitnesses: The Gospels as Eyewitness Testimony* (Grand Rapids: Eerdmans, 2006).

22  D. C. Allison, 'A Plea for Thoroughgoing Eschatology', *JBL* 113 (1994): 651–68, here 665.

# Chapter 3

1  Useful historical summaries of this period can be found in E. Schürer (rev. by G. Vermes and F. Millar), *History of the Jewish People in the Age of Jesus Christ* (Edinburgh: T & T Clark, 1973), vol. I; and L. L. Grabbe, *History of the Jews and Judaism in the Second Temple Period* (London: T & T Clark, 2004). On Herod the Great, see P. Richardson, *Herod: King of the Jews and Friend of the Romans* (Columbia: University of South Carolina Press, 1996); and on the Herodians more

generally, see N. Kokkinos, *The Herodian Dynasty: Origins, Role in Society, and Eclipse* (Sheffield: Sheffield Academic Press, 1998).

2  On Jewish messianic hopes in the first century, see further, G. E. Nicklesburg and J. J. Collins (eds), *Ideal Figures in Ancient Judaism: Profiles and Paradigms* (Chico: Scholars Press, 1980); J. Neusner, W. S. Green and E. Frerichs (eds), *Judaisms and Their Messiahs at the Turn of the Christian Era* (Cambridge: CUP, 1987); and J. J. Collins, *The Scepter and the Star: The Messiahs of the Dead Sea Scrolls and Other Ancient Literature* (New York: Doubleday, 1995).

3  Similar ideas are found in Zech 4.14, Sir 45.24–5, 50.1–21 and the Greek translation of Ezek 21.30–2.

4  On the Zealots, see M. Smith, 'Zealots and Sicarii: Their Origins and Relation', *HTR* 64 (1971): 1–19; on this topic more generally, see R. A. Horsley and J. S. Hanson, *Bandits, Prophets and Messiahs* (Harrisburg: Trinity Press, 1985). On peasant resistance, see J. C. Scott, *Weapons of the Weak: Everyday Forms of Peasant Resistance* (Yale: Yale University Press, 1985).

5  *See War* 2.258–60, 264–5, *Ant.* 20.160–1, 167–8, 172, 188.

6  *War* 6.285–6. For useful discussions of all these men, see P. W. Barnett, 'The Jewish Sign Prophets' in J. D. G. Dunn and S. McKnight (eds), *The Historical Jesus in Recent Research* (Winona Lake: Eisenbrauns, 2005): 444–62; and R. Gray, *Prophetic Figures in Late Second Temple Jewish Palestine* (Oxford: OUP, 1993): 112–44.

7  *Ag. Ap.* 1.41, see also 1Macc 4.45–6, 9.27, 14.41, *tos.Sotah* 13.2–6, for discussion see R. Gray, *Prophetic Figures*, 7-34.

# Chapter 4

1  The best study of the birth narratives is still R. E. Brown, *The Birth of the Messiah* (London: Chapman, 1992; rev. ed.).

2  J. Schaberg, *The Illegitimacy of Jesus* (Sheffield: Sheffield Academic Press, 1995); G. Lüdemann, *Virgin Birth? The Real Story of Mary and her Son Jesus* (London: SCM, 1998); B. Chilton, 'Recovering Jesus' Mamzerut' in Charlesworth, J. H. (ed.), *Jesus and Archaeology*, (Grand Rapids: Eerdmans 2006): 84–110.

3  See Origen, *Against Celsus* 1.2; *b. Shabbat* 104b, paralleled *in b. Sanh* 64a. So R. Van Voorst, *Jesus Outside the New Testament*, 104–34.

4  See G. Theissen and A. Merz, *The Historical Jesus: A Comprehensive Guide* (London: SCM, 1998): 196.

# Chapter 5

1   R. A. Horsley, *Galilee: History, Politics, People* (Valley Forge: Trinity
    Press International, 1995) and *Archaeology, History and Society in
    Galilee* (Valley Forge: Trinity Press International, 1996).

2   S. Freyne, *Galilee from Alexander the Great to Hadrian* (Wilmington:
    Notre Dame, 1980), and *Galilee, Jesus and the Gospels* (Dublin: Gill
    and Macmillan, 1988).

3   See especially, J. L. Reed, *Archaeology and the Galilean Jesus:
    A Re-Examination of the Evidence* (Harrisburg: Trinity Press
    International, 2000). Also, M. Chancey, *The Myth of a Gentile
    Galilee* (Cambridge: CUP, 2002), and *Greco-Roman Culture and the
    Galilee of Jesus* (Cambridge: CUP, 2005).

4   On the synagogue, see H. C. Kee, 'The Transformation of the Synagogue
    after 70 CE: Its Import for Early Christianity', *NTS* 36 (1990): 1–24;
    J. S. Kloppenborg, 'The Theodotus Inscription' and J. D. G. Dunn
    'Did Jesus Attend the Synagogue?' both in J. H. Charlesworth (ed.),
    *Jesus and Archaeology* (Grand Rapids/Cambridge: Eerdmans, 2006):
    206–22 and 236–82.

5   D. E. Oakman, *Jesus and the Economic Questions of His Day*
    (Lewiston: Mellen, 1986); R. A. Horsley, *Jesus and the Spiral of
    Violence* ( San Francisco: Harper and Row,1987); R. Horsley and J.
    S. Hanson, *Bandits, Prophets and Messiahs*; K. C. Hanson and D. E.
    Oakman, *Palestine in the Time of Jesus: Social Structures and Social
    Conflicts* (Minneapolis, Fortress, 2008); G. Theissen and A. Merz,
    *The Historical Jesus*, 162–83.

6   See the critiques of J. A. Overman, 'Jesus of Galilee and the Historical
    Peasant' in D. R. Edwards and O. T. McCullough (eds), *Archaeology
    and the Galilee: Texts and Contexts in the Greco-Roman and
    Byzantine Periods* (Atlanta: Scholars Press, 1997): 67–74; and M.
    Sawicki, *Crossing Galilee: Architecture of Contact in the Occupied
    Land of Jesus* (Harrisburg: Trinity Press International, 2000).

7   J. L. Reed, *Archaeology and the Galilean Jesus;* M. A. Chancey, *Myth
    of a Gentile Galilee*; L. Levine (ed.), *The Galilee in Late Antiquity*
    (New York: Jewish Theological Seminary of America, 1992); D. R.
    Edwards and O. T. McCullough (eds), *Archaeology and the Galilee*; D.
    R. Edwards (ed.), *Religion and Society in Roman Palestine* (London:
    Routledge, 2004).

8   On Pilate's standards, see *War* 2.169-71, *Ant.* 18.55–9; on Gaius's
    statue, see *War* 2.184–203, *Ant* 18.261–308, and *Leg* 207–333.

9 M. H. Jensen, *Herod Antipas in Galilee: The Literary and Archaeological Sources on the Reign of Herod Antipas and Its Socio-Economic Impact on Galilee* (Tübingen: Mohr Siebeck, 2006). Further on Galilee at the time, see E. P. Sanders, 'Jesus in Historical Context', *Theology Today* 50 (1993): 429–48; and 'Jesus' Galilee' in I. Dunderberg, C. Tuckett and K. Syreeni (eds), *Fair Play: Diversity and Conflicts in Early Christianity* (Leiden: Brill, 2002): 3-41. On the relative tranquillity of Judaea in Jesus' time, see J. S. McLaren, *Turbulent Times? Josephus and Scholarship on Judaea in the First Century CE* (Sheffield: Sheffield Academic Press, 1998).

10 For a firsthand description of Galilee, see Josephus *War* 3.35–44, 506–21.

11 Mt 2.23, Mk 1.9, Lk 2.39–40, 51-2, 4.16, Jn 1.46.

12 See J. D. Crossan, *Historical Jesus*, 46; D. Flusser, *Sage*, 12–13; C. A. Evans, 'Context, Family and Formation' in M. Bockmuehl (ed.), *Cambridge Companion to Jesus*, 11–24, here 21.

13 Philo, *De Legatione* 210; Josephus, *Against Apion* 1.60, 2.176, 178, 204. See also, *T. Levi* 13.2; and Jesus' continued 'have you not read' in Mk 2.25, 12.10, 12.26 etc. On this debate, see C. Keith, *Jesus' Literacy: Education and the Teacher from Galilee* (London: T & T Clark, 2011).

14 Mk 1.29–31, 1Cor 9.5 and Mk 10.28–30.

15 Num 13.37–39, Deut 6.8, 11.18, 22.12.

# Chapter 6

1 Translation by L. H. Feldmann, *Josephus* (Loeb Classical Library XII), 81–5.

2 Mk 1.4 and pars.; Lk 3.7–8//Mt 3.7-8.

3 J. E. Taylor, *The Immerser: John the Baptist within Second Temple Judaism* (Grand Rapids: Eerdmans, 1997). See also, R. L. Webb, *John the Baptist and Prophet: A Socio-Historical Study* (Sheffield: JSOT Press, 1991).

4 The texts are Mt 3.10, 12//Lk 3.9, 3.17, and Mk 1.8, Mt 3.11//Lk 3.16.

5 Mal 3.2–3, 4.5; see also, Sirach 48.10.

6 J. D. G. Dunn, *Jesus Remembered*, 350.

7 Jn 3.22–23 says quite clearly that Jesus and his disciples were baptizing, while 4.2 (a later addition?) claims that Jesus himself did not baptize. In Acts 2.38, Peter and the remaining disciples baptize after Pentecost; it is unlikely they would have done this unless it had been a feature (however marginal) of Jesus' own ministry. On possible rivalries between adherents of Jesus and the Baptist, see P. J. Tomson, 'Jesus and His Judaism' in M. Bockmuehl (ed.), *Cambridge Companion to Jesus*, 25–40, here 30.

# Chapter 7

1 For a useful overview of Jesus' teaching, see G. Stanton, 'Message and Miracles' in M. Bockmuehl (ed.), *Cambridge Companion to Jesus*, 56–71. For the concept of 'Kingdom of God', see D. C. Duling, *Anchor Bible Dictionary* vol. IV: 49–68.

2 1Chr 28.5, 2Chr 13.8, Ex 15.18, and especially Pss 22, 47, 93, 96–9, 103 and 145.

3 For further discussion of the apocalyptic Jesus, see R. L. Webb, '"Apocalyptic": Observations on a Slippery Term', *JNES* 49 (1990): 115–26; D. C. Allison, 'A Plea for Thoroughgoing Eschatology', *JBL* 113 (1994): 651–68; B. Ehrman, *Jesus, Apocalyptic Prophet of the New Millennium* (New York: OUP, 1999); and A. J. Levine, 'The Earth Moved: Jesus, Sex and Eschatology' in J. Kloppenborg and J. Marshall (eds) *Apocalypticism, Anti-Semitism and the Historical Jesus: Subtexts in Criticism* (Edinburgh: T & T Clark, 2005): 83–97.

4 For fuller discussion, see C. C. Rowland, *Christian Origins: An Account of the Setting and Character of the Most Important Messianic Sect of Judaism* (London: SPCK, 1985).

5 For example, Lk 12.39–40//Mt 24.43–4, Lk 12.35–8//Mt 25.1–13, Mk 13.17; Lk 10.12–15//Mt 11.20–4, Lk 6.24–6, Mk 1.15, 13.28–9, 33, 37; Lk 21.36//Mt 25.13; Lk 18.1–8 and 21.34–6.

6 C. H. Dodd, *The Parables of the Kingdom* (London: Nisbet & Co, 1935); M. J. Borg, 'Reflections on a Discipline: A North American Perspective' in B. Chilton and C. A. Evans (eds) *Studying the Historical Jesus: Evaluations of the State of Current Research* (Leiden: Brill, 1994): 9–31.

7 See particularly Mk 13.34–6//Lk 12.35–8, Mt 24.43–4//Lk 12.39–40//G.Th 21, Mt 24.45–51//Lk 12.42–6, Mt 25.1–13.

8  See particularly Amos 5.18–27, Joel 2.1–11, Zeph 1.7–18, Is 13.6–9, Ezek 13.5, 30.3, and Mal 4.5.

9  The parables have attracted much attention in recent years, see for example, J. D. Crossan, *In Parables: The Challenge of the Historical Jesus* (New York: Harper and Row, 1973); R. Longenecker (ed.), *The Challenge of Jesus' Parables* (Grand Rapids: Eerdmans, 2000); K. Snodgrass, *Stories with Intent: A Comprehensive Guide to the Parables of Jesus* (Grand Rapids: Eerdmans, 2008); and A. Jack, 'For Those on the Outside, Everything Comes in Parables': Recent Readings of the Parables from the Inside', *ET* 120 (2008): 8–15.

10  On this passage see, for example, M. Hooker, *The Gospel According to St Mark* (London: A & C Black, 1991): 125–9.

11  M. Casey, *The Solution to the 'Son of Man' Problem* (London: T & T Clark, 2007); and for an overview, L. W. Hurtado and P. L. Owen (eds), *Who Is This Son of Man? The Latest Scholarship on a Puzzling Expression of the Historical Jesus* (London: T & T Clark, 2010).

# Chapter 8

1  Useful discussion of Jesus' miracles can be found in G. Stanton, 'Message and Miracles', in M. Bockmuehl (ed.), *Cambridge Companion to Jesus*, 56–71; G. Twelftree, *Jesus the Exorcist: A Contribution to the Study of the Historical Jesus* (Tübingen: Mohr Siebeck, 1993); G. Theissen, 'The Intention of Primitive Miracle Stories' in J. D. G. Dunn and S. McKnight (eds), *The Historical Jesus in Recent Research* (Winona Lake: Eisenbrauns, 2005): 350–60; P. J. Achtemeier, *Jesus and the Miracle Tradition* (Oregon: Cascade, 2008); and E. Eve, *The Healer from Nazareth: Jesus' Miracles in Historical Context* (London: SPCK, 2009). A useful collection of primary texts can be found in W. Cotter, 'Miracle Stories: The God Asclepius, the Pythagorean Philosophers, and the Roman Rulers' in A. J. Levine, D. C. Allison, and J. D. Crossan, *Jesus in Context*, 166–78.

2  For Honi, see *b.Ta'anith* 19a, 23a and Josephus (who calls him Onias) *Ant.* 14.3.1. Hanina ben Dosa lived a century later and left a more extensive record; see *b.Sotah* 49a, *Berakoth* 34a-b, and *Ta'anith* 24b, 25a. For fuller discussion of these two holy men, see especially G. Vermes, *Jesus the Jew*, 58–82.

3  1Sam 16.14–23; *Psuedo-Philo* 60.1, Josephus, *Ant.* 3.166.

4  *Genesis Apocryphon* 20.16–17, 29; 11Q11.

5 The texts are: Mk 1.32–3 and pars, Lk 13.31–2 (both summaries); Mk 1.21–27 and pars., Mk 5.1–13 and pars., Mk 7.25–30 and par., Mk 9.14–27 and pars., Mt 9.32–4//Lk 11.14–15, Lk 8.2.

6 J. D. Crossan, *Historical Jesus*, 336–7; see also the useful discussion in E. Eve, *Healer from Nazareth*, 51–69.

7 On this, see P. W. Hollenbach, 'Jesus, Demoniacs, and Public Authorities: A Socio-Historical Study', *JAAR* 49 (1982): 567–88.

8 Is 29.18–19, 35.5–6.

9 B. J. Malina, *The New Testament World: Insights from Cultural Anthropology* (Louisville: Westminster John Knox, 3ʳᵈ edn. Rev. 2001): 58–80.

# Chapter 9

1 See Jn 19.25–27 and Acts 1.14; 1Cor 15.7.

2 J. L. Reed, *Archaeology and the Galilean Jesus*, 149–52.

3 Mk 1.29, though John suggests that Peter and Andrew came from nearby Bethsaida, 1.44.

4 The texts are: Mk 2.13–17//Lk 5.27–32, Mt 9.9–13; Mk 1.21–8//Lk 4.33–7; Mt 17.24–7; Mt 8.5-13//Lk 7.1–10; Mk 2.1–12 and pars.; Mk 1.32–4 and pars.

5 Useful studies on this topic include the classic work by E. S. Fiorenza, *In Memory of Her: A Feminist Theological Reconstruction of Christian Origins* (London: SCM, 1983), and more recently, R. Kraemer and M. R. D'Angelo (eds), *Women and Christian Origins* (New York/Oxford: OUP, 1999); T. Ilan, *Jewish Women in Greco-Roman Palestine* (Peabody, MA: Hendrickson, , 1996) and *Integrating Women into Second Temple History* (Tübingen: Mohr Siebeck, 1999); and K. Corley, *Women and the Historical Jesus: Feminist Myths of Christian Origins* (Santa Rosa, CA: Polebridge Press, 2002).

6 See the discussions of Mary Magdalene in S. Haskins, *Mary Magdalene: Myth and Metaphor* (London: Harper Collins, 1993) and J. Schaberg, *The Resurrection of Mary Magdalene: Legends, Apocrypha, and the Christian Testament* (New York: Continuum, 2002).

7 For a useful discussion, see E. Eve, *Healer from Nazareth*, 113–16; also G. Theissen and A. Merz, *The Historical Jesus*, 285–313.

8 Ps 107, 23–32, Job 9.8, 38.8–16 and Hab 3.15.

9 See the texts assembled by W. Cotter, 'Miracle Stories, the God Asclepius, the Pythagorean Philosophers, and the Roman Rulers' in

A. J. Levine, D. C. Allison and J. D. Crossan (eds), *The Historical Jesus in Context*, 166–78, here pp. 175–7.

# Chapter 10

1 *Ant.* 13.298, 18.20, 17.42.

2 *Life* 191, *War* 1.110, Acts 26.5, Phil 3.5.

3 *Ant.* 13.298, 18.15, 17.

4 See E. Rivkin, *A Hidden Revolution* (Nashville: Abingdon, 1978); M. Hengel and R. Deines, 'E. P. Sanders' "Common Judaism," Jesus and the Pharisees. A Review Article', *JTS* 46 (1995): 1–70; S. N. Mason, 'Priesthood in Josephus and the "Pharisaic Revolution"', *JBL* 107 (1988): 657–61. More generally, see A. Saldarini, *Pharisees, Scribes and Sadducees in Palestinian Society: A Sociological Approach* (Wilmington: Glazier, 1988); E. P. Sanders, *Judaism: Practice and Belief, 63 BCE – 66 CE* (London: SCM, 1992); and J. Neusner and B. Chilton (eds), *In Quest of the Historical Pharisees* (Waco: Baylor, 2007).

5 Lk 16.15; they also appear to be the 'elder son' in the parable of the Lost Son, Lk 15.11–32.

6 For an example of the first tendency see, Mt 8.24, 9.11, 14; for the second, see Mt 12.24.

7 See the discussion in M. Hooker, *Mark*, 172–81.

8 On purity, see the discussion and texts in J. Klawans, 'Moral and Ritual Purity' in A. J. Levine, D. C. Allison, and J. D. Crossan (eds), *The Historical Jesus in Context*, 266–84.

9 Suggested by G. Theissen and A. Merz, *The Historical Jesus*, 178 (with rabbinic texts).

10 For a fuller discussion of Jesus' attitude towards the Jewish Law, see J. G. Crossley, *The New Testament and Jewish Law: A Guide for the Perplexed* (London: Continuum, 2010).

11 Lk 7.36–50, 11.37–44, 19.1–10.

12 See the full discussion of Sanders' position in M. A. Powell, 'Was Jesus a Friend of Unrepentant Sinners? A Fresh Appraisal of Sanders's Controversial Proposal', *JSHJ* 7 (2009), 286–310; and also J.D. G. Dunn, 'Pharisees, Sinner and Jesus' in J. Neusner et al. (eds), *The Social World of Formative Christianity and Judaism* (Philadelphia: Fortress, 1988): 264–89.

13 On the location, see Lk 9.10; Jn 6.1 and Mk 6.31 are less clear.

14  See the discussion in M. Hooker, *Mark*, 256. Longer analyses of chronological difficulties can be found in J. Finegan, *Handbook of Biblical Chronology* (rev. edn, Peabody, MA: Hendrickson, 1998): 349–53 and J. P. Meier, *A Marginal Jew*, 1:372–433.

# Chapter 11

1  There may be some exaggeration in Acts 2.7–11, but the range of nationalities assembled for the feast is broadly matched by a list in Philo's *Embassy to Gaius*, 281–2.

2  On Jerusalem, see L. Levine, *Jerusalem: Portrait of the City in the Second Temple Period (538 BCE – 70 CE)* (Philadelphia: Jewish Publication Society, 2002); also *Judaism and Hellenism in Antiquity: Conflict or Confluence* (Peabody, MA: Hendrickson, 1998): 33–95.

3  For example, *Letter of Aristeas* 83, *Jubilees* 8.17–19, *War* 3.52, *Leg* 37, and *1 Enoch* 85–90. For more detail, see S. Freyne, 'The Geography of Restoration: Galilee-Jerusalem Relations in Early Jewish and Christian Experience', *NTS* 47 (2001): 289–311.

4  Hosea married a prostitute and gave each of their three children symbolic names (Hos 1.2–9); Isaiah walked barefoot and naked for three years (Is 20.1–6); and Jeremiah ruined a linen waistcoat on the rocks of the Euphrates (Jer 13.1–11), broke an earthen flask (Jer 19), and put a yoke around his neck (Jer 27).

5  For a useful discussion, see J. J. Collins, *Scepter*, 206–7.

6  On sacrifice, see J. Klawans, *Purity, Sacrifice, and the Temple: Symbolism and Supersessionism in the Study of Ancient Judaism* (Oxford: OUP, 2006).

7  1Cor 10.14–21, Rom 15.25–32, 16.4, Phil 2.17 and 4.18.

8  See the treatment of this in C. A. Evans, 'Jesus' Actions in the Temple: Cleansing or Portent of Destruction?' in B. Chilton and C. A. Evans (eds), *Jesus in Context* (Leiden: E. J. Brill, 1997): 395–439.

9  Amos 5.21–24, Hos 6.6, Mic 6.6–8, Is 1.11–17.

10  For a fuller account of ben Ananias's activity, see R. Gray, *Prophetic Figures*, 158–63.

11  For fuller discussion of the high priests, and Caiaphas in particular, see H. K. Bond, *Caiaphas: Friend of Rome and Judge of Jesus?* (Louisville: Westminster John Knox, 2004); also J. VanderKam, *From Joshua to Caiaphas: High Priests after the Exile* (Minneapolis: Fortress, 2004).

12  Neh 9.26, Jer 2.30, 26.30–23, Jub 1.12.

13  See in particular, Pss 10, 22, 31, 38, 41, 69 and 118.

14  For the former, see Justin Martyr, *Dialogue* 16; Origen, *Against Celsus* 1.47, 4.73, Eusebius, *Church History* 2.23.20; for the latter, see the references in D. R. Schwartz, *Studies in the Jewish Background of Christianity* (Tübingen: Mohr Siebeck, 1992): 245, n.6.

15  On this, see J. Finegan *Handbook of Biblical Chronology*, 353–69 and J. P. Meier, *A Marginal Jew*, 1: 386–402.

16  Mk 14.17–20 and pars.; Jn 13.18–19, 21–27.

17  For a sympathetic portrayal of Judas, see W. Klassen, *Judas: Betrayer or Friend of Jesus?* (London: SCM, 1996).

# Chapter 12

1  See in particular, R. E. Brown, The *Death of the Messiah: From Gethsemane to the Grave* (New York: Doubleday, 1994; 2 vols), and 'The Gospel of Peter and Canonical Gospel Priority', *NTS* 33 (1987): 321–43.

2  For an excellent discussion of the Markan trial scene, see D. Juel, *Messiah and Temple: The Trial of Jesus in the Gospel of Mark* (Missoula, MT.: Scholars Press, 1977). My own two books explore the interests of all four evangelists in these scenes: H. K. Bond, *Pontius Pilate in History and Interpretation* (Cambridge: CUP, 1998) and *Caiaphas: Friend of Rome and Judge of Jesus?* (Louisville: Westminster John Knox, 2004).

3  See A. E. Harvey, *Jesus on Trial: A Study in the Fourth Gospel* (London: SPCK, 1976); A. T. Lincoln, *Truth on Trial: The Lawsuit Motif in the Fourth Gospel* (Peabody, MA: Hendrickson, 2000).

4  See H. K. Bond, *Caiaphas*, 154–9 for the two likeliest sites.

5  A point made by P. Fredriksen, *Jesus of Nazareth: King of the Jews* (New York: Vintage Books, 1999): 221.

6  See, for example, M. Goodman, *The Ruling Class of Judaea* (Cambridge: CUP, 1987): 113–18; E. P. Sanders, *Judaism*, 472–90; D. Goodblatt, *The Monarchic Principle: Studies in Jewish Self-Government in Antiquity* (Tübingen: Mohr-Siebeck, 1994). See my study of the historicity of John's trial narrative, 'At the Court of the High Priest: History and Theology in Jn 18.13–24' in P. Anderson, T. Thatcher and F. Just (eds), *John, Jesus and History, vol 2: Aspects of Historicity in the Fourth Gospel* (SBL): 313–24.

7  For a vigorous defence of Mark's blasphemy charge, however, see D. L. Bock, *Blasphemy and Exaltation in Judaism and the Final Examination of Jesus* (Tübingen: Mohr Siebeck, 1998).

8  On this contentious issue, see the full discussion in R. E. Brown, *Death*, 1:363–72.

9  *War* 2.169–74, *Ant.* 18.55–59.

10  Philo, *Embassy* 299–305; Josephus *War* 2.175–77, *Ant.* 18.60–62.

11  For fuller discussion of the texts involving Pilate, see H.K. Bond, *Pontius Pilate*, 24–93.

12  Other Gospels remember Jesus' last words differently; see Lk 23.46 and Jn 19.30.

13  See Suetonius, *Augustus* 13.1–2; Tacitus, *Annals* 6.29; Petronius, *Satyricon* 111–12. On crucifixion generally, see M. Hengel, *Crucifixion in the Ancient World and the Folly of the Cross* (London: SCM, 1977).

14  See N. Haas, 'Anthropological Observations on the Skeletal Remains from Giv'at ha- Mivtar', *IEJ* 20 (1970): 38–59; and J. Zias and E. Sekeles, 'The Crucified Man from Giv'at ha-Mivtar: A Reappraisal', *IEJ* 35 (1985): 22–27.

15  1Kgs 13.21–22, Jer 22.18–19, Josephus, *Ant.* 5.44.

16  In Mark's gospel, Jesus is buried on the day of the Passover; for further discussion of this curious chronology, see Chapter 11. Useful discussions of the burial of Jesus can be found in M. Myllykoski, 'What Happened to the Body of Jesus?' in I. Dunderberg, C. M. Tuckett, and K. Syreeni (eds), *Fair Play: Diversity and Conflicts in Early Christianity* (Leiden: Brill, 2002): 43–82; B. R. McCabe, *Roll Back the Stone: Death and Burial in the World of Jesus* (Harrisburg: Trinity Press, 2003); and J. Magness, 'Ossuaries and the Burial of James', *JBL* 124 (2005): 121–54.

17  R. E. Brown, 'The Burial of Jesus (Mark 15.42-7)', *CBQ* 50 (1988): 233–45.

# Chapter 13

1  See for example Rom 1.3–4, Phil 3.10–11, 1Thess 1.9–10.

2  Useful studies of resurrection include A. Segal, *Life After Death: A History of the Afterlife in the Religions of the West* (New York: Doubleday, 2004); G. W. E. Nicklesburg, *Resurrection, Immortality,*

*and Eternal Life in Intertestamental Judaism and Early Christianity* (Cambridge: Harvard University Press, 2006); P. Perkins, 'Resurrection' in C. A. Evans (ed.), *Enclyclopedia of the Historical Jesus* (New York: Routledge, 2008): 498–505; and A. Yarbro Collins, *Mark: A Commentary* (Minneapolis: Augsburg Fortress, 2007): 782–97.

3   On the Pharisees, see *War* 2.163 and *Ant.* 18.14. See Martha's declaration in Jn 11.24, and also the *Community Rule* and *Messianic Apocalypse* from Qumran.

4   See Mk 9.43, 45, 47; Mt 5.22, 29, 30, 10.28, 18.9, 23.15, 33; and Lk 12.5.

5   For detailed discussion of both these traditions, see G. Theissen and A. Merz, *The Historical Jesus*, 474–511.

6   R. Bultmann, *New Testament and Mythology and Other Basic Writings*. Selected, edited and translated by M. Ogden. (Philadelphia: Fortress, 1985): 36–41.

7   See, for example, W. Marxsen, *The Resurrection of Jesus of Nazareth* (London: SCM, 1970); G. Lüdemann, *The Resurrection of Jesus: History, Experience, Theology* (London: SCM, 1994). Also R. B. Stewart (ed.), *The Resurrection of Jesus: J. D. Crossan and N. T. Wright in Dialogue* (Minneaopolis: Augsburg Fortress, 2005).

8   See J. D. G. Dunn, *Jesus Remembered*, 825–79; N. T. Wright, *The Resurrection of the Son of God* (Minneapolis: Fortress Press, 2003); and M. Bockhuehl, 'Resurrection' in M. Bockmuehl (ed.), *Cambridge Companion to Jesus*, 102–18.

9   I am particularly indebted here to the work of D. Allison; see his 'A Plea for Thoroughgoing Eschatology', and his book, *Constructing Jesus*, 31–220.

10   1Cor 15.51-6; see also, 1Thess 4.13–18, 2Cor 1.9, Rom 6.3–4.

11   On this, see L. W. Hurtado, *Lord Jesus Christ: Devotion to Jesus in Earliest Christianity* (Grand Rapids: Eerdmans, 2003).

# BIBLIOGRAPHY

Allison, D. C. *Jesus of Nazareth: Millenarian Prophet* (Minneapolis: Fortress, 1998).

— *Constructing Jesus: Memory, Imagination, and History* (Grand Rapids: Baker Academic, 2010).

Bockmuehl, M. (ed.) *The Cambridge Companion to Jesus* (Cambridge: CUP, 2001).

Borg, M. J. *Conflict, Holiness, and Politics in the Teachings of Jesus* (Harrisburg: Trinity Press International, new edn 1998).

Charlesworth, J. H. (ed.), *Jesus and Archaeology* (Grand Rapids: Eerdmans, 2006).

Crossan, J. D. *The Cross That Spoke: The Origins of the Passion Narrative* (San Francisco: Harper and Row, 1988).

— *The Historical Jesus: The Life of a Jewish Mediterranean Peasant* (San Francisco: Harper Collins, 1991).

— *The Birth of Christianity: Discovering What Happened in the Years Immediately after the Execution of Jesus* (Edinburgh: T & T Clark, 1999).

— *Who Killed Jesus? Exposing the Roots of Anti-Semitism in the Gospel Story of the Death of Jesus* (New York: HarperSanFrancisco, 1995).

Dunn, J. D. G. *Jesus Remembered. Christianity in the Making*, vol I. (Grand Rapids: Eerdmans, 2003).

— *A New Perspective on Jesus: What the Quest for the Historical Jesus Missed* (Grand Rapids: Baker Academic, 2005).

Evans, C. A. and N. T. Wright (ed. T. A. Miller), *Jesus, the Final Days: What Really Happened* (Louisville: Westminster John Knox, 2009).

Flusser, D. with R. S. Notley, *The Sage from Galilee: Rediscovering Jesus' Genius* (Grand Rapids: Eerdmans, 4th edn. 2007).

Fredriksen, P. *Jesus of Nazareth, King of the Jews: A Jewish Life and the Emergence of Christianity* (New York: Knopf, 1999).

Freyne, S. *Galilee, Jesus, a Jewish Galilean: A New Reading of the Jesus Story* (London: T & T Clark, 2004).

Funk, R. W., R. Hoover and the Jesus Seminar, *The Five Gospels: The Search for the Authentic Words of Jesus* (New York: Maxwell Macmillan, 1993).

Horsley, R. and J. S. Hanson, *Bandits, Prophets and Messiahs: Popular Movements in the Time of Jesus* (Harrisburg: Trinity Press, 1985).

Horsley, R., *Jesus and the Spiral of Violence: Popular Jewish Resistance in Roman Palestine* (San Francisco: Harper and Row,, 1987).

— *Sociology and the Jesus Movement* (New York: Crossroad, 1989).

Jesus Seminar, *The Once and Future Jesus* (Santa Rosa Ca.: Polebridge Press, 2000).

Johnson, L. T. *The Real Jesus: The Misguided Quest for the Historical Jesus and the Truth of the Traditional Gospels* (New York: Harper Collins, 1996).

Meier, J. P. *A Marginal Jew: Rethinking the Historical Jesus*, vol 1. The Roots of the Problem and the Person (New York: Doubleday, 1991).

— *A Marginal Jew: Rethinking the Historical Jesus*, vol 2. Mentor, Message and Miracles (New York: Doubleday, 1994).

— *A Marginal Jew: Rethinking the Historical Jesus*, vol 3. Companions and Competitor. (New York: Doubleday, 2001).

— *A Marginal Jew: Rethinking the Historical Jesus*, vol 4. Law and Love (New Haven: Yale University Press, 2007)

Powell, M. A., *Jesus as a Figure in History* (Louisville: Westminster John Knox, 1998).

Sanders, E. P. *Jesus and Judaism* (London: SCM, 1985).

— *The Historical Figure of Jesus* (London: Penguin, 1993).

Schüssler Fiorenza, E., *Jesus and the Politics of Interpretation* (New York: Continuum, 2000).

Smith, M. *Jesus the Magician* (London: Harper and Row, 1978).

Theissen, G. *The Shadow of the Galilean: The Quest of the Historical Jesus in Narrative Form* (London: SCM, 1997).

Theissen, G. and A. Merz, *The Historical Jesus: A Comprehensive Guide* (London: SCM, 1998).

Theissen, G. and D. Winter, *The Quest for the Plausible Jesus: The Question of Criteria* (Louisville: Westminster John Knox, 2002).

Vermes, G. *Jesus the Jew: A Historian's Reading of the Gospels* (London: Collins, 1973).

— *Jesus and the World of Judaism* (London: SCM, 1983).

— *The Religion of Jesus the Jew* (London: SCM, 1993).

— *The Authentic Gospel of Jesus* (London: Penguin, 2003).

— *Jesus in the Jewish World* (London: SCM, 2010).

Witherington, B. *Jesus the Sage: The Pilgrimage of Wisdom* (Edinburgh: T & T Clark, 1994).
— *The Jesus Quest: The Third Search for the Jew of Nazareth* (Carlisle: Paternoster, 1995).
Wright, N. T. *Who Was Jesus?* (London: SPCK, 1992).
— *Jesus and the Victory of God* (London: SPCK, 1996).
— *The Resurrection of the Son of God* (Minneapolis: Fortress, 2003).

# INDEX